Lanzarote

with

David & Ros Brawn

DISCOVERY WALKING GUIDES LTD

Walk! Lanzarote
Second Edition - July 2009

Published by
Discovery Walking Guides Ltd
10 Tennyson Close, Northampton NN5 7HJ, England

Maps
Maps are adapted from Lanzarote Tour & Trail Map (ISBN 9781904946540) published by **Discovery Walking Guides Ltd**

Photographs
All photographs in this book were taken by the authors, Ros & David Brawn.

Front Cover Photographs

Caldera Blanca

La Geria

Montaña Corona

On Corona's Northern Tour

ISBN 9781904946533

The author and publishers have tried to ensure that the information and maps in this publication are as accurate as possible. However, we accept no responsibility for any loss, injury or inconvenience sustained by anyone using this book.

Walk! Lanzarote

CONTENTS

Contents 3
Acknowledgments 6
Preface 7
The Authors 8
Background 9
'Thingys' 10

INTRODUCTION

First Impressions 14
When To Go 14
Where To Stay 14
Getting Around The Island 14
César Manrique 15
Parque Nacional de Timanfaya 15
Lanzarote's Salt 16
Cacti & Cochineal 16
Goats 17
Things To Do 17
Plant Life 18

2CSK - The Linear Solution 19
Symbols Rating Guide & Notes on Walk Descriptions 21
Map Information
Location Maps 22
Map Notes & Legend 24
Walking Equipment 26
The Routes - and Safety 28

THE WALKS

1 **Coastal Promenade - Puerto Del Carmen to Arrecife** 29
2/3 walker, 2 hours, 9½km, ascents & descents negligible, 2 refreshments (linear)

2 **Coastal Discovery** 32
3 walker, 3½ hours, 16km, ascents & descents 100 metres, 2 refreshments (linear)

3 **Coastal Promenade - Costa Teguise** 36
1 walker, 1¼ hours, 6km, ascents & descents negligible, 3 refreshments (linear)

4 **Sunday Market Special - Camino el Charco** 39
3 walker, 2½ hours, 12½km, ascents 70 metres, descents 350 metres, 0 refreshments (linear)

5 **Montaña Corona** 43
3 walker, 2 hours, 5½km, ascents & descents 220 metres, vertigo risk, 0 refreshments (circular)

6 **Coastal Promenade - Playa Blanca West** 46
1 walker, 1½ hours, 7km, ascents & descents 40 metres, 2 refreshments (linear)

7 **Coastal Promenade - Playa Blanca East** 48
1 walker, 1 hour, 4½km, ascents & descents 50 metres, 1 refreshments (linear)

8 **Montaña Roja** 50
3 walker, 1 hour, 3km, ascents & descents 150 metres, 0 refreshments (circular)

9 **Papagayo Beach** 52
3 walker, 1½ hours, 6km, ascents & descents 100 metres, 4 refreshments (linear)

10 **Peña del Rubicón** 55
3 walker, 3 hours, 11km, ascents & descents 50 metres, 0 refreshments (linear)

11 **Yaiza's Volcanic Gardens** 60
1 walker, 1 hour, 3½km, ascents & descents 60 metres, 1 refreshments (circular)

12 **Atalaya de Femés (Linear route)** 62
5 walker, 4 hours, 16km, ascents & descents 500 metres, 3 refreshments (linear)

13 **Atalaya de Femés Circuit** 66
4 walker, 2½ hours, 9½km, ascents & descents 350 metres, 3 refreshments (circular)

14 **The Hidden Barrancos** 68
4 walker, 3 hours, 10km, ascents & descents 300 metres, vertigo risk, 0 refreshments (circular)

15 **Femés Ridge** 72
4 walker, 3 hours, 8km, ascents & descents 550 metres, 0 0 refreshments (circular)

16 **Femés to Playa Blanca** 76
4 walker, 6 hours, 22km, ascents 150 metres, descents 550 metres, vertigo risk, 4 refreshments (linear)

17 **Femés to Playa Quemada** 79
3 walker, 1½-2 hours, 7km, ascents 200 metres, descents 480 metres, vertigo risk, 1 refreshments (linear)

18 **Tremesana Guided Walk** 81
2 walker, 2 hours, 3km, ascents & descents 50 metres, 0 refreshments (linear)

19 **Montaña Cuervo - A Gem in Lanzarote's Crown** 83
1 walker, 1 hour, 4km, ascents & descents 20 metres, 0 refreshments (circular)

20 **A Path Between Two Seas - The Timanfaya Coastal Path** 85
3 walker, 3 hours, 13km, ascents & descents 100 metres, 0 refreshments (linear)

21 **La Geria** 88
3 walker, 3 hours, 12 kilometres, ascents 170 metres, descents 440 metres, vertigo risk, 1 refreshments (linear)

21A **La Geria and Tinasoria** 91
3 walker, 2 hours, 9.5km, ascents & descents 270 metres, 1 refreshments (circular)

22 **Playa del Pozo** 94
3 walker, 2 hours, 5km, ascents & descents 150 metres, 0 refreshments (linear)

23 **Teguise - The Ancient Capital** 97
1 walker, 1 hour, 4km, ascents & descents negligible, 3 refreshments (circular)

24 **The Forgotten Trail** 100
3 walker, 2 hours, 8km, ascents & descents 280 metres, 1 refreshments (linear)

25 **Barranco del Malpaso** 102
3/4 walker, 2½ hours, 9.5km, ascents & descents 350 metres, 1 refreshments (circular)

26 **Circuit of Haría** 105
4 walker, 2 hours, 9km, ascents & descents 270 metres, 1 refreshments (circular)

27 **Capital Route - Haría to Teguise** 108
4 walker, 4 hours, 16km, ascents 370 metres, descents 320 metres, 2 refreshments (linear)

28 **Mala to Teguise** 111
5 walker, 4-4½ hours, 21km, ascents 600 metres, descents 300 metres, 2 refreshments (linear)

29 **Helechos Circular** 114
3/4 walker, 3½ hours, 15km, ascents 400 metres, descents 400 metres, 0 refreshments (circular)

30 **Máguez to Yé** 117
3 walker, 2½ hours, 10km, ascents 240 metres, descents 170 metres, 2 refreshments (linear)

31 **Corona's Northern Tour** 119
3 walker, 2½ hours, 9km, ascents & descents 230 metres, vertigo risk, 2 refreshments (circular)

32 **Salinas del Río** 122
4/5 walker, 3 hours, 9½km, ascents & descents 440 metres, vertigo risk, 0 refreshments (linear)

33 **Risco de Famara** 124
5 walker, 5½ hours, 17km, ascents 100 metres, descents 480 metres, vertigo risk, 0 refreshments (linear)

34 **Famara Circular** 127
3 walker, 1½-2 hours, 8km, ascents & descents 150 metres, 0 refreshments (circular)

35 Caldera Blanca 129
3 walker, 3 hours, 10km, ascents & descents 240 metres, vertigo risk, 0 refreshments (circular)

GPS Waypoints Lists 132

The Hidden Barrancos - Additional Walking 136

La Geria - Additional Walking 139

Height Profiles 142

Bibliography 143

Glossary 146

Cycling on Lanzarote 148

Bus Timetables 150

Place Names Index 156

ACKNOWLEDGEMENTS

Our research on the 'Fire Island' has been greatly helped by the Lanzarote aficionados amongst our DWG client family, who have kept us updated on the local developments, including David Gibbons (Montaña Roja), Peter Williams (Barranco de Quiquere), Jeffery Jennings (Buses) amongst many – Montaña Cuervo still attracting praise from everyone.

Lanzarote experts Andreas Kern (The Bike Station, Costa Teguise) and Carmen Portella Ernest (lanzaroteactiveclub.com) provided the suggestions for our new routes, Carmen guiding us round our new Walk 31 Montaña Corona. Andreas and Carmen are passionate for La Graciosa and presented convincing arguments for including the full island map on the new edition Lanzarote Tour & Trail Map; they were possibly motivated by wanting an accurate map of the island for their own use but it was nevertheless a very good idea!

Thanks to the island authorities for their initiatives in La Geria, the Hidden Barrancos and at Caldera Blanca to encourage walking, plus thanks to the willing staff in the Costa Teguise, Arrecife and Puerto del Carmen tourist information offices for their enthusiasm for their island.

PREFACE

Returning to the Fire Island, we were filled with a mixture of excitement and trepidation - while our DWG client family keeps us informed of change, we never quite know what to expect until we arrive, and in recent years some islands have suffered walking route closures due to unhelpful landowners. We returned to the Sol Lanzarote in **Matagorda**, a good value hotel with courteous staff, good food and masses of car parking making for a good value stay far enough away from the all-night delights of **Puerto del Carmen**.

We need not have worried. Our DWG client family's updates checked out; new building encroaching on the start of our **Montaña Roja** route (not so good), a new crossing of the **Barranco de Quiquere** (good news on Walk 2), the appearance of 'traffic light' wayposts in the 'Hidden Barrancos' and PR wayposts in **La Geria** (interesting). On arrival we discovered that it's all good news for leisure walkers with a new 'thingy' near our hotel, coastal promenades now completed in **Playa Blanca** and upgraded on Walk 1, while our Walk 2 'Coastal Discovery' has been upgraded beyond our wildest expectations with a new 'rope & slope' start complimented by immaculate paths, *barranco* crossings and cliff-top stone seating. Out in the countryside it's good news with new routes suggested by Carmen Portella Ernest of **lanzaroteactiveclub.com** for **Caldera Blanca**, **Barranco del Malpaso** and **Montaña Corona** while we've extended our Walk 10 'Pena del Rubicon' out past the **Atlante del Sol** to **Las Salinas** with a finish at the **La Hoya** bus stop. **Puerto del Carmen** has a new golf course along with an 'inner bypass'(complete with speed humps and pedestrian seating!) which are part of the comprehensive updating for our new **Lanzarote Tour & Trail Map**.

Walk! Lanzarote new 2nd edition now features dedicated map sections for each walk - only the waypoints for that walking route are shown making it easier for you to follow the route. Lanzarote's excellent bus service gets more emphasis with 'Bus Access' being updated for every route plus extensive bus information. We've included sections on the new routes produced by the island (*Cabildo*) and local (*Ayuntamiento*) governments for **La Geria** and the 'Hidden Barrancos' regions.

Lanzarote Gazette magazine is into walking and is recommending Walk! Lanzarote as 'currently the best guide in print'. When we called at the Book Swop (Puerto del Carmen) to ask about walking the owner pointed to Walk! Lanzarote 'that's the best by far, knocks the socks off anything else'. Well the 'Best' just got even better and a bit bigger at 160 pages, so we hope you enjoy your adventures as much as we enjoyed researching them.

David & Ros Brawn

P.S. The Not So Good

A new villa development has disrupted the start of **Montaña Roja** (Walk 8), we say 'new' but it's still unfinished (and unsold) after four years. Climbing to the peak of **Montaña Roja**, our views north and south are as they were but to east and west we look down on an ugly sea of developments in all states of construction except finished where greedy developers over extended themselves expecting an endless supply of gullible foreigners willing to buy identikit-villas 'off-plan'. Millions, possibly billions, of Euros have been invested trying to create profits out of the desert but both buyers and developers have fled leaving behind a concrete landscape of appalling ugliness. The east of **Playa Blanca** has suffered to a smaller degree, as has **Costa Teguise**, but nowhere else in the Canary Islands comes close to this level of depredation. All this happened long before the 'credit crunch' but if you ever wondered what 'toxic debt' looks like, here it is spread out below us, a testament to greedy developers and the foolishness of buying 'off-plan'.

THE AUTHORS

David and Ros Brawn lived and worked in England, Papua New Guinea and the Seychelles before settling for a number of years in Tenerife.

They've been walking and writing for Discovery Walking Guides since it began, researching on most of the seven Canary Islands, the Balearic Islands, Malta, Gozo, Madeira, the Alpujarras and Aracena. In addition to walking many kilometres to gather the information for their walking guides, they also surveyed and mapped a number of these regions using satellite navigation equipment combined with cartographic software.

David & Ros have researched and produced publications to various destinations including:

CANARY ISLANDS
Tenerife
Gran Canaria
La Gomera
La Palma
El Hierro
Lanzarote

SPANISH MAINLAND
The Alpujarras
Sierra de Aracena

BALEARIC ISLANDS
Mallorca
Menorca
Ibiza

Malta
Gozo

Madeira

David is also author of:

GPS The Easy Way

HISTORY

Lanzarote and Fuerteventura's first inhabitants were the *Majos* (or Mahos), the approximate equivalent of the *Guanches* in the western Canary Islands. It is thought that they led a relatively uneventful existence until 1402, when the Norman *conquistador* Jean de Bethencourt arrived, befriending the *Majo* leader and taking peaceful control of the island from a camp in **Rubicón**, soon passing power to his nephew Maciot, the founder of the island's original capital **Teguise**.

.. 'coloured hills' as seen from the west coast ..

The *Majos* named the island 'Titerroygatra', which translates as 'coloured hills', a name which would be just as appropriate today, though its current name is an adaptation of the name of an influential immigrant, Lancelotto Malocello.

GEOGRAPHY

Lanzarote is the most northerly and least mountainous of the Canary Islands, its highest point being 675 metres, **Peñas del Chache**, unfortunately taken over by the military and off limits to walkers. Its 169 kilometres of coastline varies between yellow and black beaches, cliffs and lava *malpaís*, offering some photogenic scenes. The island has been repeatedly shaped by volcanic activity, the most famous being the 1730-36 eruptions which formed **Timanfaya**, and the last in 1824 which created the volcanoes of **Tinguatón**, **Tao** and **Nuevo del Fuego**.

CLIMATE & AGRICULTURE

Lanzarote's close proximity to Africa is apparent in its weather. The dry, desert-like climate is interrupted by a few rainy days, typically in winter and early spring, but not amounting to much; for this reason the island's water supply comes from desalination plants. The modest height of Lanzarote's hills is insufficient to benefit from the humidity of the trade winds, but even so the lack of rain has not deterred the islanders from devising methods of growing a wide range of fruits and vegetables.

Particularly remarkable are the *zocos*, notably in **La Geria** where the black volcanic *picón* (ash) filters moisture to the roots and mulches the soil beneath, while keeping the plants cool. This is a windy island, and the agricultural plots are often protected from the prevailing winds by horseshoe shaped walls. When easterly winds blow they bring hot, dust-laden *calimas*, best avoided by staying indoors.

thi´ngy (noun)

1. Inanimate object that the speaker has temporarily forgotten the name of.
2. Large, or over large, man-made object of no discernible use prominently displayed in a public place, notably in the centre of large roundabouts. Associated with the Canary Island of Lanzarote and its most famous citizen César Manrique (artist, 1919-1992).

César Manrique's legacy to Lanzarote is apparent in many aspects of the island's life, visibly in the squat white painted houses with green or blue window shutters but most notably in the 'sculptures' adorning roundabouts on the island's main roads. Whether you consider these constructions as art seems open to question. Is the huge green tin-can cactus, outside the gardens in **Guatiza**, art or simply an advertisement in the same genre that American and Australian businesses use, equivalent to a giant 'hamburger' outside a burger bar? Some residents are defensive over these Thingys, believing that anything César Manrique promoted must be good for the island. You'll have plenty of opportunities to form your own Thingy opinion as you travel round.

When our 'Thingy' comments appeared in the first edition of this book we thought we might be deluged with complaints that we were being too flippant in our approach to the island's large scale art. Reality is quite the reverse; we've been praised for making people think about the sculptures as unique pieces of art along with introducing 'Thingy' to the local language and encouraging the production of new Thingys. We soon bumped into our first new Thingy a few metres along the **Matagorda** promenade from our hotel which now features in Walk 1 (see below). We rate Thingys as:-:

Recommended

'Madonna' wind measurement Thingy on the **Arrieta** roundabout. The workings of this Thingy are missed by car drivers so park nearby and walk back to the roundabout to see it in action. Sadly the 'Madonna' was badly damaged in the 2007 winter storms and two years later is still in for repairs.

Manrique's Monumento al Campesino

'Monument to the Campesino' on the first LZ1 roundabout north of the **Arrecife** circumvalacion. Build on a big scale, and even the most unlikely of objects assumes a life of its own. César Manrique's big, bold structure epitomises the artist's ideas; ironic then that he should have been killed in a car crash at this junction. Missed by most including us first time round is the 'Little Brother' of the real thing situated just off the roundabout on the LZ34 road to **Costa Teguise**.

'Rock Finger' at the western end of the new **Matagorda-Playa Honda** promenade; see Walk 1. An elegant post-Manrique Thingy, if a bit on the small size compared to the dictionary definition.

'Rotating Pipe' new thingy installed on the **Matagorda** promenade; see Walk 1. Interestingly interactive thanks to its hydraulically damped rotating base but again, rather small for a Thingy.

Rock Finger Thingy on Walk 1

Airport Radar Thingy

'Radar' Thingy on the airport road system. A post César Manrique installation usually missed by drivers attempting to negotiate the lane-switching required to escape from the airport.

toast rack thingy at junction of LZ1 and LZ34

'Toast Rack/Wind Chime' on the **Tahiche** LZ1 roundabout. Promoted from 'Art or Junk' for the second edition but shouldn't a Thingy be rather more solid and less ethereal?

'Hold-Up' Thingy at the junction of LZ35 and LZ301. New roundabout Thingy that looks sturdy enough to survive Lanzarote's famous winds, if not that inspiring.

'Hold-Up' thingy at junction of LZ35 and LZ301

"Art, or junk?" the jury is out

'Twin pillars' on the end of the **Costa Teguise** dock; Walk 3. Certainly tall enough to count as thingys but is their weathered intergalactic nature in the César Manrique mould?

'Defunct R2D2' beside the Twin Pillars; Walk 3. Rendered insignificant by the towers?

'Sailing Dingy' on roundabout at **Puerto**

Calero; Walk 2. Modern concrete sculpture but perhaps too lifelike and not abstract enough to rank as a Thingy.

'Giant Hill Sculpture' in the **Barranco de la Higuera**; Walks 17 & 22. Certainly big enough, and sufficiently devoid of discernible use to count as a Thingy, but only a small number of adventurous walkers will get to see it.

In the bin, or Paul Merton's Room 101

'Giant Sun Lounger' east of **Costa Teguise** dock; Walk 3. Rusting steel and crumbling concrete do not a true Thingy make.

Giant (fake) cactus marks the Jardín de Cactus

'Tin-Can Cactus' outside the **Guatiza Cactus Garden**. Surely this Lanzarote equivalent of the giant glass-fibre Lobster placed on top of a sea food restaurant, or giant cockroach on a pest exterminator's van, cannot be considered art as it is an advertising symbol. The idea of a Thingy is that it has no discernible use.

'Iron Horse' on the western sea front of **Arrecife**; Walk1. An example of the modernist Spanish Thingy style possibly encouraged by César Manrique's original Thingys.

'Ladder going Nowhere' modernist shelter with seating on the promenade between **El Cable** and **Arrecife** (see Walk 1) ; interesting but could be much more extreme in design.

'Muse' alongside the promenade of **Arrecife**'s sea front park; see photo, Walk 1. A surprising arrival on the scene as it is classical sculpture quite in contrast to the Thingy concept.

'Ship's Ventilator' rubbish bins on the sea front park; Walk1. Not really Thingys but why waste a chance to have a go at a good idea which becomes an eyesore due to a lack of maintenance?

Lobster Traffic Island

'Lobster' traffic island between **Punta Mujeres** and **Jameos del Agua**. As with the Cactus, an advertisement.

Thingys - the future

Thingys are now firmly embedded in Lanzarote culture and are proliferating as more large roundabouts are being built. Private examples can be seen as you travel around the island and while these clearly have no discernible use, they are neither large enough, nor prominently displayed in a public place, to count as Thingys.

'Huey Helicopter' Thingy, Casita de Femes

There are many 'artistic' style houses around the island adorned/decorated with many 'no discernible use'items. Currently we do not classify these as Thingys, not even when they have an old Huey helicopter fuselage as part of the 'construction' (**Casitas de Femés**).

Dieter and his giant trowel

Driving the LZ703 up through **Las Breñas** as part of our road survey (two new km markers) we came upon the surprise of a giant pick in the garden of a house; at the next house a giant trowel leaned against the building dwarfing the structure. Islands have always attracted artists; it was good to see some new local Thingy initiative taking place from a modern artist. Returning to photograph these new Thingys we met the creator Dieter Noss, a most affable person who then invited us to his local exhibition of work in **Yaiza**.

Dieter spent 25 years at the cutting edge of graphic design working for Der Spiegel and Stern amongst other quality magazines before retiring to 'do his own thing', now splitting his time between Munich and Las Brenas. His art spans a range of techniques perhaps described as modernist with a leaning towards metal but this is far too narrow a definition if you have seen his exhibitions in Munich and Berlin. His metal pictures in welded angle iron frames radiate the power of industrial furnaces but as with all artists he has his own statement to make. He never names a piece nor prices any work; you make an offer and if Dieter thinks its reasonable he'll accept, if not no sale.

We anticipate that the previously quiet LZ703 from **Las Breñas** centre towards **Femés** could become busier with people wanting to see Dieter's Thingys; the trowel and pick are impressive and also look out for the three metre 'wire coat hanger'; please restrict yourself to viewing from the roadside.

INTRODUCTION

FIRST IMPRESSIONS

If you are used to Mediterranean island destinations, or you've visited the western Canary Islands, your first arrival on the island might come as a bit of a shock. As your plane approaches the airport, you'll have an impression of barren starkness, relieved only by clusters and scatterings of cloned, squat white buildings, clustered thickly here and there on the coastline.

But, give yourself a few hours to adapt, and you should begin to appreciate the subtleties of what is a chunk of African desert, overlain with volcanic spewings. The lava fields themselves have a certain weird beauty, and once you get over the withdrawal symptoms caused by the lack of trees, you'll find that Lanzarote is an island offering more colour and contrast than you might have assumed. The volcanic cones come in a variety of hues, and many parts of the coastline are dramatic and photogenic. Although Lanzarote might not appear at first glance to offer much variety or challenge for walkers, this book will change your opinion.

WHEN TO GO

If you want to walk, avoid the summer months of July, August and September. It's hot, dusty and suitable for beach and water sports only. Be aware that, although Lanzarote has very little precipitation, you can hit some wet days; while completing research from February to April, there were four or five wet days. There were also a couple of *calimas*, the unpleasant hot, dust-laden east wind which picks up half the African deserts and then dumps it on the island. The skies darken with the suspended dust, and if you are a contact lens wearer or an asthma sufferer, you'll feel miserable. We wouldn't recommend walking in a *calima*, which can last anything from a couple of days to a week.

WHERE TO STAY

Almost all the accommodation is in the tourist resorts of **Costa Teguise**, **Puerto del Carmen** and **Playa Blanca**. The first two of these have the advantage of being close to the airport, having a reasonable bus service, and plenty of the usual tourist things, such as beaches, bars and shops. **Playa Blanca** is the place for you if you want to be near the ferry port for Fuerteventura, but it's a long way from everywhere else, and has a limited bus service. Sporting types can stay on the north coast at **Club La Santa** although there is not much distraction apart from within the complex itself.

GETTING AROUND THE ISLAND

There's a bus timetable in the back of this book, but be aware that these can change, so check when you arrive, either at the Biosphere Information Office which faces you as you emerge from the baggage hall at the airport, or in the **Puerto del Carmen** tourist office. Some bus routes operate only on work days, or only on Sundays (market specials), and some towns and villages have only three or four buses a day. If you intend to use buses to access and return from walks, check the times first, and be prepared to use taxis.

Easiest is to hire a car, easily available and at reasonable rates. When using a car for linear walking routes, try to link up with like-minded walkers with another hire car and use the 2CSK method - see page 19. If you need a taxi when you are not near a tourist resort, ask in a bar and they will usually phone for you - but do buy a drink as well.

CÉSAR MANRIQUE

Within hours of the visitor's first arrival on Lanzarote, the influence of César Manrique will already be obvious. The plain white, low-level buildings in traditional, unadorned style with their dark green doors and windows, and the sometimes startling sculptures that form traffic roundabouts, all bear witness to the singular effect this individual had - and still has - on the development of the island.

Born in **Arrecife** in 1919, he was a volunteer with Franco's troops during the Spanish Civil War of 1936-39 before he became an artist, holding his first exhibition in his home town at the age of 21. Moving to the mainland, he studied at the Academia de Belles Artes de San Fernando in Madrid where he developed his abstract art ideas. Enthusiastic reactions to his first serious exhibition of 1954 led to its tour of galleries in many European cities, followed by a tour of the USA following the invitation of Nelson Rockefeller. Returning home in 1968 he expounded ideas for the conservation of Lanzarote, and for the development of the island in a controlled manner. He was responsible for the banning of roadside advertising hoardings in the countryside, and urged the powers that be to lay down strict building rules to encourage traditional low level development. Under his guidance, the **Jameos del Agua** caves were turned into a tourist attraction and an underground theatre. He was also the force behind the **Jardín de Cactus**, which although it contains the real thing, is oddly marked by an outrageously fake giant cactus in its car park. He had more than a hand in many other projects on the island, including the **Mirador del Río**, and the **Restaurante del Diablo** inside the **Montañas del Fuego** where volcanic energy is used to cook the food.

His main residence during these years was **Taro de Tahiche**, north of **Arrecife**, now the **Fundación de César Manrique**, since his surreal death in a road traffic accident in 1992 on the very roundabout that he had alerted the authorities to as dangerous. His vision continues under the auspices of the El Guincho environmental group. In 1993, UNESCO recognised his efforts in preserving the natural environment of the island by declaring the entire island a World Biosphere Reserve.

PARQUE NACIONAL DE TIMANFAYA

An incredible eruption of cataclysmic proportions and lasting six years began on 1 September 1730. Centred in the south of the island, the **Montañas del Fuego** or Mountains of Fire, caused devastation to an area of 200 sq. km. The ground is still hot to the touch in places, and a party trick by the guides is to toss a dry bush into a crevasse whereupon it is instantly consumed by fire. The feeling is that the boiling molten magma is still close enough for discomfort. The **Restaurante del Diablo** built on the **Islote de Hilario** area within the park, uses the power of the volcano to barbecue the food, though it tastes no different to other forms of cooking and you do pay extra for this novelty.

Access to the park is restricted to cars and tour coaches (entrance fee payable), although there are guided walks available. If you would like to join one of these, apply at the **Centro de Visitantes** (Visitors' Centre) on the LZ 67 road, south of **Mancha Blanca**, in person or by phone on 928 840839. See Walk 18, 'Tremesana Guided Walk' for details. There's a tougher 'Ruta del Litoral' lasting about five hours and covering a distance of 9 kilometres which is arranged according to demand.

You can also take a coach tour from the parking area, taking in the weird volcanic landscapes, though you might find the multi-lingual commentary and taped music which accompany the tour irritating, and it is frustrating not to be have the freedom to walk independently in these unique surroundings.

LANZAROTE'S SALT

Salinas del Janubio

Lanzarote produces about one third of the salt it needs, but the industry is not as important as it once was. The **Salinas del Río**, (see Walk 30, 'Salinas del Río') almost on the island's most north-westerly point, are thought to have been constructed in the 15th century and are shown on maps drawn in 1590. The quantities of salt produced here were more than sufficient to serve the island's needs and the excess was sold to La Palma and Tenerife.

Until 1775, these salt pans were the only ones on Lanzarote, but from that time on several were constructed to cash in on the growing market. **Salinas del Agujero** were constructed in 1940, near **Los Cocoteros** which , together with the **Salinas del Janubio** are the principal remaining commercial salt pans on the island. The most scenic of the *salinas* are **Salinas del Janubio** which exists thanks to the volcanic eruptions of 1730, when molten lava formed the walls of the natural lake of **Laguna de Janubio**. Although salt production has declined in the last few decades, the *salinas* have become important as havens for bird life.

CACTI & COCHINEAL

Naturalised in all the Canary Islands, Prickly Pear cactii (opuntia) were introduced as a hedging plant whose edible fruits are collected by those prepared to risk being impaled on its sturdy spikes; you may see Canarians collecting these bright red or orange fruits with the aid of wooden tongs.

Cactus farm near Guatiza

Prickly Pears also proved to be the most popular host plant for the cochineal beetle, which led to a thriving cottage industry in the valuable dark red dye harvested from these insects which are dried and ground. The development of artificial colourings almost killed the industry, but in recent years some manufacturers - especially of drinks, foodstuffs and cosmetics - have returned to this natural dye.

The cochineal beetles give away their presence by the protective white powder that they exude around themselves as they feed off the cactus sap. There are few naturalised cacti in the Canaries without a few of these telltale signs of infestation, and in a few villages including **Guatiza** and **Mala** they are still farmed despite the extremely labour-intensive nature of the industry, each tiny bug being collected by hand.

GOATS

Goats are survivors, and can live quite happily on a diet of tough, wizened and spiny plants at which any sheep would turn up its nose. The ideal livestock for an arid and unforgiving landscape, they have been part of the way of life for many generations, and although the estimated numbers have varied between the 14,000 of the 1970s and a low of around 3000 or fewer in the 1990s, their numbers are now on the increase, with an estimated 15,000 or so surviving perfectly happily on what might appear to be barren desert. It would be easy to make the assumption that these are wild creatures, but most have owners, as the presence of goatherds proves.

Traditionally a source of meat, milk, cheese, wool, skins, tallow for candles and a host of herbal cures and remedies, the goat was historically an essential factor in the survival of Lanzarote's early settlers. These days there is a healthy market for goat's cheese and meat, and a limited demand for crafts using goat's wool and skins, mainly for souvenir items. You would be unlucky not to see a herd of these multi-patterned creatures while walking on the island, and you'll probably envy them their sure-footedness and easy tackling of slippery slopes.

THINGS TO DO

If you want a change from walking (or the beach) there are several attractions to visit. The island's best natural wonders have been turned into profit making ventures, including the **Montañas del Fuego** inside the **Parque Nacional de Timanfaya**, the **Jardín de Cactus**, the **Mirador del Río**, the **Jameos del Agua**, a huge volcanic tube inside which is a lake, restaurant, bars and a theatre, and the **Cueva de los Verdes**, another part of the same massive volcanic tube which has been kept in a more natural state.

There are several museums of anything from traditional and contemporary art, wine, agriculture, Lanzarote emigrants and local crafts. There's a wide choice of boat trips from sightseeing to diving or fishing, and you can hop over to Fuerteventura from **Playa Blanca** in 25-40 minutes depending on the ferry, or see the tiny island of **La Graciosa**, reached by ferry from **Orzola** in about 25 minutes. Camel treks and horse riding are available, and the relatively flat terrain and quiet roads are ideal for cycling, with bicycle hire offered by several companies. **Costa Teguise** and **Puerto del Carmen** have golf courses.

Free attractions include the **Salinas del Janubio** (see notes on the island's salt industry earlier in this introduction), the coastline at **Los Hervideros** (the boiling springs), north of the salt pans where the sea boils and spouts through lava fissures. The jagged lava has been tamed into a series of narrow paths which lead among the lava and caves, and if the sea is rough expect to get a shower as the sea is forced up through natural blowholes. Also worth a visit is

Los Hervideros

Charco de los Clicos

the half volcanic crater of **Charco de los Clicos** near **El Golfo**.

PLANT LIFE

Trees are scarce on Lanzarote, and where they do grow, it is thanks to careful planting and sustained watering. Some of the best plantings are in hotel gardens, where they provide a valuable mini-habitat for bird and insect life.

Because the volcanic history of the island is still relatively recent, swathes of its surface are still littered with lava in one of its forms. These areas of *malpaís* show signs of the process of breaking down into smaller particles that will eventually become soil, as the colourful colonies of lichen prove.

In other areas where volcanic ash rather than rock and lava streams covered them, (such as **La Geria**, Walks 21&21A), fertile soil lies beneath black duvets of fine ash, which serve to protect the roots of Malvasia grape vines, figs and other crops while drawing moisture from the cooler night air, which then percolates downwards. This method of mulching with a thick layer of ash has been adopted for agriculture of all kinds often used with the horseshoe-shaped low walls or *zocos* which give additional protection from the prevailing winds.

The Haría Valley

The dampest part of Lanzarote, the north, has the deepest and most workable soil. The little town of **Haría** (Walk 24, 'The Forgotten Trail', Walk 25 'Barranco del Malpaso' and Walk 26, 'Circuit of Haría'), sits in a fertile bowl where many types of fruit and vegetable crops are grown. The whole valley is dotted with Phoenix canariensis palms, and the roadsides are sparsely lined by white or pale pink Tamarix africana.

Look in the north of the island, especially around the **El Risco de Famara** and **Haría** areas, for the island's own endemic miniature version of sea-lavender, Limonium puberulum. Easier to spot is the white tajinaste, Echium decaisnei which can reach 1½ metres in height, and the bright yellow Sonchus pinnatifidus which resembles a giant dandelion. Another yellow giant is the fennel, Ferula lancerottensis, also an endemic. Mesembryanthemum crystallinum is a big name for the small, ground-hugging ice-plant which is common in many parts of the island, once used in the production of a type of soda.

The bibliography at the back of this book suggests further reading on Lanzarote's plant life.

2CSK - THE LINEAR SOLUTION

We've worked hard to ensure that our routes are as accessible as possible, though Lanzarote's landscape means that on our long linear routes we inevitably find ourselves a long way from our starting point. Walks 10, 12, 16, 18 (unofficial version), 20, 27, 28, and 33 are just such routes.

The very energetic might consider walking there and back again, or you could plan bus connections for Walks 10, 12, 16, 27 & 28 while on Walk 33 you could invest in a taxi for the return. You could swap Walk 12's slog up from **Yaiza** or **Uga** for our Walk 13 circular route based on **Femés**.

2CSK is our recommended solution to the problem of accessibility on linear routes. Basically you need two walking couples/groups, each with its own hire car (2C).

- The couples/groups get together and agree which linear routes they will walk, and when.
- On the day of the walk each group drives to one end of the linear route, locks the car, and starts walking the route.
- When the two groups meet, you swap/exchange car keys (SK), and at the end of the walk drive the waiting hire car back to your agreed meeting point.

2CSK is the method normally used for the Tremesana/Timanfaya official guided walk, when the guides drive to the ends of the walk, swap keys when they meet, and at the end you return in the other minibus.

In practice, though, never underestimate the ability of the other group to become confused as to what they should be doing. You will only know if things have gone 'belly up' when you arrive at the end of that long route, having crossed with nobody, to find no car!

Among the things that can go wrong are:-

- The other group get lost and never find the other end of the route.
- The other group believe that you are walking a different linear route and start out on the wrong route.
- One, or both groups get lost during the route and miss each other.
- After swapping keys one, or both groups forget the car description, and/or parking place, spending hours searching for a car that fits the key.

These are the main causes of 2CSK failure though we are sure there are plenty of others. However, when it works, it's a great way of seeing otherwise inaccessible regions of the island.

The key to success is planning. Write everything down. Make sure both groups have a good map (**Lanzarote Tour & Trail Map**) and guide book. If you have mobiles, make sure each has the other's number. Write down the details of the other hire car and ask precisely where it has been parked when you meet.

If you get the choice of which end to start the 2CSK routes, then our advice is as follows:-

2CSK Walk 10. Start from the **Las Salinas** car park off the LZ701 to walk the route in reverse.

2CSK Walk 12. Start at **Femés**; a stiff unrelenting ascent but wonderful descent down to **Yaiza/Uga**.

2CSK Walk 16. Start at **Femés**, and after a stiff ascent it's all downhill. Be aware that it's very easy to miss each other amongst the wonderful bays and wastelands at the south of the **Rubicón** desert.

2CSK Walk 18. Either start point is equally agreeable.

2CSK Walk 20. Start from **Playa de la Madera**, then you're close to refreshments in **El Golfo** or **Yaiza** when you finish.

our rating for effort/exertion:-
1 very easy **2** easy **3** average
4 energetic **5** strenuous

approximate **time** to complete a walk (compare your times against ours early in a walk) - does not include stopping time

approximate walking **distance** in kilometres

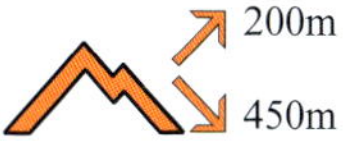

approximate **ascents/descents** in metres (N = negligible)

circular route

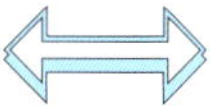

linear route

risk of **vertigo**

refreshments (may be at start or end of a route only)

Find information on how to access walks by bus (if available) at the start of each walk description.

Bus timetables can be found at the back of this book.. Please note that timetables are subject to change; check in the Tourist Offices or bus station in **Arrecife** on arrival for up to date information.

Walk descriptions include:

- timing in minutes, shown as (40M)
- compass directions, shown as (NW)
- heights in metres, shown as (1355m)
- GPS waypoints, shown as (Wp.3)

LOCATION MAPS

The Canary Islands lie approximately 100 kilometres west of North Africa's Atlantic Coast, and approximately 1100 kilometres south-west of the Spanish Mainland.

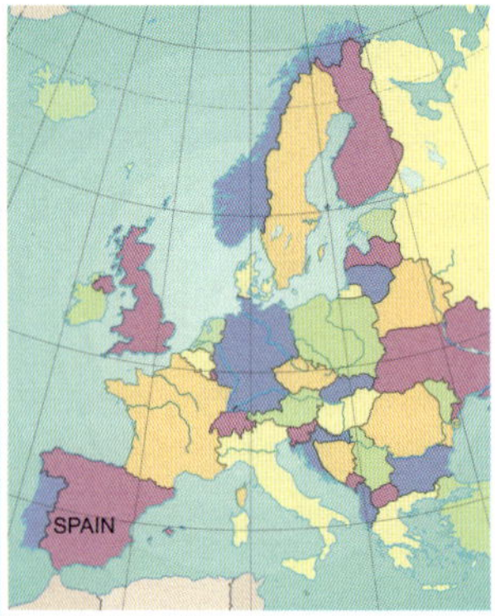

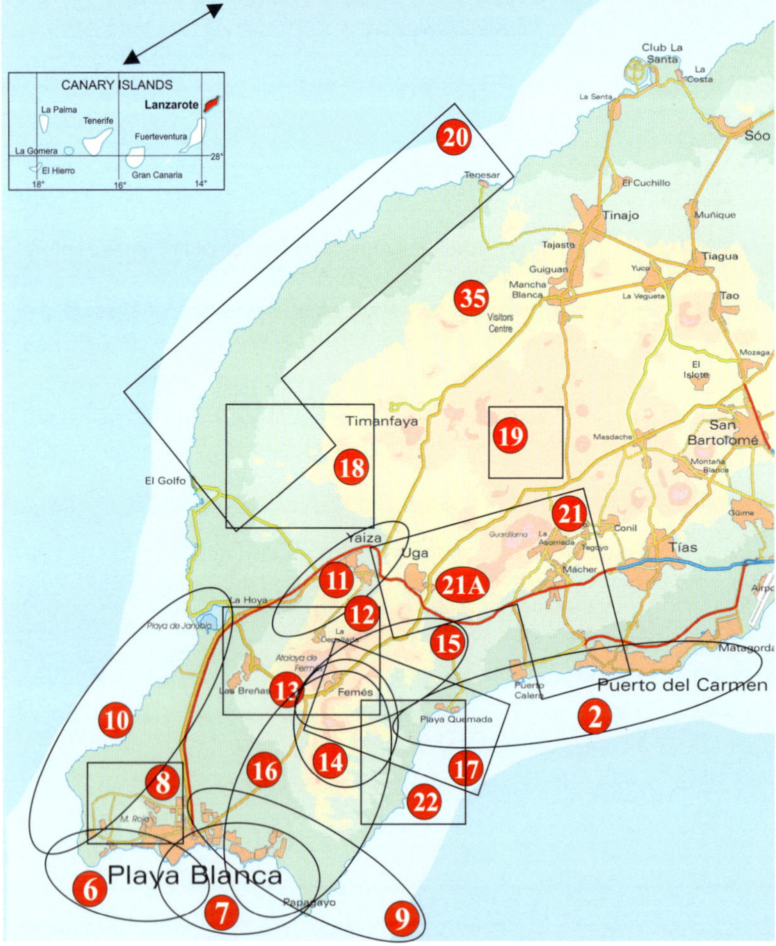

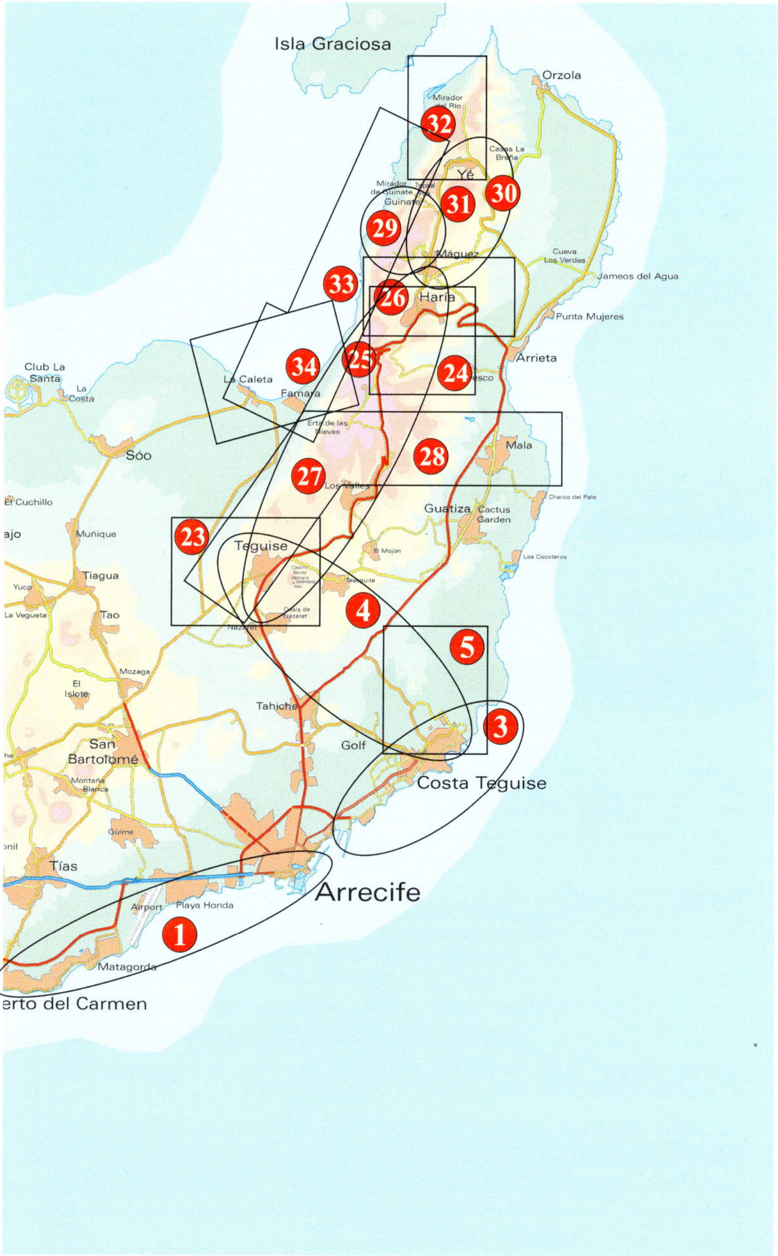
Isla Graciosa
Orzola
Mirador del Rio
Casas La Breña
Yé
Mirador de Guinate
Guinate
Máguez
Cueva Los Verdes
Jameos del Agua
Haría
Punta Mujeres
Arrieta
Club La Santa
La Costa
La Caleta
Famara
Erta de las Nieves
Mala
Sóo
Los Valles
Charco del Palo
El Cuchillo
Guatiza
Cactus Garden
Munique
Teguise
El Mojón
Los Cocoteros
Tiagua
Tao
La Vegueta
Nazaret
Mozaga
El Islote
Tahiche
San Bartolomé
Golf
Costa Teguise
Montaña Blanca
Güime
Tías
Arrecife
Airport
Playa Honda
Matagorda
1
3
4
5
23
24
25
26
27
28
29
30
31
32
33
34

The map sections used in this book have been taken from **Lanzarote Tour & Trail Map** (ISBN 9781904946540 on Map-Paper, ISBN 9781904946588, Super-Durable) published by Discovery Walking Guides Ltd. All map sections are aligned so that north is at the top of the page. In the interests of clarity, not all waypoints referred to in the walk descriptions are shown in the map sections. Dedicated map sections are produced for each walking route so that only the waypoints for that route are shown on the map for that route, making it easier to follow the route on the map section and to know where you are on the route.

Lanzarote Tour & Trail Map is a 1:40,000 scale full colour map. For more information on DWG publications, write to DWG Ltd., 10 Tennyson Close, Northampton NN5 7HJ, England, or visit:

www.walking.demon.co.uk **www.dwgwalking.co.uk**

Tour & Trail Map Legend

ROADS, STRAßE, CARRETERA, ROUTE

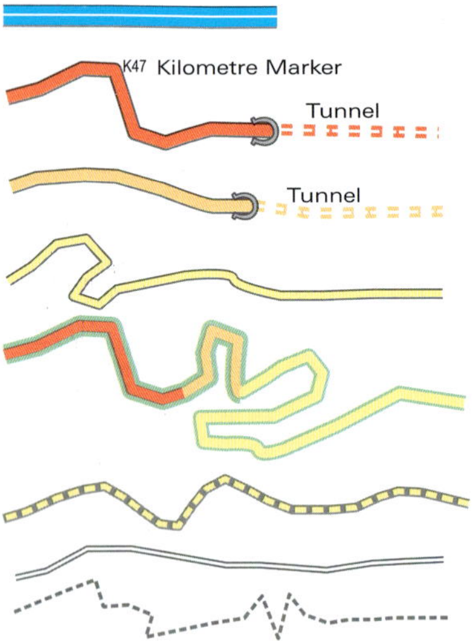

Motorway, Autobahn, Autopista.

Main road, Haupstraße, Carretera principal, Route à grande circulation

Secondary road, Regionalstraße, Carretera, Route

Minor road, Lokalstraße, Carretera, Route secondaire

Scenic Driving Routes
Landschaftlich schöne Strecke
Recorrido pintoresco
Parcours pittoresque

Narrow road, Fahrweg, Camino Rural, Chemin carrosable

Dirt road, Fahrweg, Camino, Chemin carrosable

Path, Fußweg, Sendero, Sentier

Walking Routes, Wanderweg, Sendero, Chemin.

ALTITUDE, HÖHE, ALTITUD, ALTITUDE

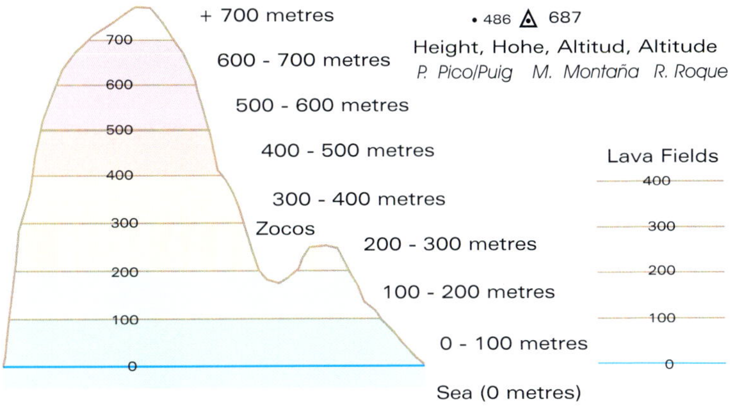

Lighthouse, Leuchtturm, Faro, Phare · Mirador · P Parking, Parkplatz

Tower, Turm, Torre, Tour · Spring · Information · Hotel · Petrol

Church, Kirche, Iglesia, Église · Chapel, Kapelle, Ermita, Chapelle

Picnic area, Rastplatz, Zona Recreativa, Pique-nique · Golf Course

Cemetery, Friedhof, Cementario, Cimetière · Bar/Rest

Sports Ground, Sportplatz, Campo deportivo, Terrain de sport

Camping, Campingplatz, Camping, Camping

Wind Turbine, Windkraftwerk, Eólica, Éolienne · Urban Area

Commercial Building · House · Important House · Ruin/Barn/Corral

Regional Boundary

WALKING EQUIPMENT

Lanzarote's climate and landscape can be extremely harsh. Remorseless sunshine combines with very low (zero) humidity, and a barren rock/lava/grit landscape covers much of the island. Protection against sunburn, sunstroke and dehydration should not be relaxed for even the easiest of routes.

BACKPACK

A 25-30 litre day pack should easily cope with all the equipment you think you will need for a day's walking. A design with plenty of outside pockets to give easy access to frequently used items, such as ½litre water bottles, is a good starting point. Well padded straps will spread the load and a waist strap will stop the pack moving about on the more adventurous routes. A ventilated back panel will help clear sweat on hot days and tough routes; a design with a stand-off frame is best for ventilation and worth the small increase in weight. Do spend time adjusting the straps so that you get the most comfortable fit.

As an alternative to traditional backpack designs, you might find the cyclist's packs produced by Nikko (which we use), and similar companies, a good compromise of stand-off frame, capacity, pockets and weight.

FOOTWEAR

While the coastal promenades provide easy strolling, the country walking underfoot conditions range from comfortable dirt tracks to walking trails, and some 'open ground' walking, on rock/lava, usually uneven. Whether you choose boots, shoes or sandals they must be up to the task. You will need a hard sole with plenty of grip and a well padded foot-bed. After wearing my Clarks sandals on the first day, and finding that my walking style was scooping up loads of grit I (David) used a pair of Bestard Race K shoes, worn with thick mountain socks, for all the remaining research. Bestard boots and shoes are not widely available in UK, but if you are on Mallorca call in at their factory shop in Lloseta. Ros completed all the routes in sandals, alternating between her Merrell, Cats and Clarks designs.

Whichever footwear you choose, do make sure that you have covered plenty of kilometres in them before coming to Lanzarote.

SUN PROTECTION

Lanzarote is famous for the intensity of its sunshine. Just look around at the 'booze and snooze' set to see examples of bad sunburn. Wear comfortable loose clothing and always carry a comfortable sun hat. Choose a design that gives you plenty of shade, is comfortable to wear, and stays on your head in windy conditions; we like 'Legionnaire' style caps which protect neck and ears too. As you'll be spending several hours a day outdoors, use a high-factor sun cream on all exposed skin and carry some in your pack for topping-up en-route.

We favour wrap-round sunglasses which, as well as reducing UV radiation, protect from getting grit in our eyes on windy days, of which Lanzarote has a surplus. When you do take a break sit in the shade and leave the sunburning to the 'booze and snooze' visitors.

WATER & FOOD

Dehydration, like sunburn, is a real danger on Lanzarote, particularly on the longer, more energetic routes. When the sand laden *calima* wind is blowing from the Sahara, humidity drops to zero and the wind leeches moisture from you. In these conditions you might not recognise that you are sweating, because the moisture immediately evaporates.

Always carry as much water as you think you might drink and have a long drink before beginning the walk. A couple of ½-litre water bottles, a few pence each from local shops, is the minimum, and add extra for longer and more strenuous routes.

Even on short routes, we advise that you carry some survival rations. Rural *tipico* bar/restaurants are mostly designed to cater for the 'coach potato' trade, and survival rations of chocolate bars and the like can provide welcome comfort when out in the wild.

MEDICAL KIT

Antiseptic wipes, antiseptic cream, plasters and bandage are supplemented by lip salve, which can seem like a life saver in Lanzarote's hot dry conditions. Also include tweezers, which you will soon appreciate if you catch a splinter or cactus spine, and a whistle to attract attention if you get into difficulties.

NAVIGATION

Don't compromise - buy the best guide book and the best map, and carry them with you. A compass is useful to orientate yourself at the start of a route and for general directions, but a GPS unit is far more useful - see Using GPS on Lanzarote.

CLOTHING

Choose loose comfortable clothing and add a lightweight jacket to your back pack; Lanzarote is justly famous for sunshine, but we were very grateful for our jackets when pioneering the Walk 15 'Femés Ridge' route; see photos. The island might be mostly desert, but it does rain sometimes so it helps if your lightweight jacket is waterproof.

OTHER EQUIPMENT

You won't want to be carrying excess weight during your walking, especially on the longer routes with major ascents/descents. Digital cameras generally weigh far less than their film equivalents, and a monocular is half the weight of a pair of binoculars. A mobile phone, and money (refreshments, taxis, public telephones, drinks machines etc.) are also recommended.

THE ROUTES, and SAFETY

There are plenty of routes to choose from in Walk! Lanzarote to suit a range of fitness levels, varying in distance from 3 to 22 kilometres and in walking time from 1 hour to the big 6 hour hike of **Femés** to **Playa Blanca**. However, bear in mind that the times given are the actual walking times that we recorded while walking the routes ourselves - you might cover the ground more quickly or slowly. Check your progress against ours early in the walk, and you will soon be able to estimate the time you'll need relative to ours. Also remember that the times given are for continuous walking, so you'll need to add more time for rest stops, picnics, admiring the views, taking photos etc.

If you are new to walking, or out of condition, then we suggest that you choose one of the coastal promenade walks (Walk 1, **Puerto del Carmen** to **Arrecife**, Walk 3, **Costa Teguise**, Walks 6&7, **Playa Blanca**). A couple of other routes will also break you in gently; Walk 19 to **Montaña Cuervo**, or Walk 23 around the old town of **Teguise**. In many cases, there's the choice of a short version of longer or more challenging routes.

To experience the strange volcanic desert landscapes, try Walk 10 on the **Rubicón** plain, or Walk 20 which combines lava fields with the coastline of **Timanfaya**. There are some beautiful beach routes, for example to **Papagayo** on Walk 9, and **Playa del Pozo** on Walk 22. If mountains are more your style, there's the easy **Montaña Roja** one hour route, or routes out of **Femés** taking in the peaks in this beautiful region; one 'mountain route not to miss' is our new Walk 35 **Caldera Blanca**. And if you thought Lanzarote was lacking in lush vegetation, we're confident that the routes in the north of the island, for example Walk 24 'The Forgotten Trail', our new Walk 25 'Barranco del Malpaso' or Walk 29 'Helechos Circular', will change your opinion.

Whichever route you choose, read it through a couple of times before setting out, and make sure you have appropriate clothing, equipment and refreshments with you.

SAFETY

- Don't attempt high altitude routes in severe weather. Be prepared to abandon a route and turn back if bad weather closes in.
- Don't walk alone - or at least let someone know where you are planning to walk.
- Wear appropriate clothing and footwear, and carry the right equipment (see Pages 26-27)
- Take frequent drinks of water.
- Shade is scarce on Lanzarote. Protect yourself from the sun.
- Start out early enough - allow plenty of time to complete the route before dark.
- Stay on the route. If it is impassable, retrace your steps.

1 COASTAL PROMENADE - PUERTO DEL CARMEN TO ARRECIFE

Since opening back in 2004 the coastal promenade linking **Matagorda** to **Arrecife** has been improved: the original boardwalk has been replaced by a broad tarmac path for walkers and cyclists along with the addition of seating and even a new 'thingy'. These improvements have helped make this Lanzarote's most popular easy walking and strolling route requiring no more than suitable footwear, clothing and sun protection. Beach side bars **at Playa Honda** mean you can conveniently stop for refreshment at the half way stage of the route. If you find 9+ kilometres of walking more than enough, your arrival in **Arrecife** close by the bus terminus makes it easy to catch a **Puerto del Carmen** bus back for your return.

The new 'thingy'

Access by bus:
Take the N°2 **Puerto del Carmen** bus from **Arrecife** and alight at the first stop in **Matagorda**, then walk down past the **Sol Lanzarote Hotel**. From **Puerto del Carmen**, alight at the first stop after the roundabout at the end of the beach road and follow the coastal pavement (west, and add 0.7 kilometres) or at the stop by **Sol Lanzarote** (see appendices at the back of this book for timetables).

Access by car:
When you see the **Sol Lanzarote Hotel**, take the road running down the western side of the hotel, **Calle Agonal** where we've always found plenty of on-street parking, even at weekends.

On foot from Puerto del Carmen:
Simply walk down to the sea front and follow the beach-side pavement eastwards to meet our official start. You can walk from the 'old town' on promenade and the beach road pavement, adding 5.5 kilometres and 1 hour to distance and time above.

From the end of **Calle Agonal** (Wp1 0M) we follow the broad beachside promenade east; this section was once a road, pedestrianised for over a decade now. An easy stroll - the whole route is easy strolling - brings us to a rotating 'thingy' (Wp.2 6M) installed since our first edition of this route. Our next feature is a lava tower (lifeguard and red cross station) shortly before coming to the start of the upgraded section of walkway (Wp.3 12M) beside a grey rock 'thingy' set in a roundabout at the end of the road.

Now we're striding out to leave tourism behind, past stone seats set in the lava wall to pass an aerial-bedecked building before coming to the end of the runway (Wp.4 19M), a popular spot with plane watchers, the big jets making an impressive sight when taking off over us. The original spring boardwalk has now been replaced by a broad tarmac path with cycle lane but still keep an eye out for errant pedallers. It's all easy strolling along between the airport on our left and the foreshore on our right to pass the 'cozzie optional' small beach of **Playa de Guasimeta** followed by *zoco* style sunbathing shelters as we start closing with the **Playa Honda** urbanisation. Our path brings us along to cross a wooden bridge over a gully (Wp.5) to come onto the pebbledash slabs of **Playa Honda**'s promenade and the welcome sight of **Bar Mercedes** (Wp.6 44M) facing the impressive sweep of golden sand; if you do miss this refreshment opportunity, there is another at **Bar Mesana** in a few metres.

The second stage of our excursion is along the sea front of **Playa Honda**, again once a road but now more popular as a promenade - except for those owners whose garages face the beach. Our broad walkway twists along the edge of the beach, passing a pair of houses on the seaward side pre-dating the current planning laws, and a clutch of bars (Wp.7) before swinging left to round a crescent of sand. Here you can short cut across the sand, though our choice is the easy promenade stroll around the lagoon inside the sand bar, passing another beach entry before a short climb is followed by steps down to continue on a crude concrete surface - funny how the worst section of the promenade fronts the flashiest houses.

Housing ends as the concrete swings inland as we come onto a recently finished section; being much easier than our original short cut across the beach past a true beach-house before coming back onto the official walkway. Back to easy strolling, we leave the sea for a while to pass inland of **El Cable**

Yacht Club (Wp.8). Keeping straight ahead, we go right onto pebbledash slabs and then left to come onto the wide brick paved promenade for our final section into **Arrecife**.

The broad brick promenade is built directly on the sea front rocks, waves crashing against the wall and spraying our route as we close rapidly on the previously distant **Arrecife** as we pass a seating area that could pass for a 'thingy'. Passing an extensive car park and **Biosfera** centre on our left, the neo-classical *Cabildo* building comes into sight on our left along with a large rusty 'thingy'. An easy stroll brings us up to the start of the thematic park though unfortunately the 'ships vents' waste bins are still un-emptied making for a shabby entrance to the island's capital. At a 'muse' (Wp.9), which you might mistake for a 'thingy', you could short-cut left across the park, though our full route goes on past the 'shipwreck' to the prow (Wp.10 95M) of the 'boat' theme park before swinging left around **Playa Reducto** to meet the road (Wp.11 100M), just to the right of the bus stops.

.. a seating area that could pass for a thingy ..

The muse at Wp.9

Arrecife had a rather scruffy air when we were researching the original edition but has been undergoing some renovations in the interim. The shops still close religiously for the 13.00 to 16.00 siesta; even so, strolling round the pedestrianised shopping streets where modern shops jostle with traditional establishments is an entertaining experience at any hour. Following the seafront road, on the pavement, we pass the refurbished **Gran Arrecife Hotel** (previously a notable eyesore) and yacht club before coming to the Tourist Information Office whose helpful staff can give a proper insight into the town's delights.

2 COASTAL DISCOVERY

Lanzarote's southern coast provides a popular walking route from **Puerto del Carmen** to the new resort and marina of **Puerto Calero**, an easy stroll, after which we continue on to reach **Playa Quemada**, a rather scruffy coastal village though graced by *tipico* bar/restaurants. Easy rather than spectacular, this route provides a good introduction to the island's countryside and is ideal as a stroll out, taking a drink in the new marina before continuing on to **Playa Quemada** for a relaxed lunch. Repeat the procedure on the way back for a laid back day's walking.

Originally a cross-country ramble on narrow dirt trails, this is now a truly manicured route graced with wide pavements/path and frequent stone seating as far as **Puerto Calero**. New crossings of **Barranco de Quiquere** and into **Puerto Calero** avoid the 'inland diversions' of our original route so making this a good strolling route for everyone with comfortable footwear.

Access by bus:
N°2 **Arrecife** to **Puerto del Carmen**, N°3 **Costa Teguise** to **Puerto del Carmen**, N°6 **Playa Blanca** to **Puerto del Carmen**. Return by bus N°25 from **Puerto Calero** (stops at **Puerto del Carmen**, **Arrecife** & **Costa Teguise**, see appendices at the back of this book for timetables).

Short Walk
To **Puerto Calero** marina and return (2 hours, 9 kilometres).

We start out from the old port at the western end of **Puerto del Carmen** (Wp.1 0M) taking the steps up by the **El Veradero Restaurant** to **Calle Los Infantes** which we follow to its end by the **Rincón Apartments**. From the end of the cul-de-sac we climb the rope-handrailed stair to come to the start of the coastal walkway (Wp.2).

Climbing the zigzag stair

It used to be an unpromising start, climbing up a steep rock bluff, but now the 'rope/slope' zigzag ascent brings us onto

a broad pavement which runs along below villas. Passing a couple of 'gazebo' style seating areas, it's an easy stroll above the sea to the end of the paving (Wp.3), continuing on a broad dirt path heading out into the countryside. Navigation couldn't be simpler as we follow the broad path lined with low posts that runs along the top of the cliffs, before swinging inland to cross a rocky inlet (Wp.4)

.. the broad path lined with low posts ..

Our route runs out of the inlet into a flat barren landscape dotted with squat-walled villas as the path comes back to the cliffs for us to pass an abandoned cliff-side villa (N°17) before coming to the lava-walled gardens of villas at the entrance to **Barranco de Quiquere** (Wp.5 30M), a veritable oasis when set against this barren landscape. Low lava walls protect us from the cliffs as we swing into the *barranco* to discover another major improvement to this route.

Crossing the *barranco*

Originally, crossing the *barranco* involved an inland diversion or a tricky scramble down to the its floor, then another tricky climb out and around the seaward side of the villas.

Now we have a gentle stepped descent before crossing the watershed followed by a steady climb up the manicured broad path; there's even a seat half way up if you want to take a break, plus a collection of stone seats just as we reach the crest beyond the last villa - now, how thoughtful is that?

If this is your first southern walk, allow yourself the luxury of taking in the distant views. Inland, the central massif finishes at the pass to **La Geria**, while the large building set on the final ridge is a *parapente* launch point. Depending on the winds, you might see whole flocks of these colourful fragile fliers gliding down to their landing strip inland from **Puerto Calero**.

To the right of the pass is the 'pencil-point' peak of **Montaña de Guardilama** which offers Lanzarote's most spectacular viewpoint to those fit enough to brave the ascent; our **La Geria** route (Walk 21) offers the opportunity to experience those lofty delights.

Ahead are the misty southern mountains which rise almost sheer from the **Rubicón** plain. The antennaed peak of **Atalaya de Femés** sits above the pretty village of **Femés**, our centre for some adventurous walking routes amongst the peaks and *barrancos* of this little-known region. Yes, there's plenty of exciting walking ahead of you.

Our broad path takes us along low cliffs set above a lava plateau foreshore before dropping into a small *barranco* and then climbing back onto the cliffs. Originally there was a myriad of quad bikers' tracks and trails across this area but the new official path offers easier strolling.

We come up to overlook **Puerto Calero** marina at a path junction (Wp.6 54M); previously we had to detour inland and round the streets before meeting the marina's **Paseo Maritimo** promenade.

On the Paseo Maritimo

Now we take advantage of the new stone path descending into the *barranco* to cross the marina access road onto the **Paseo Maritimo**; the *paseo* climbs up to overlook the marina as we stroll along to its main entrance. (Wp.7 61M).

Puerto Calero offers a selection of shops, cafes, bars and restaurants set against a backdrop of expensive nautical hardware; just the place for a leisurely break, whether you plan to continue on to **Playa Quemada** or simply to return to **Puerto del Carmen**. There's also the option of returning by bus from Puerto Calero on bus N°25 (via **Puerto del Carmen** and **Arrecife** to **Costa Teguise**, see the appendices at the back of this book for timetables).

For our continuation on to **Playa Quemada**, we take the **Paseo Maritimo** (0M) from beside the marina entrance. We follow this wide elegant walkway as it undulates along out past the marina, a number of flights of stairs giving access down to the foreshore before the walkway turns inland up to a T-junction (Wp.8 10M) at the **Hotel Hespería**.

The rock stairway before Wp.9

Although it looks like a dead end, we go left (W) to walk past the restaurant entrance onto a small rock headland with marine rope railing. We follow the rope down steps to cross a tiny artificial beach and climb a rock stairway that brings us up to the western end of the hotel from where we come inland beside the hotel to pick up a track (Wp.9) that curves up over the next headland.

The dusty track takes us into an undulating landscape, quite adventurous compared to the manicured walkway to **Puerto Calero**. Staying on the track, we head towards the coast. This is another area used by quad bikers, resulting in a myriad of tracks and trails. To avoid confusion, keep to the coastal track/trail as we go through a series of gentle ascents and descents to head westwards across small hills and shallow valleys; when a track turns inland a walking trail links us to the next track section. Only when we walk up a longer than usual slope do we come into view of the first houses of **Playa Quemada**; this point (Wp.10) is grandly shown as a trig point of 22 metres on military maps, but is hardly noticeable on the ground.

Following the track, we come to the first houses, the track becoming tarmac for an easy stroll down the first street to a small square. Then it's downhill past the beach front houses to a restaurant (Wp.11 32M) where you could walk down the beach front instead of the road. Cutting through to the beach, we stroll along to the end of the houses to come onto the tarmac as it heads inland to the **7 Islas** and **La Casita** bar/restaurants. Sitting on one of these terraces and taking refreshment, we can absorb the charm of this informal settlement of small houses and weekender homes. Some might describe its rather disorganised style as scruffy, but there's no doubting its quaintness. Just as the track to **Puerto Calero** contrasts with the path to **Playa Quemada**, so does this settlement's casual approach contrast with the 'organised' development of the marina; in one short walk we've experienced three contrasting coastal settlements; just pick the one that seems most agreeable to yourself.

Take your time relaxing before returning to the resort by your outward route.

3 COASTAL PROMENADE - COSTA TEGUISE

The massive **Barceló Suites Hotel** complex dominates our approach into **Costa Teguise** and rather sets the tone for the resort in looking somewhat well-used and being some distance from the sea. In **Playa Blanca** and **Puerto del Carmen** most of the tourist accommodation is strung out along the sea front, while **Costa Teguise** has opted to push inland and mixes tourist and residential developments; this means that you could be staying some distance from the sea during a holiday here.

As with **Playa Blanca**, both ends of the coastal promenade are somewhat isolated, so our route finishes with an inland section to take us to the nearest taxi rank and bus stop. You can easily short cut the final section of the route; see our Short Walk alternative.

Access by bus:
N°1 **Arrecife** to **Costa Teguise** and N°3 **Puerto del Carmen** to **Costa Teguise** via **Arrecife**; both routes stop at various points within **Costa Teguise** (see appendices at the back of this book for timetables)

Short Walk
At **Playa Cucharas**, turn inland at Wp.10 into the commercial centre and turn right on its inland side, for the short step to our taxi rank finish (4 kilometres).

Access by car:
On street car parking at the western end of the promenade and along the resort's main access road, plus commercial centre's car parks.

We start at the western end of the promenade on the turning circle at the end of **Calle de los Volcánes** (Wp.1 0M); plenty of on-street car parking despite recent developments.

Taking to the broad, brick paved, promenade we head east between the lava rock foreshore and smug seafront villas until we come to the stark seaward face of the **Las Coronas Hotel** (Wp.2) which has attracted the local graffiti artists and faces a rather poor piece of beach. We pass on to the much more inviting **Playa Bastián** where a paved walkway gives access into the resort, just before we pass a lifeguard/red cross station 'martello' tower (Wp.3 14M) and pass inland of the **Villa Toldeo Bar/Rest** to come to a pedestrian roundabout (Wp.4).

The remains at Wp.5

Ahead, a track leads into the resort's commercial centre as we keep right to pass to seaward of a development and then the **Punta Jabillo** hotel left and then beach on our right, marked by a fake windmill (Wp.5) - or it was a fake windmill until the big storm of 2007. Now it's just a fake windmill base.

Round the beach, we pass the **Neptuno Commercial Centre** and car parks before coming to the second fake windmill base (Wp.6 25M), another 'storm' casualty, opposite the **Nautilus Apartments**. The brick-paved promenade now changes to eroded pebbledash slabs, as we walk between the lava foreshore and a disused building site to round the point and come to the sight of two tall 'thingies' which dominate the bay.

At Playa Cucharas

The three 'thingies'

We are heading towards the resort's main beach of **Playa Cucharas**, as we come to cross the dock's access road at a roundabout (Wp.7); There are actually three 'thingies' at the end of the dock, two tall and one squat, their redundant decayed appearance rather summing up this section of the resort.

The scene is one of a pleasant beach fronted by crass commercialism combined with urban decay as we walk past another decayed 'thingy' and abandoned commercial premises before hitting a clutch of Brit and Irish bars catering for the volume tourist; these used to include the imaginatively named 'Sunburnt Arms' but even this bright spot has disappeared since our first edition. A short flight of steps (Wp.8) takes us up across a bar terrace to swing right in front of the scruffiest piece of seafront un-development so far.

Things improve - they could hardly get worse - as we come to the access roads and bars on our left and overlarge plumbing fixtures on our right; as a collection they possibly rank as a 'thingy'. At a junction (Wp.9 41M) a path goes straight ahead, our Short Walk option to cut inland and climb up to the **Cucharas Commercial Centre**, while we go right to walk around the final section of **Playa Cucharas** where the promenade devolves into rock and sand.

Across the sand, we pass the last breakwater (Wp.10) at the end of the beach to continue on a rough track between low dunes and the lava foreshore, the way lined with very old rope handrail fencing, to come onto the end of an old road (Wp.11 49M) by a breakwater. We come back towards the resort and the pebbledash slabbed continuation of the promenade to start curving around **Playa de los Charcos**. These are much classier developments than around **Playa Cucharas**, as we pass the fake windmill (Wp.12 52M) beside an inland lagoon which is part of the **Sands Beach Villas** development, known in a previous life as Lanzarote Beach Club.

Passing the breakwater enclosing the beach we come to the end of **Sands Villas**, and the end of civilisation as **Costa Teguise** knows it, to walk past an original windmill dating from the sea salt era. The promenade, now rough concrete, passes a bleak, fenced building site and finishes just before a sea front house (Wp.13). We head inland alongside the fenced site on a dirt road, passing a track off to more distant houses before coming onto the **Avenida de las Islas** street (Wp.14 63M). Heading left (W) we walk along the pavement passing the building site's abandoned development back towards civilisation, now passing **Sands Beach Villas** inland facade.

A taxi rank is our original finishing point (a 6 euro ride back to our start point if you don't want to walk), but you will probably want to follow our example of continuing to **Cucharas Commercial Centre** (Wp.15 74M) where behind the shabby facade you will find some decent cafés facing seawards, for some well-earned refreshment. If you continue along the length of this commercial centre you'll be rewarded by discovering **Helga's Patisserie** tucked away behind the tourist office in **Pueblo Marinero**, well worth discovering. There's also a bus stop nearby for the N°1, 3 or 25 to **Arrecife**.

From the western end of the commercial centre we simply continue along the main street, turning left at a T-junction to pick up the pedestrian walkway that will bring us back to the pedestrian roundabout at **Playa Bastián** (Wp.4). From here we retrace our outward route for just over a kilometre to return to our starting point at **Calle de los Volcánes**.

4 SUNDAY MARKET SPECIAL - CAMINO EL CHARCO

With the advent of the car, many of Lanzarote's commerce routes were upgraded from donkey trails to tarmac roads. When Lanzarote was first colonised, pirate raids dictated establishing the capital at **Teguise**, protected by the **Castillo de Santa Bárbara**. From here routes ran down to the coast; one passing through the small settlement of **Teseguite** and then straight down to **Salinas El Charco**. Refrigeration largely killed the sea salt market, but this old donkey trail route is still shown on some maps. This is one old route which still survives, though the new **Tahiche-Mala** road necessitates a short diversion through a tunnel.

Sunday is the day to walk this route using a 'market special' bus, seeing the island's busiest street market before setting out on the old 'salt trail'.

Access by bus
Sunday market specials go from **Costa Teguise** (Nº11), **Puerto del Carmen** (Nº12), and **Playa Blanca** (Nº13); see appendices in the back of this book for timetables).

Short Walk
To **Castillo de Santa Bárbara** and return, (ascents/descents 110 metres).

Our starting point is at the start of the access road to **Castillo de Santa Bárbara** (Wp.1 0M). If you are coming from the market, then make your way to the main road, cross over and walk up the pavement to reach our 'official' start. With the old castle above us we have a slogging ascent up the tarmac (SE) between storm-water eroded earth banks. As we ascend we are looking for a faint dirt track leaving the tarmac (Wp.2) which comes just before the road gets even steeper.

Gratefully, we leave the steepening tarmac to stroll along the narrow track between stone walls as it contours around the hill to come to cultivated fields contrasting with the generally barren landscape. Views open up over **Teseguite** and down to the coast as our track goes right to go around another area of storm-water eroded earth banks.

...views open up over Teseguite ...

Keeping to the main track (Wp.3), we swing left towards **Teseguite** to stroll gently downhill with extensive views expanding over the valley and up to the **Ermita de las Nieves** and radomes of Walk 27 'Capital Route - Haría to Teguise'

Our track swings downhill through the sunburnt landscape to bring us onto a tarmac street (Wp.4) and the first houses of **Teseguite**.

Teseguite might be a small settlement, but it can be confusing to navigate to find our exit route. Going left, we stroll down (NNE) to the second junction (Wp.5) marked by a 'palm tree' roundabout outside the cemetry, where we go right (E). We stroll gently downhill to cross over a village street, and pass **Casarino** on our right before coming to the next crossroads (Wp.6), where we go left (E).

It is downhill again to a T-junction (Wp.7) at the end of **Calle Revuelta**, where we go left and immediately right on **Calle Cadina** to come along to another T-junction (Wp.8). Here we go right to start our exit into the country. At a junction (Wp.9) with 'Finca Luna' signed left, we go right, and where the tarmac lane swings right, we go straight ahead on a dirt track (Wp.10), the **Camino El Charco** - well, we did warn you it could be confusing.

We head out into the country between stone walls, passing a troglodyte style hut (Wp.11) to come into an area littered by a 'rain of stones'. It's downhill on the faint track, and after it swings left and right views open up across the sloping plain to **Montaña Corona** with **Costa Teguise** peeking round its base. Water erosion has washed away sections of the track as cultivated fields start on our left, just before the track runs out at a triangular field (Wp.12).

To find our onward route we go right across the edge of the field to go through a gap in a 'pile of stones' wall to find a faint trail heading down towards **Montaña Corona** along a gully. We pick our way down the shallow gully between fields to come out into the open; ahead a pair of cultivated fields stands out in the barren landscape. Keeping the water runoff on our right, we are back to easy strolling, our trail crossing the runoff (Wp.13) and becoming better defined as we come to the cultivated fields. Now we simply keep straight ahead on the track, passing a pylon and then a 'bedstead' gated

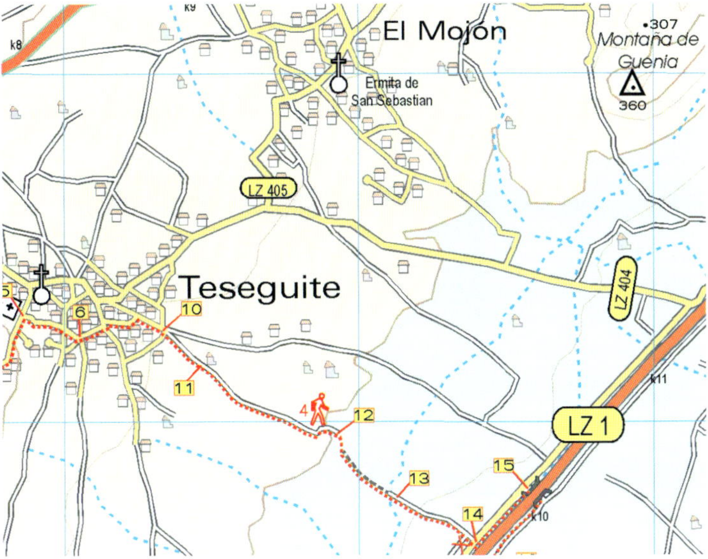

property on our right where the track becomes more used, to come down to meet the old main road (Wp.14).

Originally our route went straight across the old main road, but the new road is wider, faster and busier. To avoid any risk we go left (NE) on the old road to a tunnel under the new road (Wp.15) where we come onto remains of the old road. Going right, we continue alongside the new road on a track to come back to the line of the **Camino El Charco** (Wp.16). Obstacle passed, we are back to simple navigation as we follow a track heading towards **Montaña Corona** (SSE) and the coast, passing a minor track off to our left (Wp.17) and a pair of ruins before topping a rise where our track runs down to cultivated fields and a crossroads of tracks (Wp.18).

Coming down to the crossroads from the new road it is very noticeable how the land has changed. Above the main road the land is cheerfully barren, but below, it's as if this forgotten plain is cowering beneath the dominant heights of **Caldera** and **Tahiche**. Grey is the dominant colour, relieved a little by the spiny grey-green Lanzarote Fire Bush (Launaea arborescens) which dominates the long-abandoned fields in this harsh landscape.

At least it is easy walking, passing a minor track (Wp.19) as we come gently uphill past cultivated fields to the unexpected sight of a house. Passing the house (Wp.20) and then another track off left to a field, we walk alongside a stone wall to come over a small rise; views open up to the ocean, though **Costa Teguise** is hidden behind the bulk of **Montaña Corona**. We drop down to cross a water runoff (Wp.21) where a faint track goes straight ahead, while our track swings right.

It's a featureless *malpais* littered with stones, our track changing to a more comfortable sand base as we curve towards **Costa Teguise**. An easy stroll brings us back onto the *malpais* at a small rise which brings the sea and **Costa Teguise** into view.

Approaching Costa Teguise

Our track becomes fainter as we cross a small water runoff (Wp.22) and then come up to see our faint track running across towards the **Hotel Beatrix** reception. The track gets even rougher as we pick our way down to step gratefully onto the pavement (Wp.23) outside this large hotel.

5 MONTAÑA CORONA

While **Playa Blanca** has its **Montaña Roja**, **Costa Teguise** has **Montaña Corona**. Although the peaks differ by only 30 metres altitude, their natures are quite different. **Corona** might only be 232 metres high, but it is quite a tricky peak with a steep, pathless, final ascent and a slippery, shale-covered path descent. These two sections are joined by a ridge top walk around the rim of the *caldera* which might upset vertigo sufferers, and certainly should not be attempted in windy weather.

Those are the bad points, but for experienced walkers the views from the top fully justify the difficult ascent, and the ridge top walk is a pleasure for the confident. In windy weather, and for anyone unsure of tackling the ascent/ridge/descent, we have a low level short walk option suitable for all.

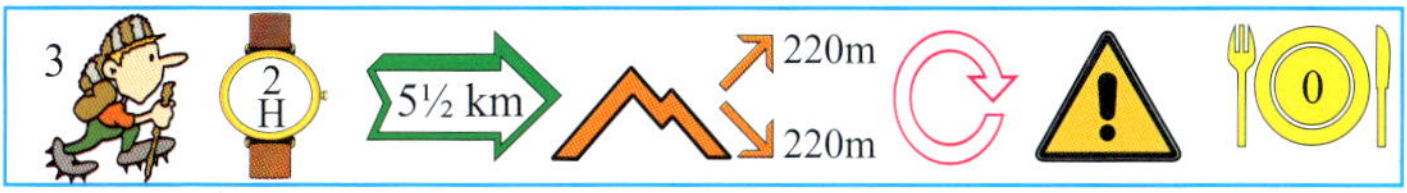

Short Walk
Follow main route to the trail crossroads at Wp.7, then turn right to follow the lower trail as it contours around the *caldera* to the trail crossroads at Wp.13; then resume the main route.

Access by car: Park on the road past the massive **Hotel Beatriz** before the road swings left.

Access by bus: N°1 **Arrecife** to **Costa Teguise**, N°3 **Puerto del Carmen** via **Arrecife** to **Teguise**, N°24/25 **Puerto Calero** via **Puerto del Carmen** & **Arrecife** to **Costa Teguise**. From the most easterly bus stop (near **Hotel Salinas** on **Avenida Islas Canarias**, off **Avenida del Mar**) take pavements approximately NW to the **Hotel Beatriz**. See appendices at the back of this book for timetables.

Starting out on the western pavement (Wp.1 0M), we walk away from the resort, a ruin ahead of us on a small spur as the road and pavement swing left to climb past a pretty valley on our right, contrasting with the harsh *malpais* elsewhere. The spiny aulaga or Lanzarote firebush (Launaea arborescens) and saltbush (Suaeda vermiculata) invade the pavement, slowly returning this failed urbanisation back to nature, as we swing right to walk through the largely barren *malpais* in a gentle ascent. On this uninteresting section even an old electricity junction box (Wp.2) merits a mention as we head toward the mountain. Our pavement climbs up to a crest, and as it curves left we step off onto a jeep track (Wp.3 14M).

Montaña Corona stands out clearly ahead

The track runs across open ground toward a gap in a stone wall. Passing a small trail off to our right (Wp.4), we climb up to the gap (Wp.5 20M) to find two large stone cairns which mark the trail to the base of **Montaña Corona**. It is easy walking along the trail to pass a large cairn (Wp.6) and stone designs, better seen from the peak, to arrive at a crossroads of trails (Wp.7 24M).

For our Short Walk, turn right here and follow the trail round the *caldera* to the large stone cairn on a spur (Wp.13).

Montaña Corona looks both big and steep from this viewpoint, so girding our loins we set off up the lower slope on the stony trail, easier as an ascent than descent. The trail zigzags, more for artistic reasons than for any practical use, as we take frequent stops on this 'puff and grunt' climb. Our path disappears as we come onto bedrock, those stone designs by the crossroads much clearer from this elevated position. Our ascent is not vertiginous in the normal sense, but is developing into a steep almost scrambling climb; face the slope not the views when taking a break. We come slowly up past small volcanic blowholes, heading for the highest point above us, until finally we come up onto the summit of **Montaña Corona** (Wp.8 50M).

After that slightly unnerving climb, we gratefully take in the extensive views. Although we are only at 232 metres altitude, the low plains give the impression of a much higher altitude. Thoughtfully the rocks on the summit make for comfortable seating allowing us to enjoy a break before tackling the descent.

From the high point our return route is along the rock ridge of the *caldera*, a far more comfortable open ground route than our earlier ascent. We set off, picking our way carefully over the rocks and edge round a large boulder (Wp.9); this is definitely a 'Stop, and look at the view' section of the route.

Montaña de Saga is a beautiful cone of reds and browns to the north of us as we cross a broad rock cap to the ridge (Wp.10) before negotiating a trench through the ridge by caves (Wp.11). We are now curving south and descending through rough terrain to the second height point (Wp.12 62M).

... Montaña de Saga is a beautiful cone of reds and browns ...

A grit/shale path leads straight down the slope towards the large stone cairn on the saddle below, the path zigzagging as it loses height but this is still a very picky, slippery descent before arriving at the crossroads of trails (Wp.13 78M) just above the big stone cairn; our short walk option arriving here from the west.

Most walkers now plunge past the cairn and down the slippery, picky, loose shale trail to the flood plain fifty metres below, but if like us you have had enough of uncomfortable descents then we have a slightly longer but much more civilised alternative. From the crossroads we go left (N) on a narrow trail which curves round the mountain to a faint path junction (Wp.14 81M) where we keep right to descend amongst the foothills as our trail curves towards the resort. A faint trail (Wp.15) goes onto a low rise as we continue down the small valley to cross its water runoff (Wp.16), where our trail is reduced to a trace crossing the flood plain towards a small cairn of stones (Wp.17 89M) where we meet the main path.

There are traces of paths almost everywhere on the flood plain, and the low ridges and big mountain offer no navigational sighting points; just the sort of country where GPS waypoint (or PNF) navigation scores highly. From the cairn we follow the sandy trail (SSW) to a junction (Wp.18) where we go right and then a path joins us from the left (Wp.19), shortly followed by a path off to our right (Wp.20). We keep straight on the main path to close with old stone walls lining the valley, where we start climbing gently up past terraces abandoned millennia ago; do not pay any attention to white painted supposed cairns, as these are land boundary markers. Despite carrying Alan's route on a second GPS we disbelieve the faint path going up by a wall to climb up onto a low ridge (Wp.21 99M) where **Costa Teguise** comes into view.

Ahead a path runs across to the wall (Wp.4 on our outward route) while we go left on a fainter trail to meet a stone wall (Wp. 22) where we swing right (S) to head towards the **Hotel Beatriz**. Our trail heads down beside a stone wall, getting stonier underfoot as we head for the ruin seen at the start of our walk. We come down to a corner of the stone walled field (sic) to take a path (Wp.23) which comes down onto a clearer trail (Wp.24) which follows a small stony valley. Our path widens to a track passing a path on our left (Wp.25) as the valley flattens out and our car comes into view ahead and we curve away from the water runoff to come back onto the pavement beside our start point (112M) at the end of our compact adventure.

6 COASTAL PROMENADE - PLAYA BLANCA WEST

Playa Blanca is Lanzarote's newest and showiest resort, but it is a resort of two halves, so for our first exploration we will test out the affluent western promenade. It's easy strolling on a paved promenade, although it would seriously benefit from a *tipico* bar at its end on the edge of the **Rubicón** desert.

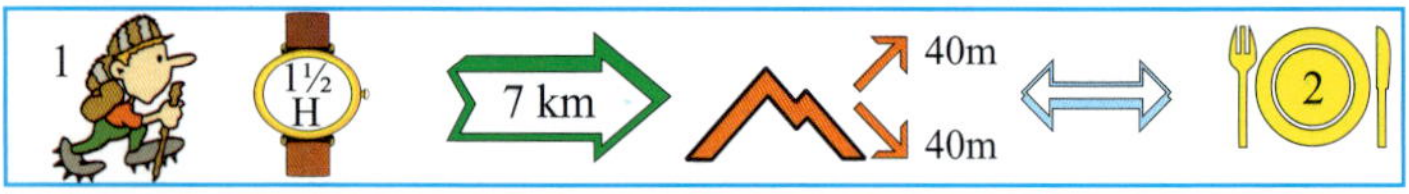

Access by bus:
Take bus N°6 from **Arrecife** via **Puerto del Carmen** or N°8 **Arrecife** to **Puerto del Carmen**, alight at the port bus stop, and walk down to the blue bar on the right where the coastal promenade starts.

Access by car:
Park either opposite **Centro Commercial Limones** or around the port area.

Extension

After the tourist commercialisation of the western promenade our route finishes in near perfect isolation - perfect, that is, if it had a cliff-top bar. If you wish to explore further then we suggest following the route of Walk 10 to waypoint 6 where we turn right (E) to follow the street through **Faro Park**, where there is a possibility of refreshments, and out onto the dual carriageway to the first roundabout with options A & B.

A: Going right, we follow the street to take the access lane to the *faro* where we rejoin our outward route.

B: Go straight over the roundabout; at the start of **Playa Bogardo** on our left, we go right on the access street to **Kamezi**. At the end of the street we walk round the western edge of the complex to come back onto the promenade near waypoint 8.

We start out on the promenade (Wp1 0M) to walk alongside bars on the seaward face of the commercial centre, now displaying a much smarter appearance than in the days before the promenade opened. The port slips behind us as the brick-paved walkway runs along the top of cliffs and curves right around the **Lanzarote Park Hotel** (Wp.2) and comes down to the beach and bars in front of **Playa Flamingo**. From the end of the beach we climb up to a viewpoint (Wp.3 15M) manufactured out of an old gun pit.

After the small climb it is up and down past the **Timanfaya Palace Hotel**, and its mini-beach, then it's past the new development of

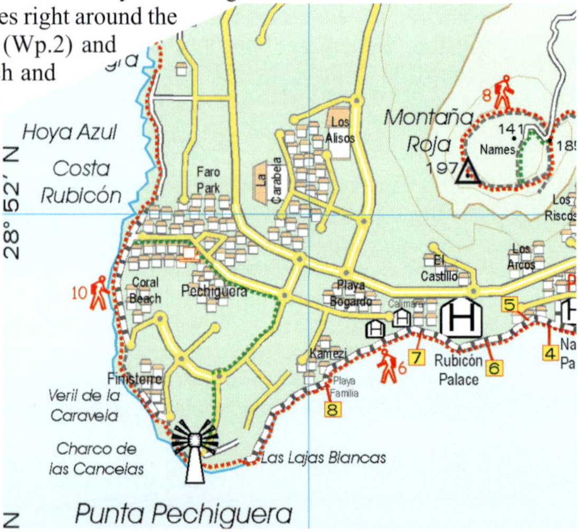

Playa Real, to stroll past the seaward visage of the **Natura Palace Hotel**, at the end of which is a walkway (Wp.4 28M) which leads up to the road serving the hotel, an alternative return route on pavements. A cute wooded bridge (Wp.5) takes us over a water runoff to start passing the extensive grounds of the **Rubicón Palace Hotel**, almost a town in itself if the size of its jacuzzi (Wp.6) is anything to go by. By comparison the seaward face of the **Hotel Club Calimera** (Wp.7) is a fussy collection of little *zocos* and tiny beaches festooned with 'hotel residents only' signs.

Montaña Roja stands out ahead

Putting the fussiness behind us, we pass another hotel before reaching the artificial beach of **Playa Familia** in front of **Villas Kamezi**, where the promenade finishes at the end of the villa development (Wp.8 44M) - well, that's where it finished when our first edition was published, but now the coastal promenade has been extended to take in the proposed new developments. As with many areas of **Playa Blanca** the money ran out leaving an extended promenade heading towards the battle-scarred lighthouse, being repainted during our visit in 2009.

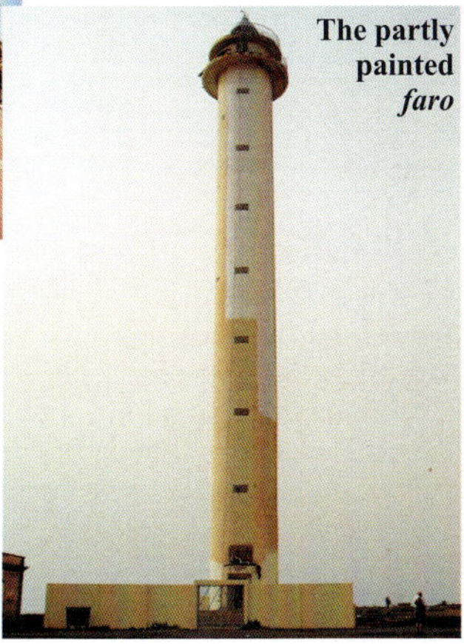
The partly painted *faro*

Strolling along this final section, we have views over the start of the **Rubicón** desert which has proved as tricky as quicksand for property developers' dreams of massive profits. We traverse the edge of the desert in Walk 10, taking in that crumbling monument to the foolishness of pursuing mammon in this desert, **Atlante del Sol**. If only that lesson had been learnt, the desecration caused by further failed developments might have been avoided.

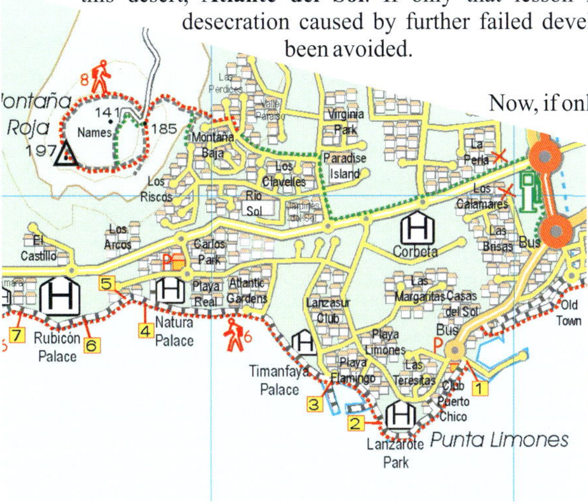

Now, if only someone had built a cliff-top bar at the end of the extended promenade, it would be the perfect easy stroll; failing such luxuries we return by retracing our outward route along the promenade and back to the port, refreshments and bus services.

7 COASTAL PROMENADE - PLAYA BLANCA EAST

Now completed, **Playa Blanca**'s eastern promenade offers comfortable strolling between the resort centre and **Playa del Afe**. There's plenty of seating along the way, the cliff-top seating overlooking **Playa del Afe** being notable, but refreshment opportunities are nil once outside the resort centre.

If arriving by bus and intending to head out to **Papagayo** on Walk 9, you can use this route to reach the start of the route.

Our choice is to drive to **Playa del Afe** and walk into **Playa Blanca** 'old town'. That way, your refreshment opportunities are improving all the time, and you have the option of a taxi back to your start if you don't feel like walking; starting out from the 'old town' offers the exact opposite!

Access by bus:
If not staying in **Playa Blanca**, take the Nº6 or 8 bus and alight at the second roundabout and walk down the road to a third roundabout, where walkways go down to link to the coastal promenade. Your route is as described below but in reverse. There's also the option of using the town's own bus Nº30 which leaves from **Playa Blanca** bus station to access the east of the town, thus walking into the old town as described.

Access by car:
Follow the road down through the third roundabout and head west. After going straight across three roundabouts take the next road right, go straight over two roundabouts onto the cul-de-sac serving **Playa del Afe** and our start is 150 metres away eastwards.

The eastern promenade finishes at the **Playa del Afe** (Wp.1 0M), a once-popular cozzie-optional pebble beach before development arrived. Note that, although the 'Playa Papagayo' blue sign points inland, the traditional walking route to this beautiful beach is along the **Playa del Afe** promenade to paths leading up the headland on the seaward side of the **Papagayo Arena Hotel**.

From the eastern end of **Playa del Afe** we take the promenade away from the beach to head uphill then a little dink left and a dink right sees us walking up past the seaward side of the **Iberostar Papagayo Hotel** to the cul-de-sac on our right (Wp.2) to come onto the plateau above the cliffs.

It's now easy strolling along the broad path to a junction (Wp.3) with **Castillo Coloradas** access and a road on our right where our view is held by the lava mountain, or 'slag heap', of the **Volcán Lanzarote Hotel**. Continuing on the path past houses, we come to a *mirador* viewpoint overlooking the **Rubicón Marina** (Wp.4 19M). Much vaunted as a millionaire's playground during its construction, the marina's reality is empty berths and a closed commercial centre, a nautical 'white elephant'. Down the steps (right), or slopes (left), we have a choice of following the paved walkway (our GPS track), or making our way through the shut marina.

Views from the promenade

The Rubicón Marina

Keeping to the walkway we pass the front of the **Volcán Lanzarote Hotel** plus some unoccupied premises before reaching a bar/restaurant (Wp.5) - important as it is the last refreshment opportunity if walking out from the resort - before we cross the marina's access road to come back onto seafront promenade (Wp.6) to continue alongside the lava foreshore, passing a house engulfed in trees (Wp.7) before coming back to hotel developments.

The promenade twists down to pass **Playa Coloradas** beach (Wp.8) and then climbs to bring the 'old town' into view. For the final stage, we are squeezed between bars and the sea, passing stairways up to the main road should you wish to escape at any time. Keeping straight ahead on the promenade we finally leave the bars behind as we come to overlook the port and the paved walkway swings right to take us up to the road (Wp.9 60M).

8 MONTAÑA ROJA

197 metres might not sound like much of a mountain, but located where it is in the flat deserts of **Playa Blanca**, this counts as a high summit. Easy way-finding on well marked paths with enough of a climb for a sense of achievement, this is a popular ascent, perhaps because it is such a contrast to the featureless resort development. A route for all ages; we were accompanied by a three year old boy and his parents on our latest visit.

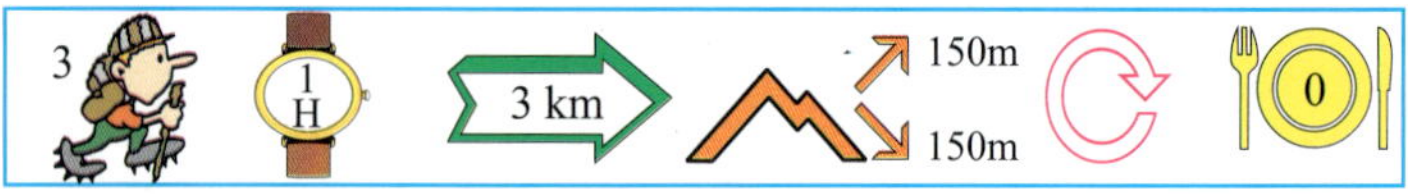

Short Walk option - this *is* the short walk.

Access by bus:
N°6 or N°8 **Arrecife** via **Puerto del Carmen** to **Playa Blanca** bus station, from where there are two choices. Either walk inland (N) along the main road to pass the CEPSA petrol station and go left (W) at the roundabout, strolling along the **Avenida Faro Pechiguera** pavement to the second roundabout where we go right on **Calle Francia** (N) to come gently uphill to **Paradise Island Club**,where we turn left (W) onto **Avenida Noruega** to our official start at Wp.1. Adds 2½ km to the route.

Alternatively, take the N°30 **Playa Blanca** town bus from the town's bus station (a rather roundabout route) to **Virginia Park** which is 2 stops after the school (Colegio). Walk south towards the sea for a few metres, then first right is **Avenida Noruega.** Check with the driver first as there are two different town routes, both number 30.

Access by car:
If you are driving, we suggest parking at the outer fringes of the development.

At last we are heading for the mountain, passing **Los Clavelles** on our left as we head uphill to the road junction alongside **Montaña Baja** development; drivers should park on the road in this general area.

The giant pebble points the way

The 'Al Volcan' sign (Wp.1 0M) points us up the road, to a street junction (Wp.2). Development scourge has meant that the old start to the path has been cut off by an abandoned development so we walk up the street to the end of the fence where the path now starts.

It's a dusty sloping path that winds its way up towards the ridge, passing a path coming from the left (Wp.3, and an alternative start route) and bringing us onto the broad back of the ridge (Wp.4 15M) to meet a dirt road coming in from the north.

Our ascent of Montaña Roja lies ahead.

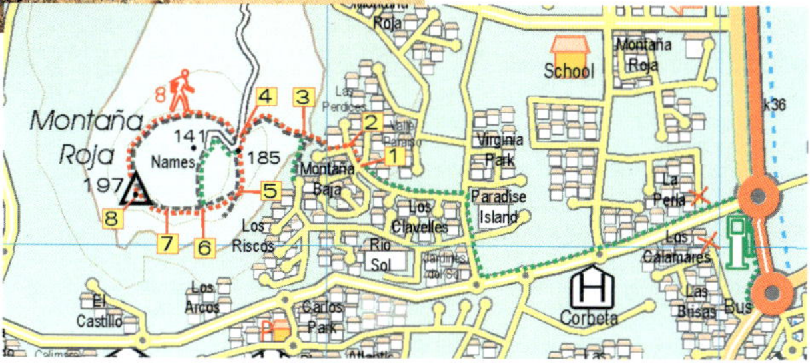

Stone names decorate the floor of the *caldera.*

Our choice is to go left to circle the crater clockwise, gently uphill overlooking a large array of 'stone names' which have been laid out on the floor of the *caldera*.

Following our ascent, we now have an easy stroll with views over the new hotels to **Papagayo**. At a path junction (Wp.5) we have an optional peak to visit on our left, or can go down to a saddle (Wp.6) where a path descends into the *caldera*, an optional steep short cut. Continuing round the crater rim, we have a climbing section alongside lichen-covered rocks to a saddle viewpoint (Wp.7) and then a moderately serious ascent up to the trig point (Wp.8 27M).

After the trig point we pass another saddle viewpoint, after which our trail descends, curving right and flattening out for an easy stroll along to the dirt track into the *caldera*. Now it is gently up to meet our upward path (Wp.4 40M) on the wide ridge, and back down the dusty trail to our car - or if using the bus, a longer stroll back into the resort or to await the town bus N°30 back to the bus station.

9 PAPAGAYO BEACH

Playa de Papagayo is one of the most photographed locations on Lanzarote, and in our view the one that truly lives up to its image when you arrive there. The easy option is to drive there, following the road signs onto the dirt roads on the southern **Rubicón Plain**, pay your 'gate' fee and park in the extensive parking area near the bars; you are then left with only the steep descent to, and ascent from, this cliff-enclosed perfect beach.

The easy 'car' option is eschewed by aficionados like us, who feel that the beauty of the beaches in this isolated region is enhanced by expending a bit of effort in gaining the reward. **Playas Mujeres** and **Pozo**, which we cross on the way to **Papagayo**, and **Playa Congrio** are also beautiful beaches with the added attraction of being cozzie-optional. So to make a day of it, take your cozzie - or not, as the mood takes you - and enjoy the best beaches on the island, their beauty enhanced by the barren surroundings in which they are found.

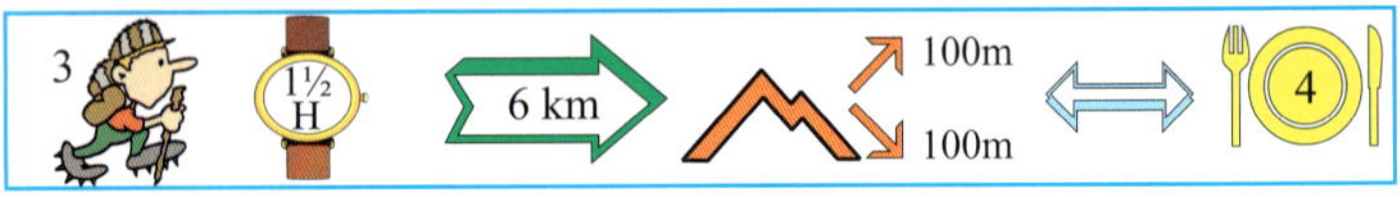

Access by bus:
Alight from the Nº6 or Nº8 bus at the roundabout after the petrol station, and walk down into the 'old town' to join the Extended Walk.

Access by car:
On the LZ2, go straight over the petrol station roundabout and the next roundabout to a third roundabout at the edge of the old town. Here, go left (there is no other way) to head east on **Avenida Papagayo**, keeping on the main road until you encounter blue (walker) **Playa Papagayo** signs; yellow signs will direct on the dirt road and 'gate' route for drivers. When you see the sign directing walkers onto a cinder track, blocked to vehicle access by large boulders, look for an on-street parking place on the road up to the **Papagayo Arena Hotel**.

Short Walk
To **Playa Mujeres** and return.

Extended Walk
Take Walk 7, Coastal Promenade - Playa Blanca East from the 'old town' to the start of this route and return the same way. When you reach the end of the last stretch of coastal promenade blue signs direct you inland to our official start point, but you could cross the shingle beach to paths that climb up the headland on the hotel's seaward side; see map section.

So many people have walked this route over the years, in all its possible forms, that we have literally a confusion of tracks and trails, most of which will eventually lead you to **Papagayo**; for a description we could simply say "Go east into the wilderness, and stop when you find paradise", but you probably expect a bit more than that. For GPS users, loading up our waypoints will be a great help, while PNF users with both track and waypoints will consider wayfinding a doddle. For those without the benefit of satellite technology, do follow our outward route; it may not always the best, but it's the way we arrived at paradise.

We start out from the street below the **Papagayo Arena Hotel** where a blue 'Playa Papagayo' sign (Wp.1 0M) directs us up a cinder track. Past the boulders barring vehicle access, we climb up to a junction (Wp.2) behind the hotel and take the faint track to the left to come up onto a featureless desert plateau - featureless except for the pointless trig point on our front left that supposedly marks the peak of **Papagayo**, but do not be drawn towards it.

Keeping to the faint track we come up a rise that brings the beaches into view, car windscreens acting like mirrors in the large car parks as our route curves right past a cairn to a faint junction (Wp.3) where we keep straight on towards the distant car park.

Papagayo beach

Strolling over the headland, we have various trails on our right as we come to the top of a steep trail (Wp.4) which gives us a skittery descent down to the back of **Playa Mujeres** (Wp.5 16M) beside the first car park. Walking across the rear of the beach behind the dunes, we pass the second car park (Wp.6) to a choice of a steep sandy path which runs up from the beach, or we can continue ahead up a sandy *barranco*, followed by an open-ground ascent over rock onto the next headland - our choice.

Cairns provide approximate direction markers to the start of a path (Wp.7) dropping down to **Playa del Pozo**, the path finishing in a small rock scramble to drop us onto the beach (Wp.8 30M).

Straight across the beach, we head for a path (Wp.9) climbing the sloping rock face onto the next headland. We climb up the path, the sand changing to purple rock as we come onto the headland, the car park now much closer as we cross a water-eroded gully (Wp.10) followed by an ascent, and crossing a second gully before coming up to the bars above **Papagayo** beach (Wp.11 45M).

Past the bar's generator, a manicured walkway is signed to the beach taking us between the bars. There's a choice of three bars for refreshments and, given their spectacularly isolated position, prices are very reasonable; regard a refreshment stop on their terrace as compulsory, and enjoy the views down onto Lanzarote's best beach. If you are planning on sunbathing, take one of the steep paths which lead down to the perfect beach, though take care on their slippery surfaces, and it will be (of course) an equally steep climb back up.

Playa Mujeres behind us on the return.

For our return we chose an inland wandering route from the car park, crossing those gullies higher up (much easier to cross) and taking in the wooden cross (Wp.12) and line of boulders before meeting the access track to **Playa Mujeres** at its junction (Wp.13) before rejoining our outward route at Wp.5.

There are so many tracks and trails through this desert landscape that you could navigate back by simply heading north and avoiding any pitfalls. If you do not have a compass or GPS, then use the trig point pillar as your general direction marker.

10 PEÑA DEL RUBICÓN

"Deserts have a strange unreality all of their own. Driving across the **Rubicón** desert, there's a sense that nothing has happened here in aeons; walking there gives an even greater sense of timelessness - it's easy to imagine that whole civilisations might have disappeared under the wastes of the world's great deserts. Our excursion is along the seaward margin of the **Rubicón**, passing some beautiful rock pools set in the lava foreshore, to the 'peña' of this desert, the long-abandoned **Atlante del Sol Hotel**, a monument to the foolishness of investing in the desert." - that was our original summary, though the foolishness of property developer greed is obvious amongst **Playa Blanca**'s recently abandoned developments, the **Atlante del Sol**'s dramatic isolation still stands as a monument to the failure of 'desert dreams' decades after its ill-fated construction.

Originally a 'there & back' walk, we've now extended it into a linear route taking in the desalination plant and **Las Salinas** salt pans before arriving at **La Hoya** to catch the bus back to **Playa Blanca**. An adventurous but easy route skirting the dramatic lava cliff coast between the wild Atlantic (on our left) and the **Rubicon** desert (on our right), it has a wilderness feel all the way until we overlook **Las Salinas**. Sun protection and plenty of drinking water are essential, especially in the summer months. It's best to do this route on a weekday as buses calling at **Rotónda La Hoya** are rare on Sundays/holidays.

Access by bus:
Bus Nº6 to the port in **Playa Blanca** and follow our western coastal promenade route (Walk 6) to its end where Wp.8 of that route becomes Wp.1 of this route; add 1 hour to your total time. Bus Nº6 stops at **Rotónda La Hoya** on both its inward and outward journeys between **Arrecife** and **Playa Blanca**; see appendices at the back of this book for timetables.

Shorter Option
To **Atlante del Sol** and return to the *faro* (11km, 3 hours).

Access by car: 2CSK Route (see P.19)
Given that this is a long linear route you might consider parking near the main bus stop in **Playa Blanca** and following Walk 6 to our official start - see Access by Bus - add one hour to our walking time.

Our start point is the western end of the coastal promenade (Wp.1 0M) where we step round the end of **Villas Kamezi** and cross open ground to come onto the remains of a tarmac road. At the end of the tarmac we go left on the dirt base of a new road, and then right on a smaller track to come to the twin light houses of **Faro de Pechiguera**, one small and squat and one tall and imperious, (Wp.2 11M). We work our way round the lighthouses to leave on a small path beside a low wall (Wp.3) which widens to a track which brings us up to a turning circle by the **Finistere** development (Wp.4 16M). Now we have the luxury of a promenade, but it doesn't last long and we are back on dirt track and trail until we climb over a boulder mound to come onto another turning circle (Wp.5 20M). Now we're back on a better financed promenade, strolling between foaming foreshore and lifeless houses before coming to the access into **Faro Park** development (Wp.6 28M). Shortly, in 190 metres, the promenade finishes along with the houses, and we have a scruffy little section before coming onto a track, then taking a minor track ahead when the main track swings right, to cross a water runoff and come to a junction (Wp.7 40M) where a track goes right to the tarmac access road.

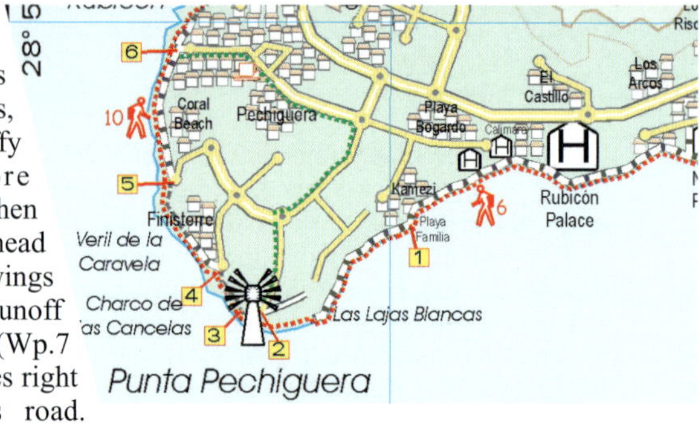

Continuing ahead, we pass an isolated house on its seaward side, the track ending for us to negotiate the end of the property's wall and a runoff before coming onto a trail paralleling the coast. Our trail widens to a track and views open up over the nothingness of the **Rubicón** desert as we head for another isolated house, recognisably scruffy even at this distance. As we close with the scruffy house, getting even scruffier as we close with it, the monstrous ugliness that is the **Atlante del Sol** comes into view. Approaching the house (Wp.8 50M), we find a motley collection of caravans and vans seemingly attached to it, and a street name 'Cala Malva 1', obviously owned by an optimist still awaiting the arrival of **Playa Blanca**'s outskirts.

As is the way of deserts, it's a surprise to find ugliness or nothingness, standing alongside something of great beauty - think of those **Papagayo** beaches backed by featureless, barren desert. It's the case here as, opposite the house, metal steps lead down the cliffs to a exciting lava foreshore containing beautiful rock pools.

From the house we continue along the track running above the cliffs, a branch going out onto a 'table' headland (Wp.9), the track becoming sandy as we pass a small lava peak (Wp.10), just after which is a bulldozed area where rocks have been heaped up and also a lava rock wall which serves no obvious purpose. It's almost as if we've passed into an illogical unreality as our track goes left in front of the wall while we go left on a trace of a track which soon peters out among the lava-topped cliffs. Ahead, our destination of **Atlante del Sol** seems close as we come inland to seek a route amongst the tracery of faint tracks and trails which dissect the rock-littered sandy desert.

We weave our way across the plain, passing a walled farm on our right to come on the unexpected sight of a swampy lagoon in front of the fire darkened shell of the hotel. Skirting the noisome waters we pass on the seaward side of the first wing and walk across the open ground to the far wing (Wp.11 78M) where we happen upon signs of occupation in the form of beds and a kitchen set up amongst the ground floor rooms; not our choice of 'weekender' accommodation in the shadow of the hotel's brooding ugliness, but then it takes all sorts!

'Peña' is strange Spanish word which doesn't translate well into English. The best we can offer is 'punishment' or 'inner pain', or 'torment', as when deciding between two unpleasant options. Standing by this financial and physical ruin that once was someone's expected boom town, the power of the desert and the ability of its nothingness to absorb even the best laid plans and investments is palpable. Of course there are now far bigger monuments to developers' greed littering the southern edge of the desert, but it's a chilling

thought that **Atlante del Sol** has stood abandoned for over three decades; how long will it be before the abandoned developments of **Playa Blanca** finally disappear?

Our original route, now our Shorter Option, is to return from here to the *faro*, but today we're off across the desert heading for **Las Salinas** and the **La Hoya** bus stop to catch a ride back to **Playa Blanca**.

From the hotel's northern corner (0M) we walk out over the open ground (approx. E) to come onto a faint track, just slightly more cleared than the surrounding desert, which curves away from the sea (E) and gradually becomes more track-like as we come into onto a well-used track (Wp.12 8M). That's the difficult navigation over as we turn left to follow the rough track (don't even think of bringing your hire car here) as it heads towards the coastline (NE). Its easy strolling along the undulating track which flattens as we progress, and splits for a short section before passing a *zoco* style wind shelter (Wp.13 21M); deserts have lots of natural features but anything man-made is a rarity, even a dry stone wind shelter.

.. Atlantic rollers crashing ..

With Atlantic rollers crashing into the lava cliffs on our left, this section can seem like strolling through sea mist accompanied by whale-like noises created by hidden blow holes, until we pass a second *zoco* style shelter (Wp.14 27M) our track now taking a northerly aspect towards the **Punta de Piedra Alta**, rather a grand name for a trig point set on top of the cliffs.

Just after our track divides (Wp.15 35M), you might like to walk over to the cliffs to see rock-climbing fittings that allow cliff mountaineers to absail down to the lava-shelf foreshore by the **El Convento** cave –two climbers were in action - very impressive - when we were last here.

Black cubist rocks decorate the cliff top plateau on the section before we come opposite the trig point (Wp.16 42M) to walk across the open ground and from beside the trig point (Wp.17) we have a superb view of lava shelf foreshore and sea-delved cave with the Atlantic rollers crashing over the shelf in a foaming mass, one of the most spectacular sea views on the island.

Back on our track, we head for the desalination plant directly ahead, after a particularly rough section the track smooths out for us to make easy progress. As we close on the plant the track divides, the right hand track is clearer but both sections will lead us up to the parking area from where we walk up to the northern face of the plant (Wp.18 74M).

Atlante del Sol to the desalination plant (5km) has been easy walking, but looking north towards **Las Salinas** we now face a broken landscape as the desert runs out. Despite first appearances, it is an easy section only requiring more concentration on where we're putting our feet as we stroll across (NE) to a track junction (Wp.19) where we keep ahead (NE) on a degraded rough rock track overlooking a small disused quarry; if you take the left fork at Wp.19 you'll be walking across the floor of the quarry to its wall of tumbled rocks where a cairn marked path climbs up to join our main route (Wp.20).

We stay on the rough track; in 120 metres a path goes down to our front left. We can either stay on the higher rough track or take the lower trail, both options rejoining 280 metres later (Wp.21) after the high route has come onto a better track which runs out at this point. Ahead of us (NE) is the welcome sight of a narrow walking trail snaking up and down, in and out, of the tumbled landscape. After all that walking on desert tracks it's very satisfying to be on a trail that's the only choice of route. We wind our way towards the small car park above the **Las Salinas** sand bar. As we close with the car park there are higher and lower options which come together again as we step off the trail at the bottom of the dirt road access from the LZ701 (Wp.22 97M).

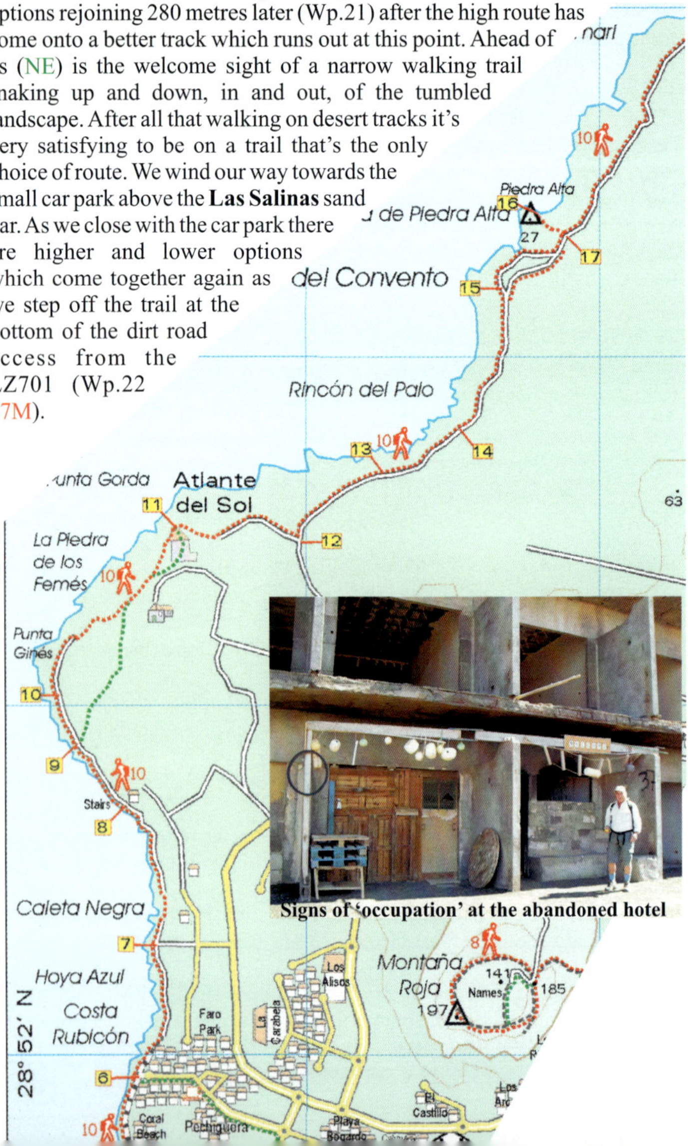

Signs of 'occupation' at the abandoned hotel

On the narrow trail towards Las Salinas

Below us, trails lead down onto the sand bar that protects the **Las Salinas** salt pans from the fury of the Atlantic, and across the bar to another car park on the far side. The bar runs down to an exciting beach but on no account should you be tempted to swim here as the currents can be treacherous. Across the salt pans is the inviting sight of a bar/restaurant that isn't on our route but you could be tempted into a diversion if the bus timetable allows.

It's been an interesting route so far and it would be good to say that the excitement lasts right up to the end but sadly, we're now into the boring piece of getting to the bus stop. You could try cutting across the hills up to the road but more straightforward is an uphill slog to the LZ701 road (Wp.23 105M), then turn north to walk along the road to the roundabout – be careful as although this is a quiet road, what traffic there is whizzes along as though its trying to outpace vehicles on the LZ2 main road. Across the roundabout, it's just 180 metres to the **La Hoya** bus stop and shelter (Wp.24 123M). If your timing and the bus schedule allows it is an easy stroll down from the roundabout to the bar/restaurant picturesquely situated overlooking the salt pans but allow a good fifteen minutes uphill return in time to catch your bus back to **Playa Blanca**.

11 YAIZA'S VOLCANIC GARDENS

To commemorate the devastating volcanic eruptions of 1730-1736, in which the **Yaiza** region suffered the worst depredations, the local government built an elevated walkway and gardens running around the base of **Montaña Cinta**. This makes for easy strolling combined with views over the town to the lava sea and **Timanfaya**.

Unfortunately, they forgot to complete the centre section of the walkway, thus requiring us to do a little traditional path walking to join the two sections. They also forgot to tell anyone that these gardens exist, so although tour buses park near our start, you are likely to have the **Volcanic Gardens** and their views to yourself.

Access by bus:
The Nº6 takes you into **Yaiza**.

Access by car:
Park off the old main road through **Yaiza** behind the church, where there is plenty of on-street parking and an official car park in front of the police station.

Short Walk
This is a short walk, but you can shorten it further by taking the stair access down to the old main road opposite **El Campo Bar/Restaurant**.

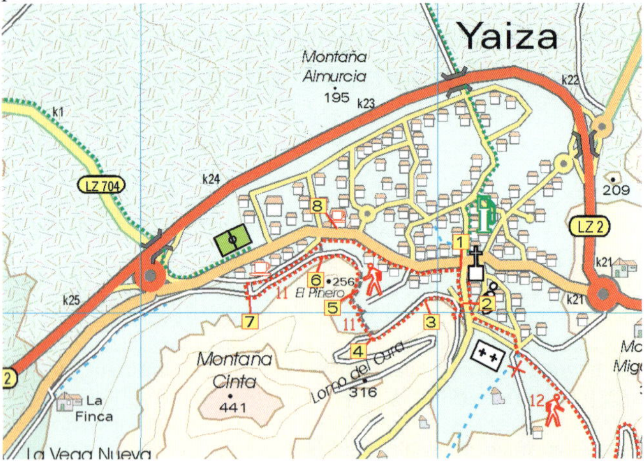

We start out from the church (Wp.1 0M) to walk south past government administration buildings (note the 'Educación, Cultura y Festivos' office on the left, where you may be able to pick up their 'Ruta de Cabellos' leaflet) to a multi-street junction with a confusion of traffic arrows painted on the roadway. On our front right is a lava wall containing planted gardens and a wide rock stairway, which we climb to come onto a broad red cinder track (Wp.2). The most energetic section of the route is already completed, as we turn right to stroll along the elevated walkway taking in the views over **Yaiza** town.

... views over Yaiza ...

Our stroll curves around the hillside to the end of the first section of gardens (Wp.3), the second section of gardens facing us across a valley as we continue on a dirt track along the southern side of the valley. The fields on the valley floor are edged with earth mounds, and at the end of the second large field (Wp.4 10M) the track continues ahead while we go right onto a path which runs along the top of an earth mound (NW).

Views to Montaña Cinta from the path

At the northern side of the field we swing right, dropping down to cross a gully between the mounds, and then left (NW) along another mound to come up onto a disused track (Wp.5). Going right, we come down the track, which narrows to a trail after an earth mound to reach the red cinder track at the second section of the 'Volcanic Gardens' (17M).

Aloes along the route

With the cross-country section behind us, it is back to easy strolling as we curve round the mountain to come above the **El Campo Bar/Rest**, where an access stairway drops down to the road (Wp.6); our Short Walk option.

Both sections of the **Volcanic Gardens** have been well planted,;the Aloe plants and Euphorbia varieties that line the track are particularly fine specimens, so it is a great disappointment when this planting runs out and the final section resembles a scene of crucifixion rather than a garden, with young saplings staked out to die without water on the barren slopes.

At the end of this depressing section a dirt track continues round the mountain to **La Finca**, while we go right (Wp.7 25M) down a steep track that drops us down to the access road for the outlying houses of **Yaiza**. Once on the access track, we head right towards the old main road and **El Campo**, passing some scruffy houses before reaching the main road where we choose to take a refreshment stop in **El Campo Bar/Rest.** (Wp.8 30M). Our return is to simply walk along the pavement, up to our starting point at the church.

12 ATALAYA DE FEMÉS - LINEAR ROUTE

Femés remains our favourite village on Lanzarote. While we have the option of driving into the village and ascending the **Atalaya** by our unique circular route, we recognise that bus travellers and classicists like the traditional linear route. This is a long energetic ascent, as after the first kilometre every step is upwards until we reach the antennaed summit, from where we have a choice of returning by the same route to our start point or descending to **Femés**; our preference. Then to return to your start, we suggest our **Atalaya de Femés** - Circular route, until you meet up with your outward route.

While this is one of the island's wilder routes, wayfinding is very straightforward. Virtually all the route is on clear tracks and paths, and if you do have any navigation questions, the answer is always 'uphill'.

*Distances are **Yaiza/Uga** - **Atalaya** 7 kilometres, **Atalaya** - **Femés** 2.7 kilometres, **Femés** - **Yaiza/Uga** 6.2 kilometres using the 'Circular' route.

Stroll
Volcanic Gardens (30 mins, see text).

Access by bus:
Route N°5 operates a limited **Arrecife** - **Femés** service Monday to Friday but you'll need to get up early; N°6 stops at **Yaiza** church on the old main road, or entrance to **Uga**. See appendices at the back of this book for timetables.

Access by car:
2CSK Route (see P.19)
Park in the car park near the church in **Yaiza**.

Starting from **Yaiza**.
From outside the church (Wp.1 0M) we walk away from the old main road passing public buildings on each side; note the Cultura y Educación office on the left; to pass a large public square on our left and come to the junction at the top of the square (Wp.2). Ahead the road runs on to **La Degollada**, while on our front right are the **Volcanic Gardens**, built to commemorate the 250th anniversary of the **Timanfaya** eruption.

Stroll
Climbing the many steps, you will come onto a broad walkway which curves around the hillside giving views over **Yaiza** to the **Timanfaya**; surprisingly this gem is little visited by tourists. (See Walk 11, Yaiza's Volcanic Gardens)

From Wp.2, we follow the wide road left (ESE). When the tarmac changes to black *picon* grit (Wp.3), take a break to look up; our eyes are drawn to the massive *lomo* rising up to the **Atalaya** peak, it looks big and distant - both are true, but don't be daunted in your quest. We have easy striding across a plain before the track starts climbing, steadily at first but then steeper as a 'puff and grunt' ascent up to a junction by a giant tooth (Wp.4), once a complete windmill but seemingly more diminished each time we pass.

Starting from Uga
We start from opposite the village road junction with one of those quirky Spanish road junctions where you go right then attempt to cross the busy traffic to go right, instead of the logical turn left lane; see map. If you get off the bus at the church walk out past **Bar Gregorio** then left, right, left and up to carefully cross the main road.

From the southern side of the junction a dirt road leads up around a large house to a junction where the left hand track is 'Solo Camels'! Keeping left, we come onto a fertile plain after which our track runs along a valley floor as the ridges rise on each side of our route. Stark farm buildings, including camel farms, line the track until we come to a track off to the right heading toward a huge molar on the ridge above us. We turn up the track to climb up to a saddle and then up the line of the ridge to pass the remains of the old windmill and join our **Yaiza** route (Wp.4).

There is plenty of uphill ahead so you might want to take a first break on the windmill saddle, with views west across the **Valle de Fena** to the **Volcanic Gardens** and east down over the rather scruffy camel farms, before tackling the serious ascent ahead.

Combined Route
From the 'tooth', our black *picon* track runs straight up the spine in a steady ascent. When the black track goes down towards the **Femés** valley (Wp.5)we keep right on a rocky track, and then keep right at a second cairned track (Wp.6) which leads down into the valley, our return route. We keep right and uphill at these junctions with the **Atalaya** coming into view ahead. Surprisingly, we have a small downhill section before the ascent is rejoined, sections of **Femés** coming into sight along with views over the scattered houses and plots of **La Degollada**.

Our steady ascent brings us up onto a plateau on the wide ridge and for once the walking becomes an easy stroll as we saunter past rocky outcrops. These outcrops provide enough moisture and shelter for plant life to thrive, in contrast to the barren landscape we have been walking through. After skirting the outcrops, and with the peak's aerials ahead, our track dwindles to a path across a narrow section of the ridge and a small descent before we face a stiff 'puff and grunt' climb. The steep climb - stairs cut in the trail would be most useful - brings up onto a trackless plateau where cairns guide us front left over to the start of a faint track which takes us onto the **Atalaya**'s access road (Wp.7).

Once on the broad dirt road navigation, which has not been at all difficult to this point, becomes simplicity itself. We head up the broad track climbing up through a zigzag to look down into a 'named' *caldera*. It's then a straight uphill slog to the peak's trig point (Wp.8) beside the buildings and aerials. At the far end of the buildings we find

... the 'named' ***caldera*** **...**

a stepped path leading down to a cave house, just the place to take off your backpack and relax. The two small rooms and plastered walls appear to pre-date the transmitters, and a path leads on to a second smaller cave also shaped for habitation.

Descent to Femés

From the trig point, **Femés** village square looks both inviting and deceptively close. Our descent is so straightforward (we just head down the access track) that no description is necessary except to say, take care. The track is eroded in places and has a loose grit/dust surface in others making for a skittery descent with the possibility of being unceremoniously dumped on your bottom; we know! We pass our upward route (Wp.7 8M) and after a series of zig-zags we pass a track going steeply down to our right (Wp.9). After the chained vehicle barrier (30M) we come onto a village dirt road (Wp.10) to go right and pass the bottom of the track we saw earlier. Reaching the village houses, we come onto tarmac/concrete streets where keeping straight ahead brings us into the village square and **Bar Femés** (Wp.11).

Return to **Yaiza/Uga**

Now, most walkers climb back up the access road to walk back down the ridge to

On the peak

their start point but unless you are a deliberate masochist who enjoys boring uphill climbs, then why not try something a little bit different with the start of our **Atalaya de Femes** - Circular route? It is certainly easier than the access road, and does mean that you are not repeating yourself.

We start out from **Bar Femés** (Wp.11 0M) by walking down the road (NE) away from the village. As the pavement ends (5M) we keep to the main road passing the lower section of the village on our left as easy strolling takes us down past a decorative palm garden before we come to a dirt track (Wp.12, 19M). We take the track to come above black *picon* fields and a hut (Wp.13 25M) just before the track runs out (28M) for us to come onto a narrow walking trail running behind the northern edge of the fields. A white painted cairn marks a small gully (Wp.14, cairns ahead of us marking our trail's route to climb up onto a spur of the main ridge. Across an affluent and the trail is less distinct, as we ascend from the corner of the last field (Wp.15) to cross another affluent.

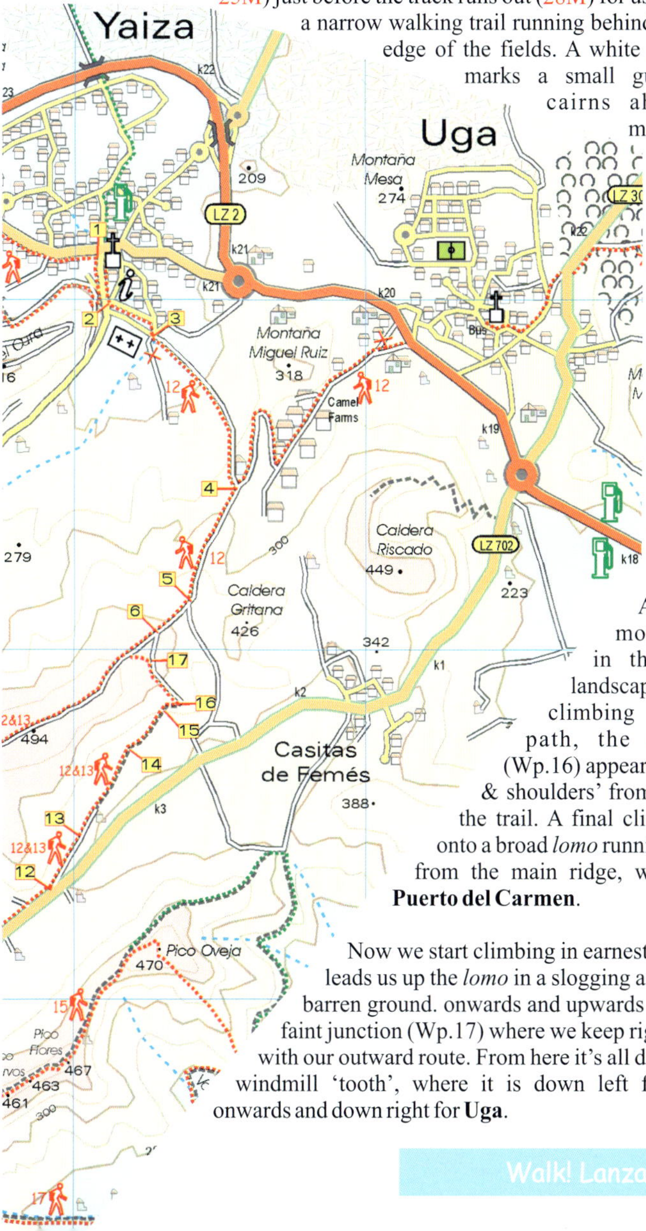

Across two more affluents in this furrowed landscape and we're climbing the cairned path, the final cairn (Wp.16) appearing as a 'head & shoulders' from lower down the trail. A final climb brings us onto a broad *lomo* running south-east from the main ridge, with views to **Puerto del Carmen**.

Now we start climbing in earnest. A faint track leads us up the *lomo* in a slogging ascent over the barren ground. onwards and upwards we come to a faint junction (Wp.17) where we keep right to connect with our outward route. From here it's all downhill to the windmill 'tooth', where it is down left for **Yaiza**, or onwards and down right for **Uga**.

13 ATALAYA DE FEMÉS CIRCUIT

Traditionally, the route up to the **Atalaya de Femés** is a linear one from either **Yaiza** or **Uga**, described in detail in our **Atalaya de Femés** - Linear Walk description. **Femés** is a beautiful village nestling in a fold at the top of the escarpment overlooking the **Rubicón** plain, easiest to reach by hire car but also accessible by bus. So here is our circular route up the **Atalaya**, definitely both the simplest and most interesting way of taking in the peak.

Access by car:
There's plenty of parking around **Femés** village square.

Access by bus:
N°5 **Arrecife** to **Femés** leaves the bus station at 8:00 Mon to Fri only, reaching the village at approx. 08.45. There's only one N°5 back to **Arrecife** from here at 18:30. See appendices at the back of this book for timetables.

We start out from **Bar Femés** (Wp.1 0M 373 metres, closed Thursdays) by walking down the road (NE) away from the village - yes, we are walking away from the mountain that we intend to climb. This seems more than a little crazy, but bear with us.

As the pavement ends (5M) we keep to the main road passing the lower section of the village on our left as we come to a bus shelter (12M). More easy strolling takes us down past a decorative palm garden before we come to a dirt track (Wp.2 19M). At last we leave the tarmac, taking to the track to come above black *picon* fields and a hut (Wp.3 25M) just before the track runs out (28M) and we come onto a narrow walking trail running behind the northern edge of the fields. A white painted cairn marks a small gully (Wp.4), cairns ahead of us marking our trail's route to climb up onto a spur of the main ridge. Across an affluent, the trail becomes less distinct as we ascend from the corner of the last field (Wp.5) to cross another affluent. Across

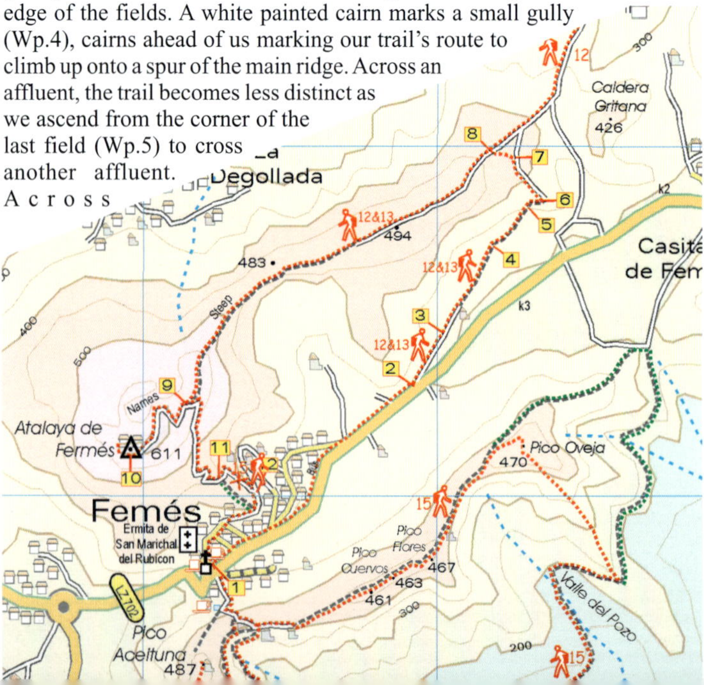

another two affluents in this furrowed landscape, and we are climbing the cairned path, the final cairn (Wp.6 44M) resembling a 'head & shoulders' from lower down the trail. A final climb brings us onto a broad *lomo* running south-east from the main ridge, with views over to **Puerto del Carmen**.

Now we start climbing in earnest. A faint track leads us up the *lomo* in a slogging ascent over barren ground. Onwards and upwards, we come to a faint junction (Wp.7). We keep straight ahead, but if returning to **Uga** or **Yaiza** swing right at the junction to connect with your outward route, the track dwindling to nothing as we cross the rock-littered open ground before coming onto the clear track of the traditional linear route running up the *lomo* (Wp.8 61M). Our steady ascent brings us onto a plateau on the wide ridge; for once the walking becomes an easy stroll as we saunter past rocky outcrops which provide sufficient moisture and shelter for plant life to thrive, in contrast to the barren landscape we have been walking through. After skirting the outcrops, and with the peak's aerials ahead, our track dwindles to a path across a narrow section of the ridge and a small descent before we face a stiff 'puff and grunt' climb. The steep climb - stairs cut in the trail would be most useful - brings us up onto a trackless plateau where cairns guide us front left over to the start of a faint track which takes us onto the **Atalaya**'s access road (Wp.9 98M).

Once on the broad dirt road navigation, which has not been at all difficult to this point, becomes simplicity itself. We head up the broad track climbing up through a zigzag to look down into a 'named' *caldera* and then straight uphill slog to the peak's trig point (Wp.10 107M) beside the buildings and aerials. Going to the far end of the buildings we find a stepped path leading down to a cave house; just the place to take off your backpack and relax. The two small rooms and plastered walls appear to predate the transmitters, and a path leads on to a second smaller cave also shaped for habitation.

Descent to **Femés**

From the trig point, **Femés** village square looks both inviting and deceptively close. Our descent is so straightforward (we just head down the access track) that no description is necessary except to say, take care. The track is eroded in places and with a loose grit/dust surface in others making for a skittery descent with the possibility of being unceremoniously dumped on your bottom; we know!

Descent to Femés

We pass our upward route (Wp.9 8M) and after a series of zig-zags we pass a track going steeply down to our right (Wp.11 23M). After the chained vehicle barrier we come onto a village dirt road (Wp.12 32M) to go right and pass the bottom of the track we saw earlier. Reaching the village houses, we come onto tarmac/concrete streets where keeping straight ahead brings us into the village square and **Bar Femés** (Wp.1 42M) with more scenically positioned refreshments available a short stroll away on the edge of the **Femés** escarpment.

Safe from the depredations of tourism is a region of barren grandeur comprising the **Higuera** and **Casita** barrancos. Fifteen years ago when we discovered this route it was little-known, though it's now become relatively popular with energetic walkers. The only development since we first walked the route consists of a basic refuge near its half way point. It might be called a refuge but it offers negligible shade, so set out well protected and with plenty of water for this adventure in the wilderness. Clear paths make for easy route finding, with the exception of finding our outward path by the goat farm.

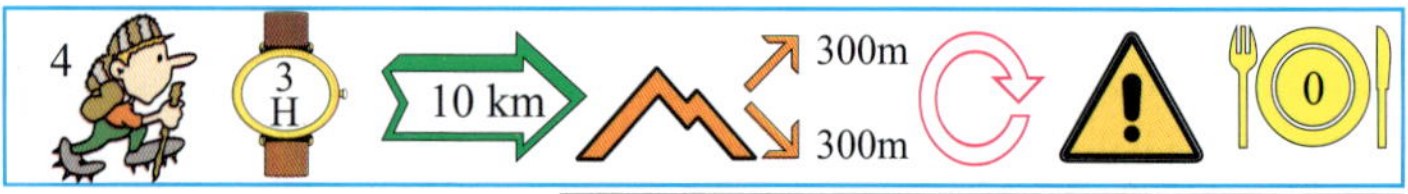

Short Walk

Follow the route in reverse to ascend **Pico Aceituna** and return the same way. 1.5 hours, 4 kilometres, 200 metres ascents/descents.

Access by car: park in **Femés**.

Access by bus:

N°5 **Arrecife** to **Femés** leaves **Arrecife** bus station at 8:00 Mondays to Fridays only, reaching **Femés** at approximately 08:45. There's only one N°5 back to **Arrecife** from here at 18:30. See appendices at the back of this book for timetables.

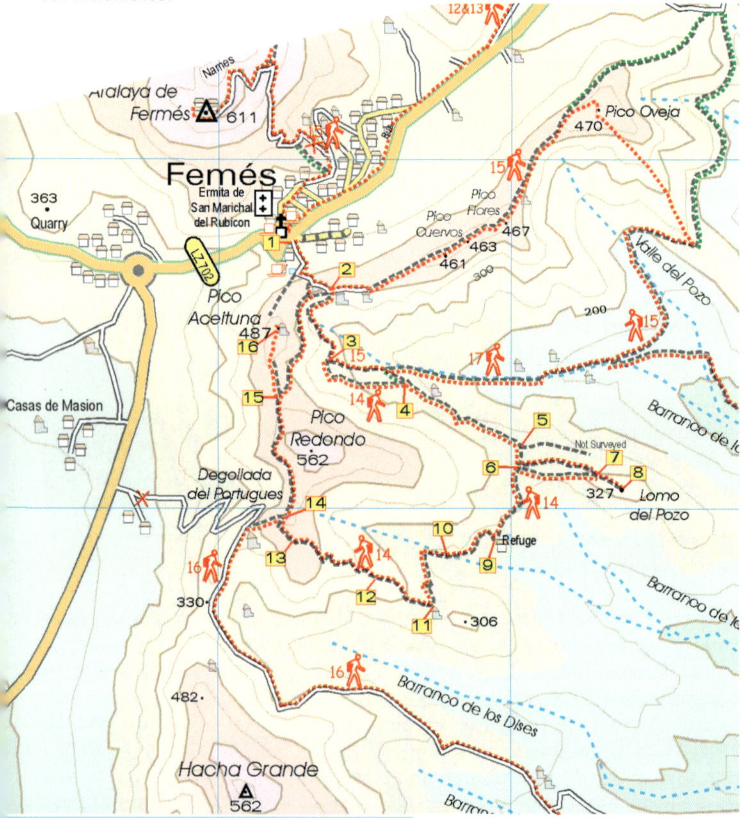

We start in the village of **Femés** outside the bar of the same name. Across the 'main' road we start out on a tarmac road (Wp.1 0M 376 metres) heading south (S) towards a ridge topped with an ugly farm. The tarmac soon gives way to dirt as we start a slogging ascent up towards the farm, passing two paths on our right before struggling up to the end of the track beside the goat farm on the ridge (Wp.2 7M) to look down into the **Barranco de la Higuera**. Here the ground is churned up by the goats which can confuse the confuse-able as to where the path is. Keeping the main farm and corral on our left, we step to the edge of the ridge.

The start of the descent

Away on our right is our return path, clearly outlined against the rock, while below us our dusty narrow path drops down into the *barranco*. It is a skittery descent on the loose, goat-churned surface, dropping past multi-hued rocks to turn below **Pico Aceituna** (and the return path) to start a zigzag descent down to a cobbled section (18M).

Now we are on an undulating easy section of path which heads towards an electricity pylon, **Puerto Calero** coming into view in the distance. We wind steadily downhill, passing Nicotiana plants struggling to survive in this barren landscape.

Passing a path to our left (Wp.3 27M) (our original route, and an option to finish in **Playa Quemada**) we start turning into and out of the affluents which feed the main *barranco* before we come under the pylon to step onto an old jeep track (30M). A path connects sections of the old track as we follow the line of the pylons; ahead we can see our trail's extension as we pass a path coming up from our left (Wp.4, our original route) before coming down to a second pylon. From the pylon, we ignore traces heading into the *barranco* as we start heading up the main path which climbs up past a crumbling corral and crossing an affluent before a slogging ascent brings us up past great swathes of Asphodels to meet the ridge's crest at a broad saddle.

On reaching the saddle we find a wide stone-littered plain, on our left another trace/path down to **Playa Quemada** (Wp.5) while our route continues ahead as a swept path through the rock litter. An easy stroll takes us over to a junction (Wp.6 55M) where a jeep track and a path head left (E) to the small peak of **Morro de la Loma del Pozo**.

Having come this far it would be foolish to ignore the extension to the *morro* (literally, the snout or nose) so we head out on the narrow path, an easy stroll until we close with the peak where the gradient increases by the first outcrop. The jeep track comes up to join us (Wp.7) - not that you'd want to drive anything on this track - for a steep ascent up to a pair of large cairns which mark the summit (Wp.8 66M). We return to the junction (Wp.6 80M) on the jeep track.

Back on the main route, we head SW on the path, the refuge coming into sight like a mirage in this barren expanse. Our path heads down through an affluent to bring us to the refuge (Wp.9 86M), perched on the edge of the **Barranco de la Casita**.

We give thanks to the authorities who have constructed a refuge in the middle of nowhere, and honour the construction with our presence for a break; if only they had put a proper roof on it to provide some meaningful shade.

Relaxing at the refuge

Relaxing at the refuge, we can appreciate the subtle variations of the rock hues in this arid environment, as well as contemplating the task ahead of us as we sit under the looming presence of **Pico Redondo**.

From the refuge (0M) we follow the path as it winds down into a gully, after which our path unwinds along the side of the big *barranco*, crossing a couple of affluents before coming into the ravine proper to run down to cross the line of the watercourse (Wp.10). Standing on the *barranco* floor, we appreciate that the next stage is of necessity energetic. All around us the land rises up to high ridges and to **Pico Redondo**, none of it vertical but all of it muscle-sappingly steep. Looking up the ravine we can see our next objective, the high saddle to the left of **Pico Redondo**, and very high up it appears from this viewpoint.

Our broad path angles up the southern slope before swinging left for a long traverse up onto the ridge which separates us from **Barranco de los Dises**, a 'puff and grunt' ascent up through zigzags bringing us onto the ridge by an old corral (Wp.11 17M 295 metres) to look longingly back to the refuge. Now our path heads straight up the ridge, getting rougher as we come up to pass a rocky peak thick with asphodels (Wp.12 343 metres). Ahead, our path zigzags up a steeper section of the *lomo*, yet another 'puff and grunt' ascent, taking breaks at each turn.

This relentless slog up the *lomo* is brightened by the flocks of goats of all shades and sizes that we always find on this ridge.

The goats are not quite pettable but give a bemused look at us strange bipeds who make such hard work of the rocky ground that they simply skip over.

... bemused goats ...

Eventually our ascent brings us up onto the saddle between **Pico Redondo** and **Hacha Grande** (Wp.13 48M 449 metres).

From the saddle, a narrow path curves right around the peak's western slopes to bring us above a goat farm set on a saddle fifty metres below us. We come down to a path junction (Wp.14 52M) where the **Femés-Papagayo** route goes down to the farm and dirt road. Keeping right, our narrow path, and a black water pipe, curve round a steep bowl (possibly vertiginous for some) past bands of soft hued rock before a short ascent takes us over a spur into a smaller bowl. **Pico Aceituna** is ahead as we come up past deep purple rock to emerge onto the saddle between **Redondo** and **Aceituna**. (Wp.15 72M).

Here we take a diversion off the main route to climb **Pico Aceituna**. A faint path leads up the lower slopes but soon disappears amongst the rocks. We simply keep climbing straight up, picking our steps over the rocks to come onto the summit (Wp.16) beside a large stone corral which has been built in this least likely location. From the northern end of the peak we look down on **Femés**, while the views over the **Rubicón** plain to **Playa Blanca** and **Fuerteventura** are a fitting reward for this small ascent.

It is possible to scramble down the northern face of the peak - possible, but not recommended, and so we retrace our upward route back to the saddle (Wp.15). We leave the saddle on a narrow path dropping down into the **Barranco de la Higuera**, our route curving round beneath **Aceituna** before climbing up to the goat farm ridge by a second building. We take a path down the slope in front of the building to join the dirt road for a relaxed stroll down to the village centre, where a choice of refreshment opportunities should not be overlooked; **Bar Femés** is closest and least touristy but also the least picturesque.

15 FEMÉS RIDGE

Femés is a favourite with us. Way back in 1995, our 'Hidden Barrancos' route pioneered walking in the **Higuera** and **Casita** *barrancos*, our route now appearing in other books and our subsequent routes being the basis of the new wayposting in this previously neglected region.

Femés Ridge is one of the few Lanzarote routes where you get close to a high mountain feeling, yet we reach the mountain peak in a relatively relaxed manner on a little-known path, plus some open ground climbing. We have magnificent views from **Pico Oveja** (Sheep Peak) over the southern peaks, before descending into the valleys. You cannot get that high - and that low - on a circular route, without the inevitable uphill finish; a long slog up through the old Majo settlement in the **Barranco de la Higuera**. Quite simply, a modern classic route for experienced walkers.

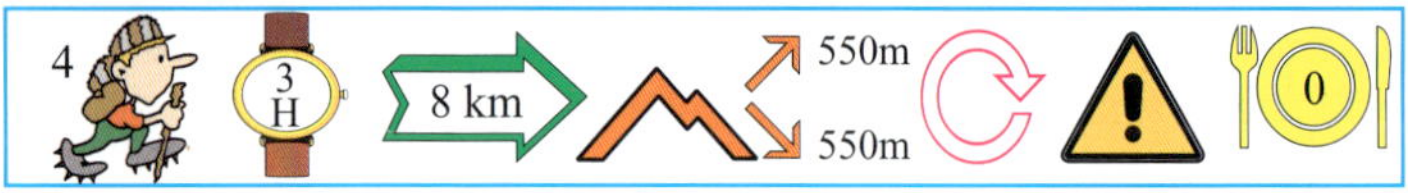

Short Walk
To **Pico Oveja** and return (3 Walker, 1¾ hours).

Access by car:
Park in the centre of Femés near the church square.

Access by bus:
N°5 **Arrecife** to **Femés** leaves **Arrecife** bus station at 8:00 Mondays to Fridays only, so you should reach **Bar Femés** at approximately 08.45. There's only one N°5 back to **Arrecife** from here at 18:30. See appendices at the back of this book for timetables.

Heading up the track at the start

From **Bar Femés** (Wp.1 0M) we cross the main road to head up the track, tarmac soon giving way to dirt, towards the ugly goat farm sat on the ridge. The slogging ascent up between the water tanks and past a trail off to our right brings us up to the farm's modern door entrance (Wp.2 7M), where we continue along the track (E) to head over a crest to a second farm (Wp.3 12M) with noisy chained dogs.

Timanfaya Fire Mountains ahead

The track ends as we continue on the northern side of the ridge following a trail - really a mere trace of a goat trail - to maintain height as we head towards the first of the peaks. When one trace finishes we simply step onto another, a path gradually emerging as we come below the first peak (Wp.4), a rocky scramble if you want to take in the views.

Black *picon* fields dot the **Femés Valley** below us, while ahead in the distance are the **Timanfaya Fire Mountains** (**Montañas del Fuego**), but no views south until the rocky ridge runs down to a 'rock free' crest where we step up from the path to marvel at the southern landscapes. Back on the path, we maintain height until our path starts running downhill to a saddle, the surface becoming rock-littered, slowing our progress before disappearing entirely in a maze of goat traces. From the saddle, we climb up to a boulder-mounted cairn on the ridge (Wp.5 28M) for more breathtaking views into the valleys.

From the cairn, we continue along the ridge saddle past a pair of *zoco* style small corrals, a faint path emerging as the ridge rises again on our right to **Pico Oveja**. Maintaining height, we see ahead that our current trail runs down, becoming more defined as it descends to meet a trail from **Casitas de Femes** on a broad saddle.

Now it's decision time. We could continue on the improving trail across the northern slopes of **Pico Oveja** and the ridge line before turning back into the 'hidden barrancos', all of it easy walking on defined trails (see map section); or we could head direct for the peak, a rather more adventurous option.

Being adventurous, we go uphill over open ground and goat traces, aiming for

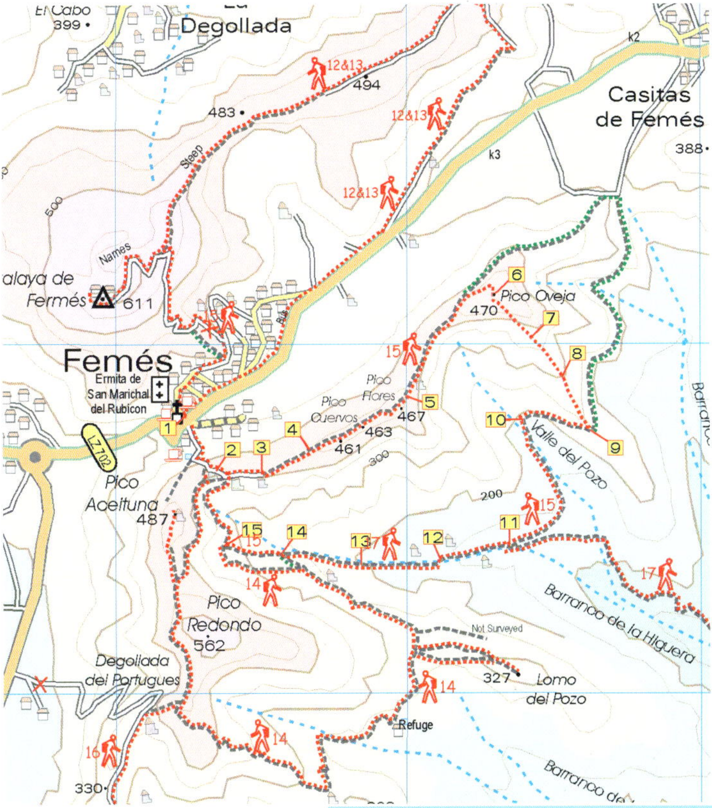

an old terrace; there are a few of these small boulder-supported terraces, but simply head for the highest one. Continuing diagonally uphill towards the line of the ridge, we cross another terrace before coming up to a low stone wall which runs up the ridge. Now we follow the wall until it gives out, from where a 'puff and grunt' ascent brings us up to **Pico Oveja** (Wp.6 55M).

Wonderful views fromPico Oveja

Stepping around the peak itself, we move from a comparatively gentle landscape to an orogenical one. After that climb it would be a waste to immediately strike off down into the valleys, and even though there is plenty of proof that the peak is popular with goats, we find some suitable ledges at a comfortable height on the southern side, on which to be seated while taking in the views.

From our vantage point on the peak we can see the trail coming over the saddle from **Casitas de Femés**, our first objective on the descent.

This is pathless country with a picky descent, steep in places before we reach the path, so if in doubt, return by our outward route to **Femés** or backtrack to the alternative path.

We strike off from the peak (0M) along the line of the ridge (SE) carefully picking our way down to where the ridge broadens into a rock-littered *lomo*. Keeping direction (SW), we stroll down the *lomo*, surrounded by superb views, to its 'nose' (Wp.7). The steep 'nose' calls for care as we pick our way down over loose rock and boulders. Taking a break on this picky descent we can see the trail from **Casitas** coming over a saddle, still a long way ahead and down from our position.

At the base of the 'nose' we look back at the line of our descent - it looks almost sheer from below (!), before resuming a strolling descent of the rock-littered *lomo* to pass the remains of a corral (Wp.8) and finally come down to the trail (Wp.9 36M), positively a 'walking motorway' in these pathless expanses. From here you could turn left for **Casitas** and return to **Femés** on the road, an easier but less spectacular route than what we have ahead.

Once on the path we follow it right, our route feeling comfortably luxurious after the *lomo*, to start dropping (NW) into the **Valle del Pozo**. After heading up the valley and gradually descending, we come down to cross a water runoff by an old stone wall (Wp.10 41M). Across the runoff, our trail swings left (SSE) down towards the main valley and a line of small electricity pylons. Our faint path crosses another runoff and follows old stone walls, this section giving a wonderful sense of spaciousness as we stroll down to cross more runoffs before swinging right (SSW) into the main valley where we come alongside a jeep track, which our path joins by an electricity pylon (Wp.11 52M).

We've been descending continuously for nearly an hour, and now we face the consequences in the form of a long uphill slog along the **Barranco de la Higuera**. Setting off from the pylon we follow the jeep track beside the broad water runoff. As we climb this relentless ascent, we start to pass old corrals and stone walls before crossing the runoff (Wp.12) which now becomes a small gorge on our right. Technically, the jeep track should be an easy section of our route, but it doesn't feel like it as we labour up past pylons, corrals and stone walls before crossing an affluent (Wp.13) which brings the hideous goat farms into view high up on the ridge ahead; and before you ask the answer is, 'Yes, we *do* have to climb up there!'.

The remains of corrals and buildings litter the valley floor, some thought to be remains of Majo settlements (the eastern Canary Islands' equivalent of the western islands' Guanches), pre-dating the Spanish invasion. A second division of this agricultural settlement was based around the mouth of the *barranco* at **Playa del Pozo**. There have been some archaeological investigations made of these ruins; their Majo heritage seems well proven.

We keep slogging up the rough jeep track, passing a trail off to our left (our original route in 'The Hidden Barrancos') (Wp.14) and crossing an affluent where the track swings up to our left and we continue ahead on a clear trail.

The path junction at 94 minutes

This trail climbs steeply up to join our 'Hidden Barrancos' route at a path junction (Wp.15 94M) which provides us with a good place to take a break before tackling the final ascent up to the farms.

From the junction, our narrow trail climbs steeply (N), though this style of ascent is more pleasing than the jeep track, and is enlivened by the wonderful geological examples that we pass before finally emerging from the head of the *barranco* beside the farm (110M). After that long and energetic ascent, we stumble back down the dirt track and across the road to fall into **Bar Femés** (Wp.1 115M) for some well-earned refreshment, where we can re-live the wonders of this modern classic that we've just completed.

16 FEMÉS TO PLAYA BLANCA

The long route out of **Playa Blanca** via **Papagayo** beach and up the dirt track to the **Degollada del Portugués**, followed by path and track into **Femés**, is one of Lanzarote's classic long distance routes. As with many of the island's long linear routes, accessibility is a problem. After an initial climb out of **Femés** we skirt around **Pico Aceituna** on our 'Hidden Barrancos' route (Walk 14) in reverse, before dropping down to the **Degollada del Portugués**. From this pass, we stroll down a dirt track to emerge from the mountains onto the far south of the **Rubicón** desert plain. Our official route then wanders along the coast, with the opportunity of testing the famous beaches of this region, before heading into **Playa Blanca** on the return route of Walk 9 and Walk 7 to reach the 'old town'.

Both Noel Rochford (Landscapes) and Paddy Dillon (Cicerone) describe this route as an energetic uphill from **Playa Blanca**. Why they should choose to travel this route by the most difficult approach is a mystery to us.

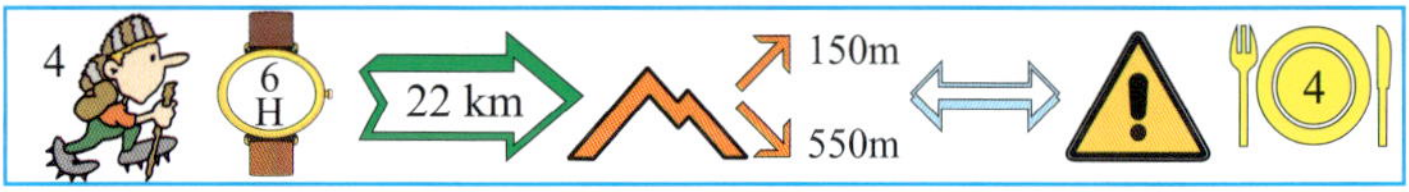

Fine views on the descent

Access from Playa Blanca: taxi to **Femés**.

Access by bus:
N°5 **Arrecife-Femés** leaves at 8:00 Mondays to Fridays only, so you should reach **Bar Femés** at approximately 08.45. There's a regular N°6 services back from **Playa Blanca** to **Arrecife** via **Puerto del Carmen**. See appendices at the back of this book for timetables.

Access by car: drive to **Femés**, and park by the village square and taxi back from **Playa Blanca**.

2CSK Route (see P.19) though make sure you start from **Femés** end of the route. Park the lower car as described for Walk 9 'Papagayo Beach', and reduce distance to 19 kilometres.

We start out from **Bar Femés** (Wp.1 0M); if you're walking our routes in order, you'll be a well-known regular in this little bar by now. Following Walks 14 & 15 up onto the ridge, we then take Walk 14 in reverse (Wp.2 11M) to come onto the pass between **Pico Aceituna** and **Pico Redondo** (Wp.3 24M). The path below **Pico Redondo** is a little trickier, and might cause vertigo sufferers a little trouble, before reaching the path junction (Wp.4) above the goat farm, where we follow the black water pipe down past the farm and onto the **Degollada del Portugués** (Wp.5 43M). A track, barred to vehicle access, climbs up from the **Rubicón** desert plain through a series of zigzags before crossing the *degollada* to run down the **Barranco de los Dises**. We stroll down the track, passing another *degollada* viewpoint at the head of the *barranco* before coming under the bulk of **Hacha Grande** to snake in and out

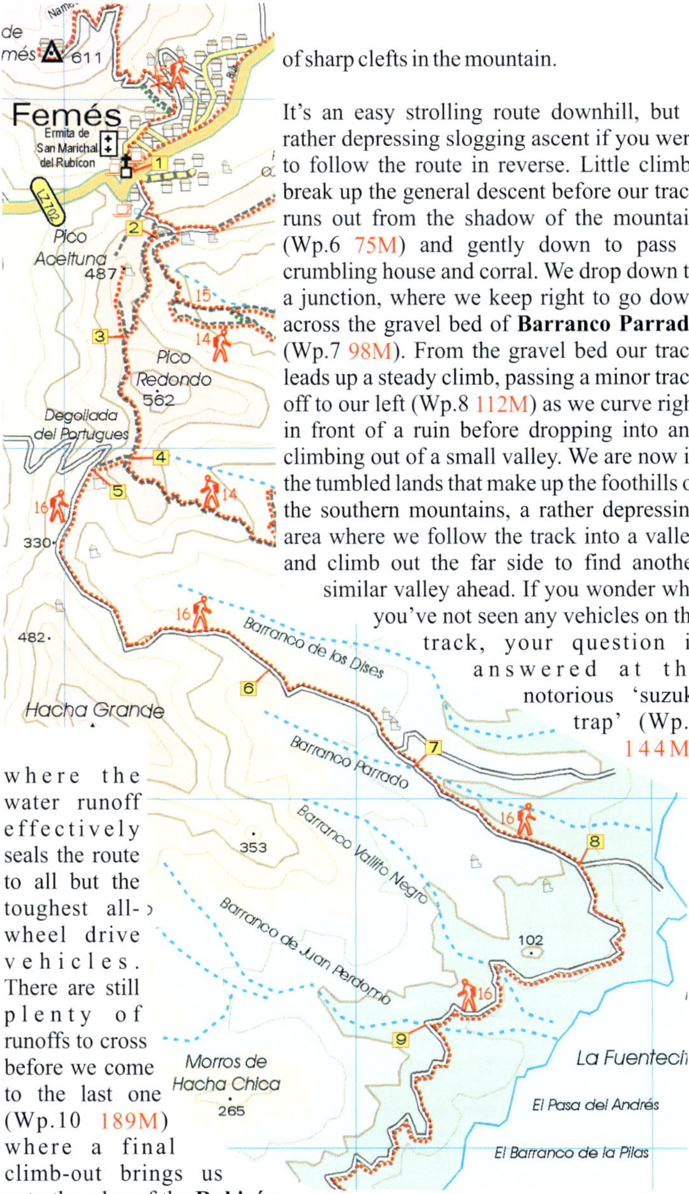

of sharp clefts in the mountain.

It's an easy strolling route downhill, but a rather depressing slogging ascent if you were to follow the route in reverse. Little climbs break up the general descent before our track runs out from the shadow of the mountain (Wp.6 75M) and gently down to pass a crumbling house and corral. We drop down to a junction, where we keep right to go down across the gravel bed of **Barranco Parrado** (Wp.7 98M). From the gravel bed our track leads up a steady climb, passing a minor track off to our left (Wp.8 112M) as we curve right in front of a ruin before dropping into and climbing out of a small valley. We are now in the tumbled lands that make up the foothills of the southern mountains, a rather depressing area where we follow the track into a valley and climb out the far side to find another similar valley ahead. If you wonder why you've not seen any vehicles on the track, your question is answered at the notorious 'suzuki trap' (Wp.9 144M) where the water runoff effectively seals the route to all but the toughest all-wheel drive vehicles. There are still plenty of runoffs to cross before we come to the last one (Wp.10 189M) where a final climb-out brings us onto the edge of the **Rubicón** desert plain at a track junction (Wp.11 197M).

From the foot of the mountains we look out over the hazy plain to the headland bar above **Papagayo** beach and the white scars that are the eastern outskirts of **Playa Blanca**, and we have a problem. Until now, wayfinding has simply meant keeping to the main track, but now we have a plethora of tracks and trails to choose from with few identifiable landmarks to guide us. If you want the quickest way to the bar, then follow a track WSW and then forking S to come onto the main track serving the **Papagayo** parking area. Our scenic route is to go SE on a track and then follow the coastal paths - plenty to choose

Our final objective, Playa Blanca, is in sight

from, to either drop into beaches such as **El Pasito** (a strange glitch caused us to lose our GPS track at this point; possibly distracted by naturists, I forgot to power up after taking a break on the beach), or pass above the bays where possible.

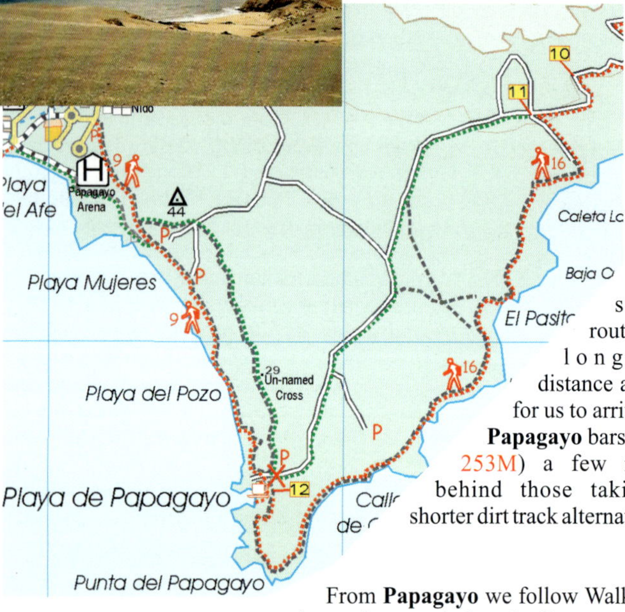

Our scenic route is a bit longer in distance and time for us to arrive at the **Papagayo** bars (Wp.12 253M) a few minutes behind those taking the shorter dirt track alternative.

From **Papagayo** we follow Walk 9 back to the road system below the **Papagayo Arena Hotel** (1.5 km 45M). On the roads follow the blue 'Papagayo Beach' signs in reverse down to a small roundabout, and then on walkways down to the pebble beach of **Playa del Afe**; you could reach this point by staying to seaward of the hotel, and descending on paths directly onto the beach.

From the end of the beach the coastal promenade (Walk 7) starts, guiding us into the centre of **Playa Blanca** at the 'old town' (4 kilometres +60M). By the time you've finished six hours of continuous hiking, you've certainly earned some reward for your efforts, and we bet you'll be glad you chose the 'downhill' option!

17 FEMÉS TO PLAYA QUEMADA - THE MISSING LINK

Having pioneered the 'Hidden Barrancos' (Walk 14) route fifteen years ago, we are pleased to add the exciting circular route 'Femés Ridge' (Walk 15), and this very pleasant linear route from **Femés** to **Playa Quemada** to our repertoire. After the ascent up to the goat farm ridge, it's all downhill along the **Barranco de la Higuera** to **Playa del Pozo** then a final section on the tracks and trails of our 'Playa del Pozo' (Walk 22) route to finish in **Playa Quemada**. There's a slight risk of vertigo in the early stages of the route (see Walk 14 'Hidden Barrancos'). We've kept our description to a minimum as once you are past the goat farm, trail finding is easy - you don't want your head in a book when you have an easy walking route through impressive scenery to enjoy.

The opening up of this easy linear route presents a myriad of opportunities to combine sections of our 14, 15 and 17 routes with other paths in the region to produce a wide variety of 'pick & mix' walking combinations.

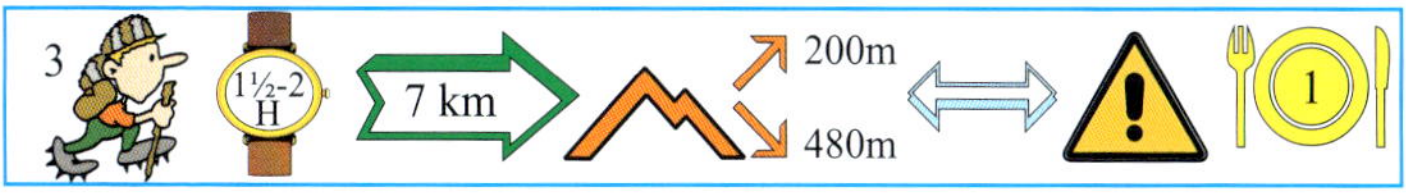

Access by bus:
N°6 **Arrecife** to **Yaiza** then taxi to **Femés**. N°5 **Arrecife** to **Femés** leaves **Arrecife** bus station at 8:00 Mondays to Fridays only, reaching **Femés** at approximately 08:45. For bus users we suggest extending this route by following Walk 2 along the coast to **Puerto Calero** where you can catch the N°25 to **Arrecife** (also stops at **Puerto del Carmen** & **Costa Teguise**. See appendices at the back of this book for timetables.

Access by car:
Park either by the square in **Femés** or in **Playa Quemada** near where the road swings right by the first restaurant. In either case you will have to re-walk the route to get back to your car; so it's probably best to start in **Playa Quemada** - then you get an easy return after lunch.

It's our usual start after coffee at **Bar Femés** (Wp.1 0M) to climb up the track to the ugly goat farm from where we take the 'Hidden Barrancos' trail (Wp.2 9M) down into the head of the **Barranco de la Higuera**. Dropping swiftly down below **Pico Aceituna**, we come to the path junction (Wp.3 16M) to go left down the *barranco* on our 'Femés

Ridge' route in reverse, a much easier option than the ascent on Walk 15.

Approaching Playa Quemada

An easy strolling descent takes us down past the remains of Majo (Guanche) settlements to the pylon path junction (Wp.4 39M) where our 'Femés Ridge' route comes in from the **Valle del Pozo**.

Keeping to the jeep track, we move away from the line of the water runoff in the *barranco* (E) until we meet the runoff from **Valle del Pozo** to swing right (SSW) towards **Playa del Pozo**. We come back to the **Barranco de la Higuera** runoff (Wp.5 50M) to head down the broad valley, crossing the mouth of **Barranco del Fraile** (Wp.6 63M) to come to the track climbing up the eastern wall (Wp.7).

Now we're on our 'Playa del Pozo' route, leaving the track to go onto the walking trail (Wp.8), and when we come to a lower path below us on our right we have a choice of following the main path on the inland route (Wp.9) or of following the lower path across the headlands and *barrancos* (Wp.10), both routes coming together again before we come to the outskirts of the **Playa Quemada** settlement (Wp.11 95M). Rather than follow the roads, we take the coastal path across to the sea front houses and restaurant (Wp.12 105M).

Extension to Puerto Calero (add 35 mins and 1.8 km)
Our finish is already on the route of Walk 2 so we simply continue east on the little access road and as we climb up to the last houses **Puerto Calero** marina comes into view. Taking the coastal path from the end of the housing, we follow Walk 2 in reverse onto **Puerto Calero**'s promenade, continuing as far as the marina entrance where we turn left up the road to the bus stop by the roundabout.

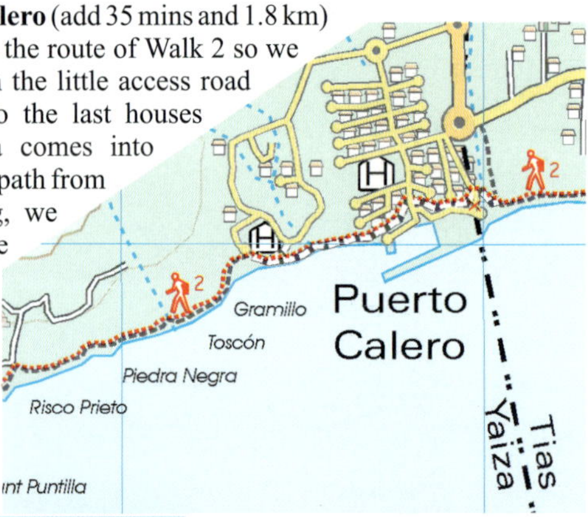

18 TREMESANA GUIDED WALK

The most difficult thing about this walk is getting a place on the walk itself. This is the official guided walk in the **Timanfaya** and you need to book by phoning the Visitors' Centre on 928-840839, or calling in person; the centre is on the LZ67 road south of **Tinajo** and **Mancha Blanca**. Numbers are limited to two mini buses, each carrying seven walkers and at the time of preparing this edition, the walks go on Monday, Tuesday, Thursday and Friday. Given the increasing popularity of this guided walk, it is getting even more difficult to secure one of the fourteen places available so we recommend phoning (00-34-928-840839 when dialling from outside Spain), well before you leave for Lanzarote. You will need to reconfirm your place on the walk the day before by phone or visit.

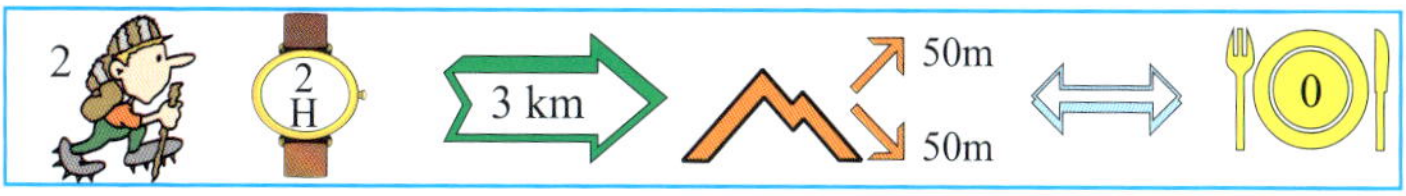

Access by car:
On the LZ67 road from **Yaiza** to **Mancha Blanca**. Drive past the entrance to **Timanfaya National Park**, and the Visitors' Centre is the next major building on your left, 3.5 kilometres further along the road. Make sure you arrive before the 10.00 start.

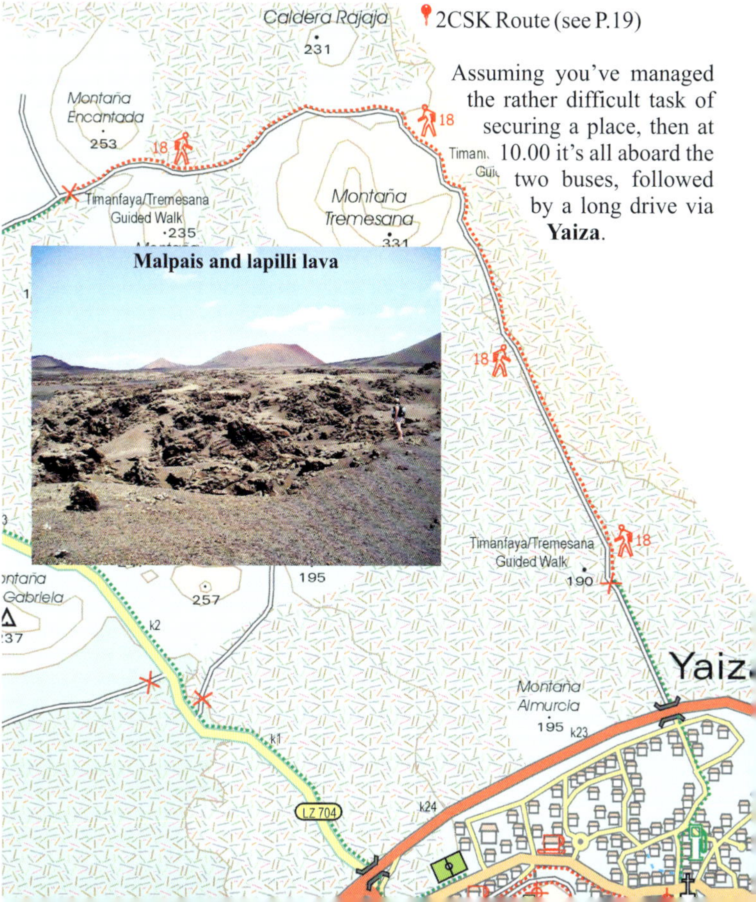

2CSK Route (see P.19)

Assuming you've managed the rather difficult task of securing a place, then at 10.00 it's all aboard the two buses, followed by a long drive via **Yaiza**.

Malpais and lapilli lava

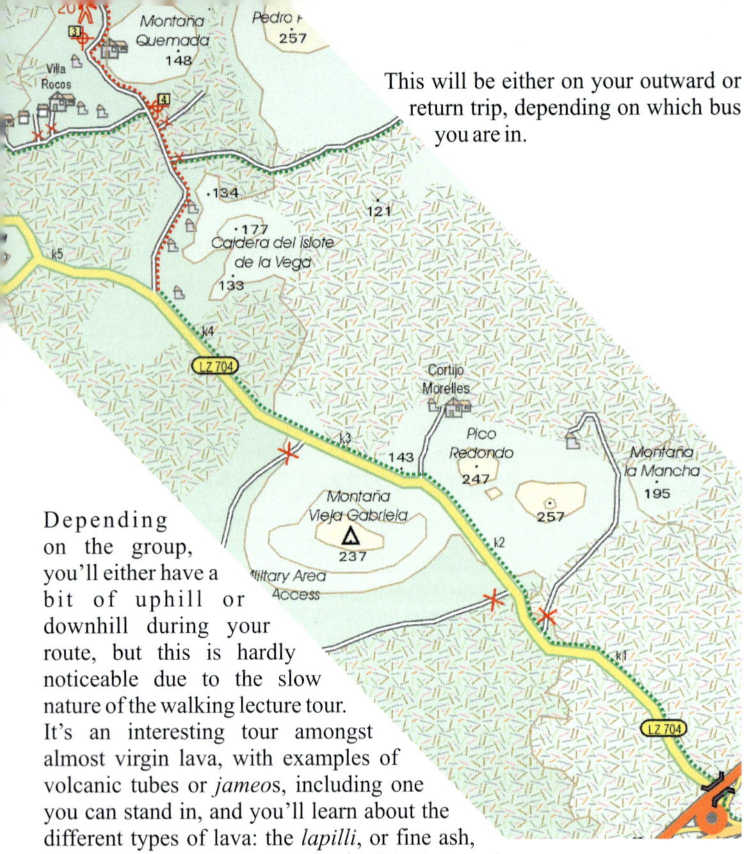

This will be either on your outward or return trip, depending on which bus you are in.

Depending on the group, you'll either have a bit of uphill or downhill during your route, but this is hardly noticeable due to the slow nature of the walking lecture tour. It's an interesting tour amongst almost virgin lava, with examples of volcanic tubes or *jameo*s, including one you can stand in, and you'll learn about the different types of lava: the *lapilli*, or fine ash, the *malpais* or 'AA' scoria lava which is sharp and jagged, the *pahoehoe* type that has set in smooth swags, and lava bombs.

The guides are well versed in the facts and myths of the **Timanfaya** as we amble through the unique landscape on this strolling lecture tour. They park the buses at each end of the manicured track (Wps. 1&2) and swap keys when they meet - wonder where they got that idea from? If they think you are capable, (basically, if all of you look like you can walk and there are no 'couch potatoes' in the group) they will do the full 'there and back' walk of six kilometres in only a little more than the one way time. For everyone interested in the historical and volcanic background of the **Timanfaya**, this is a 'Must Do' tour, though you will have to sift the fact from myth; for example, if ..."a footstep takes three years to disappear ...." then why is there no sign of the workers' footmarks who created this manicured track?

At the risk of exposing yourself to Lanzarote's 'lava police', you could walk the route yourself without guides. Just <u>saying</u> this is possibly a treasonable offence on Lanzarote, but the track is open to public access. At each end a padlocked chain bars vehicle access, for which the guides and farmers have keys, but it is open for walkers. If you cannot get a place on the official walk, or would be unhappy at the very pedestrian pace, simply park at one end of the access track and walk in and back; alternatively, be a two car group and park a car at each end and swap keys when you meet amongst the lava.

19 MONTAÑA CUERVO - A GEM IN LANZAROTE'S CROWN

Once in a while we discover an absolute gem of a walking route, something not in any other guide book, and which even the authorities have missed. **Montaña Cuervo** is just such a gem, so much so that if you miss this little route you will miss much of what Lanzarote has to offer. Vulcanologists will marvel at the condition of the exploded volcanic cone, while the rest of us simply stare in awe at the truly spectacular *caldera*.

Don't try to compare this natural wonder with the sanitised **Timanfaya** bus ride or closely guided walks - nothing compares to **Montaña Cuervo**. However, judging by the access track and car park near the cone, the authorities might be planning to make this another 'loads-a-money' attraction, so best to see this natural wonder now while it's as free as the Lanzarote wind.

The mystical Montaña Cuervo

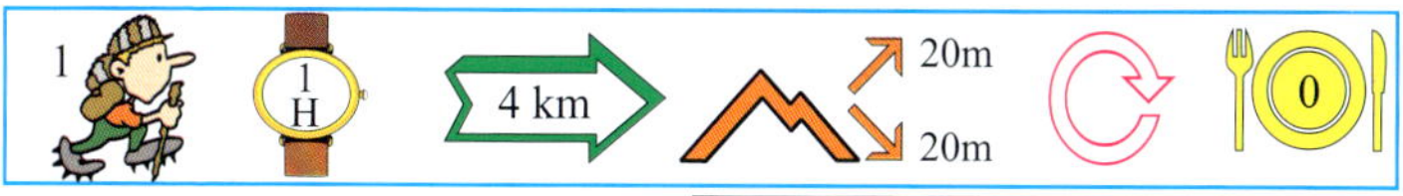

Access by car:
On the LZ56 park on the roadside just north of the **Tías/Tinajo** municipal boundary markers, or pull into the car parking area on the east of the road a few metres further north.

Short Walk
This walk is already short, but if you are only interested in the truly spectacular, then go into the *caldera* and return, remembering the path over the lava field on your return.

Extended Walk
Dirt tracks branch off our circular route enabling you to explore more of the 'lava sea' of this region. Where our track meets the cone at Wp.2, a *picon* path climbs to the lip of the crater: a gritty ascent and slidey descent, not recommended.

We leave the LZ56 on a well-stabilised track (Wp.1 0M), stepping over or round the chain barring vehicle access to head west towards the small mountain. **Montaña Cuervo** is not a big mountain, but rising up out of the lava sea, its sharp image contrasts with the fuzzy lava, lending it a mystical presence even from this distance. An easy stroll along the cinder track takes us past a faint track, off to our right, to swing left and then right to come to the base of the cone (Wp.2 6M) where another track goes off to the right (N). We shun the steep *picon* path climbing to the lip of the crater and follow our track around the cone (NNW), a lava 'wave' cutting out the views as we pass another steep *picon* path ascending the crater shortly before coming to a surprise (Wp.3 10M); not the large car parking area on the right, but the huge gash in the side of the volcanic cone which gives access to its interior.

To descend the path beneath huge volcanic boulders into the *caldera* is to enter another world. From the road, you'd never guess that this stunning interior landscape of a volcano was awaiting you. From our viewpoint on the floor of the crater (Wp.4), the geology is simply awesome, while at the western end of the crater, 110 metres away, wild pink geraniums colonise the floor and slopes, adding to the unreality of this surreal experience.

People spend hours in this crater where time has little meaning, so when you choose to depart we'll re-start our timing at the crater entrance (Wp.3 0M) as we head west around the cone on a broad *picon* trail running between the mountain and the lava 'wave' on our right. The wave is broken by a track (Wp.5) which heads towards **Timanfaya**, the break giving us a chance to look out over this great 'lava sea'.

As we circle the extended cone, we pass another track going out into lava fields (Wp.6 8M) and admire more colonies of wild geraniums blooming in the most unforgiving landscape you could imagine, particularly numerous in one floriferous area seemingly at odds with the surroundings, which also sustains Vinagrera (Rumex lunaria), Lanzarote Firebush or Aulaga (Launaea arborescens), and Nicotiana glauca. Our track runs gently downhill past a track heading out into the lava (Wp.7) and curves around the mountain (SSE), then passing a series of lava ledges (Wp.8) on our right, clearly indicating the thin, harder surfaced crusts above a softer core that you'll be warned not to step on if you take the **Timanfaya** guided walk. We crunch along the *picon* trail curving (WNW) towards the main bulk of the mountain rising above cinder dunes, the dunes and cinder slopes being replaced by bedrock (Wp.9) shortly before we come back to our outward route (21M) beside the path which climbs to the crater rim.

Inside the crater ... a surreal experience

Strolling back towards the LZ56, we notice a trail marked by an arrow of stones (Wp.10 24M), a junction we missed on our way outward. We turn off the track onto the path which then wanders through the broken crust of the lava field giving a real, up close and personal view of lava ledges and collapsed crust, before coming back to our outward track to stroll back to the parking area. Arriving back at our car, we can only marvel at this 'gem' of an easy walking route, almost literally in the middle of nowhere.

20 A PATH BETWEEN TWO SEAS - THE TIMANFAYA COASTAL PATH

Our third **Timanfaya** route has a surreal nature all of its own for most of the route, as we walk along a coastal path between the Atlantic Ocean on our right and the 'Lava Sea' on our left. It is long and linear so best suited to our 2CSK approach (see P.19).

We start at the achingly lovely **Playa Madera**, and twelve kilometres later emerge from the lava sea below a beautiful villa set on a hill in the middle of nowhere. Good walking footwear is essential for this rocky lava trail if you are to avoid bruising the soles of your feet. Note that access has to be by car.

Access by car:
From **Tinajo** take the minor road towards **Tenesar** coastal settlement. When the road turns sharp right, continue straight ahead on a wide, but corrugated, dirt road. Ignore all side turnings, and as the surface changes to picon look for somewhere to park; note this is six kilometres of bumpy dirt road from when you leave the luxurious tarmac. On no account try to drive down to the beach area at **Playa Madera**.

Short Walk
Take the path from either end and walk as far as you like as an out and back route.

From **Yaiza** take the LZ704 road to **El Golfo**. The easiest way to identify the dirt road that you need, is to drive to the junction before **El Golfo**, signed left to 'La Hoya', turn around and the dirt road is the first one on the left as you head back towards **Yaiza**.

Turn onto the dirt road and pass two chained tracks right (the first is for the **Timanfaya** guided walk) and one left and then start looking for a parking place off the track before reaching the villa set on the slopes of **Montaña Quemada**.

Playa Madera

From your parking place, walk down the track onto **Playa Madera** (Wp.1 0M), a wonderfully isolated black beach with the Atlantic waves crashing onto the edge of the 'Lava Sea', and climb up the path onto the lava sea.

This is a wonderful setting, with the ocean crashing against the lava and small lava points on our right, while on our left the 'lava sea' rolls away to the distant **Timanfaya** fire mountains. Amongst the lava sea are points of higher ground around which the slow moving lava flowed, known locally as *islotes*; these green islands harbour local flora which stand out in sharp contrast against the barren lava.

That is about as poetic as it gets, because while the setting is dramatic, with the ocean battling the lava sea, it is very much all the same. Here, they have lava in abundance forming a massive jagged plain, and the only way across this impenetrable expanse is on the coastal path. So it's onward, one step after another along the rocky path, stopping occasionally to take in the views, which all seem remarkably like the views you stopped for earlier. It is a strange combination of beauty and monotony; we can walk for what seems like ages and then look around to have the rather disconcerting feeling that we haven't moved since the last stop, the immediate landscape being ocean and jagged lava sea. This weird impression of not making any progress can be somewhat disturbing, but keep going.

We have 9.5 kilometres of this beautiful but monotonous landscape, before **Montaña Halcones** rises out of the jagged sea on our left, indicating that we will soon be leaving the sea. Our path finally turns away from the ocean and winds along (SSE) to meet a dirt track. Now the landscape starts to change as the lava sea gives way to fig trees in *zocos* and occasional cultivated plots as our route heads towards **Montaña Quemada** (SE), climbing gently to bring us up to a vehicle barrier (Wp.2 176M). Even the isolated farming plots seem like the height of civilisation after all that jagged lava, as we walk up to pass beneath a luxury villa (Wp.3 182M) set on the slopes of **Montaña Quemada** above our track. Having climbed up the slope of the mountain, the track now runs down to a junction of tracks (Wp.4 188M) marked by concrete gate posts with a small commemorative shrine set in them.

Where you go from the junction depends on where you choose to finish. 2CSK walkers (see P.16) should find the second car somewhere along the onward track (SE). If you plan to finish in **Yaiza**, then take this onward track to meet the LZ704 tarmac road, and turn left for 4.5 kilometres of road walking to the big roundabout, now taking the old main road signed for **Yaiza**, for another kilometre to find the first refreshments opposite the football pitch and showground on the town's outskirts.

If you are seeking the closest civilisation or refreshment, go right at the junction. This track undulates along past farmsteads (W) before swinging left (S) to meet the LZ704. Turn right and in under a kilometre you are in **El Golfo** with a choice of tourist style *tipicos* to choose from; you should also find a taxi or two here, or ask in a bar.

21 LA GERIA

The unique agricultural landscape of **La Geria** is one of Lanzarote's most photographed features. At close quarters the 'grape pits' do not look that impressive, but add a bit of altitude and how that perspective changes into an amazing landscape.

Originally a linear walk from **Uga** to **Puerto del Carmen**, our circular option over **Montaña Tinasoria** is now Walk 21A; there's also the option of ascending **Montaña de Guardilama** (not on windy days though) on both routes. Now you can choose the option that suits you; either bus to **Yaiza** and do the linear walk to **Puerto del Carmen** (3 Walker), or follow the main walk to the pass and then climb **Tinasoria** as you curve back towards your outward route (3 Walker); to both of these you can add in the straight forward but tough ascent of **Guardilama** for its awesome views (5 Walker). No refreshments en-route, but there are bars in **Uga** and **Bar/Rest Gregorio** near our start.

The first part of our route is on the recently wayposted PR LZ40.1 until waypoint 7 where we turn south for the coast while the PR LZ40.1 continues ahead to **La Asomada**; see leaflet PR LZ40 'Red de Senderos La Geria' available from Tourist Information Offices.

*Timings in the walk are given for the linear route direct to **Puerto del Carmen**.For the ascent of **Guardilama** add 1 hour, 2.5km and 200 metres of ascents/descents.

Access by bus:
The N°6 calls at **Yaiza** and **Uga**. See appendices for timetables.

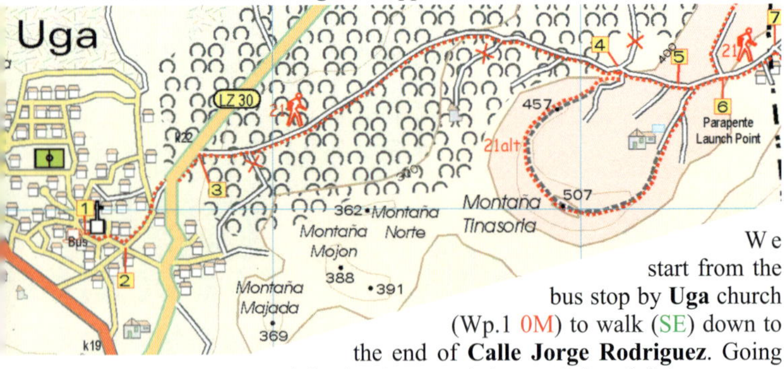

We start from the bus stop by **Uga** church (Wp.1 0M) to walk (SE) down to the end of **Calle Jorge Rodriguez**. Going straight ahead, past cul-de-sacs left and right, we come up to a junction (Wp.2) where we go left on **Calle Los Arenales**, a narrow road heading NE above a new, but unused park. After a house on our right, we take a dirt road to the right which climbs steeply up to the **Teguise** road; alongside the track are our first examples of La Geria 'grape pits'. On the narrow main road we head away from **Uga** (NW) to take the first dirt road off to the right (Wp.3 17M). Now we are into the **La Geria** grape growing area proper, though in these early stages there are more fields and terraces than the traditional grape vine *zocos* (depressions of volcanic ash enclosed in a

Turning off the tarmac at Wp.3

horseshoe-shaped walled of volcanic rock with a vine planted in its centre). As we progress, the track runs along a plateau above **La Geria** for

La Geria and Montaña Guardilama

us to look across a landscape of *zocos* backed by the volcanic peaks of the **Timanfaya**.

Figs alternate with grapes as we climb steadily past a track off to the right, the **La Geria** landscape expanding into thousands of horseshoe-shaped depressions covering the whole region. Away on our left is one of the large *bodegas* as we continue uphill past the *bodega* access track (Wp.4) towards the pass. A steady, almost slogging, ascent brings us up onto the pass (Wp.5 57M) from where we can take a break for the views over the unique **La Geria** landscape. Now, if you think these views are impressive, think what another 100 or 200 metres altitude would do.

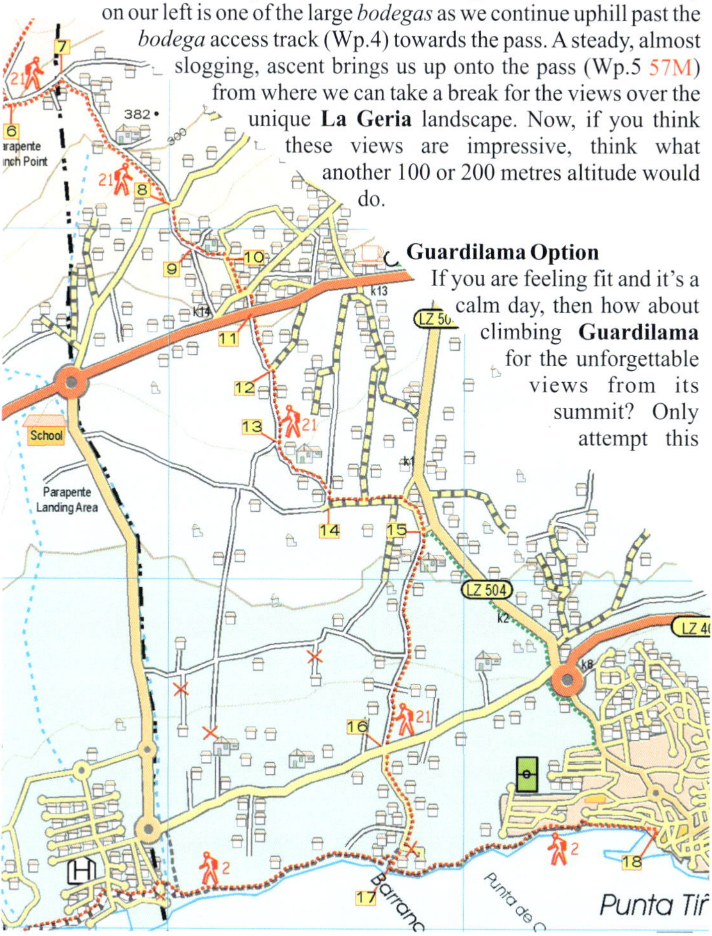

Guardilama Option

If you are feeling fit and it's a calm day, then how about climbing **Guardilama** for the unforgettable views from its summit? Only attempt this on the calmest days as the wind sheer makes this route potentially dangerous. Not recommended for vertigo sufferers.

We go over the pass and in a few metres take a track to the left (Wp.6/Wp.8 21A) to walk up past grapes enclosed by stone walls. After the last of the stone walls the track continues straight up the mountain. This truly is a 'puff and grunt' ascent, taking frequent breaks to get our breath back. The track peters out half way up, after which we follow a faint trail straight up over the open ground; another 50 metres of ascent and a few more stops for breath sees us reach the summit (Wp.9 21A). The views are simply awesome. **Guardilama** is Lanzarote's most 'pointy' accessible peak. The **La Geria** plain lies some 300 metres below us, and the views over the volcanic cones of the **Timanfaya** are unforgettable; stay as long as your vertigo will allow to enjoy the island's most spectacular views.

Take care on the steep descent, watching every step you make; it is all too easy to be distracted by the views and lose your footing on the steep ground.

Onward to Puerto del Carmen

From the pass we follow the dirt road down into the more familiar Lanzarote landscape, a steady descent bringing us down to a T-junction (Wp.7), **Camino del Mesón** track continuing ahead as we turn right to head downhill past a clutch of houses. We stay on the main track, passing a nice house and track on our left as we head down to cross the **Asomada** road (Wp.8 77M); there's a post at the junction, but its 'Camino del Mesón' sign has gone missing.

Straight over the road, and we're back on a dirt track to come down past **Villa Vistas** to a crossroads of tracks (Wp.9) to continue straight over and come down onto a tarmac lane (Wp.10). Going right (S) we stroll down to the end of **Camino Los Olivos** to go left on a narrow lane, then right onto a track to carefully cross the fast and busy LZ2 main road (Wp.11).

We're back on a dusty track running (SSE) down through the general wasteland that lies between mountains and sea, a wasteland dotted with 'exclusively desirable villa residences' in estate agent speak. At the end of **Camino La Caldarina** (Wp.12 97M) we take the track to the right (S), keeping left at the next junction (Wp.13) to pass **Finca Lomos Altos** before reaching a T-junction; here we go right to come onto the end of a tarmac lane (Wp.14) at another T-junction. Going left (E) passing a lane off to the left then one to the right, we come to a lane off left to the main road. Keeping to our tarmac lane, we come to a second lane (Wp.15 120M) linking us to the **Puerto del Carmen** road.

If at this stage you are growing tired of the bungalow-dotted wasteland you could take to the main road for an easy tarmac stroll down to the *circumvalacion* roundabout, followed by pavements down into the resort.

Those of us choosing to stick with the grit head down (S) **Camino Barranco de Quiquere** past the multi-tiered garden of **Casa la Helice** for an easy stroll down past the grandly named little track of **Camino las Casanas** before coming onto the **Puerto Calero** road (Wp.16 138M). Straight over the road, we continue on the track down to the mouth of the *barranco* where we meet the route of Walk 2 (Wp.17) From here we follow the coastal path (W) back to the 'old town' of **Puerto del Carmen** (Wp.18 172M).

21A LA GERIA & TINASORIA

Walk 21 is our original route through **La Geria**, perfect if you wish to bus out from **Puerto del Carmen** to **Uga** and then walk back to the resort. Now, for walkers who wish to experience **La Geria** as the focal point of their walking route, we present our original alternative as a walking route in its own right where 90% of the walking is amongst the famous '*zocos*'.

The first part of our route is on the recently wayposted PR LZ40.1 until waypoint 7 where we turn uphill for **Tinasoria** while the PR LZ40.1 continues ahead to **La Asomada**; see leaflet 'PR LZ40 Red de Senderos La Geria' available from Tourist Information Offices.

Uga church at Wp.1

Our starting point is from the bus stop by the church in the centre of **Uga** (Wp.1 0M); where we usually start with coffees (café con leche) at the bar facing the church, from where we walk (SE) down to the end of **Calle Jorge Rodriguez**.

Going straight ahead, past cul-de-sacs left and right, we come up to a junction (Wp.2) that's more like a tarmac village square, where we go left on **Calle Los Arenales**, a narrow road heading NE above a new but unused park. After a house on our right, we take a dirt road to the right (Wp.3) which climbs steeply up to the **Teguise** road; alongside the track are our first examples of **La Geria** 'grape pits'. On the narrow main road we head away from **Uga** (NW) to take the first dirt road off to the right (Wp.4 17M).

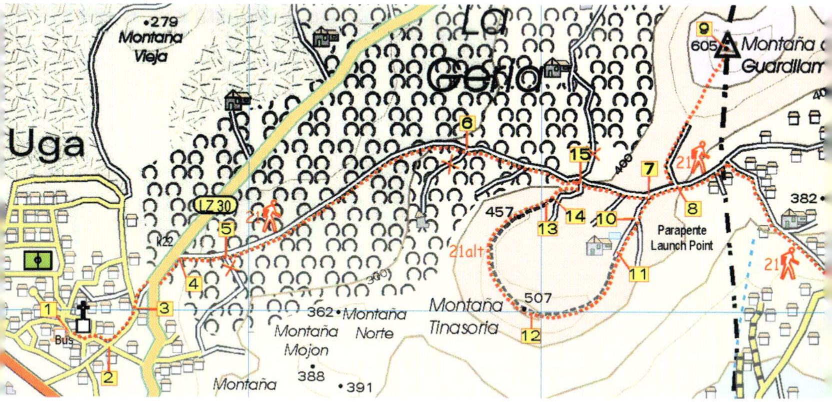

Into La Geria proper

Now we are into the **La Geria** grape growing area proper, though in these early stages there are more fields and terraces growing onions than the traditional grape vine *zocos* (depressions of volcanic ash enclosed in a horseshoe-shaped walled of volcanic rock with a vine planted in its centre).

At first it's easy strolling as our track runs along a plateau above **La Geria**, passing a chained track to our right (Wp.5), for us to look across a landscape of *zocos* backed by the volcanic peaks of **Timanfaya**. Figs alternate with grapes as we climb steadily past a track off to the right (Wp.6), the **La Geria** landscape expanding into thousands of horseshoe-shaped depressions covering the whole region. Away on our left is one of the large *bodegas* as we continue uphill past the *bodega* access track (Wp.15) towards the pass. A steady, almost slogging, ascent brings us up onto the pass, from where we can take a break for the views over this unique landscape - if you think these views are impressive, think what another 100 or 200 metres altitude would do. Over the pass we are walking past a fenced field on our left as we come to the **Tinasoria** track on our right (Wp.7 55M).

Guardilama Option

See the Guardilama Option included in Walk 21 description. The waypoints 8; turn off the main track & 9; peak of Guardilama, are included in Walk 21A's waypoint file.

The water cisterns

Climbing Tinasoria

With the main track behind us we walk gently uphill, passing a track off to our front left (Wp.10) as we head towards a relatively modern, brick-built, but abandoned farm behind which is the rising, sweeping crescent of **Tinasoria**'s crater rim. Reaching the farm (Wp.11 65M), a handy place for a break before the final ascent, we notice a collection of linked water cisterns, unusual in both their size and number given that the only ground above this altitude is the **Tinasoria** rim. Beyond the farm our track dwindles, becomes rougher, splits and rejoins, before finally coming

Views over the *zocos*

down to trail width as our curving ascent takes us towards the peak.

During the start of this climb we lose the views as our trail is just below the rim but as we get higher we start to get views over the south-west landscape. Our trail runs out at the cairn marking the peak of **Tinasoria** (Wp.12).

It's tempting to stop at the cairn for the views but if we continue a little further along the broad crater rim we come to a rough seat thoughtfully constructed from rock slabs, just the place to take a break while taking in the magnificent views.

To return to **Uga** we could simply turn round and reverse our outward route, or, as we chose, we could continue following the rim around the crater which gives a higher altitude perspective of **La Geria** than being on the main track. It is open ground walking as the rim reduces to become a broad meadow carpeted with wild flowers more reminiscent of the **Haria** valley than the dry landscape of **La Geria**.

On the descent

The gently sloping meadow brings us down alongside the *zocos* in the *caldera* on our right, and passing a notable hole on our right, before finishing at the limit of the grape *zocos*; *caldera* on our right and the top slopes of **La Geria** on our left and ahead.

We have two choices of reaching the main track:-

Option 1: we can go over to the edge of the *zocos* in the *caldera* (Wp.13) to pick our way between the *zocos* to come onto the dirt track, then turn left to walk down out of the *caldera* before joining the main track (Wp.15).

Option 2: continue to the end of the meadow (Wp.14) where we come to the edge of the *zocos* climbing up from **La Geria** where we find a narrow trail heading (NE) between the grape pits before finishing with a *picon* scree descent down to the level of the *caldera* track, from where we walk out to join the main track (Wp.15).

Both options involve walking across intensively farmed land and while we have not had any access problems you would not want to bring large groups of walkers across this ground at the risk of upsetting the farmers.

Back on the main track we have an easy relaxed stroll back down the track, quite a contrast to the earlier ascent, with just the steeper sections requiring care not to slip on the dusty/gritty surface. Returning to **Uga**, we have a choice of bars for refreshment while contemplating our next adventure, waiting for the bus, or just chilling out.

22 PLAYA DEL POZO

Playa Quemada is literally the end of the road, but this doesn't mean that it's the end of exploring - far from it. Sections of this coastal exploration route get quite busy in a rather bizarre fashion, as the many people who head for the **Playa de la Arena** beach clad in the most minimalist gear contrast wildly with the *parapentes* who labour up to their launch point with enormous back packs. Once away from the first section of the route you're into barren tranquility, strolling above the cliffs before dropping into the large **Barranco de la Higuera** to find a few cozzie-optional hikers enjoying the isolated beach of **Playa del Pozo**.

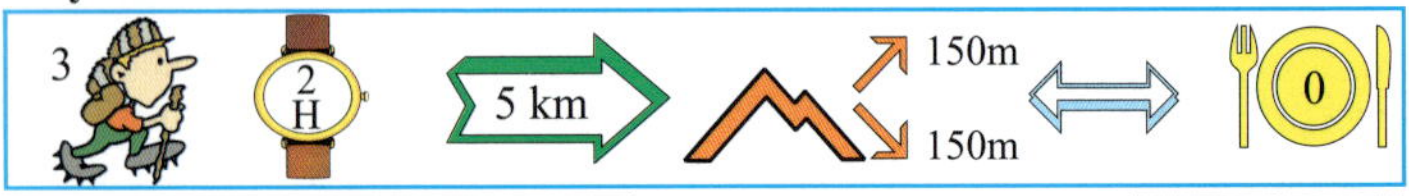

Extension
This route can be extended into an ascent up to **Femés**, 7km, Ascents 550 metres; see Walk 17.

Short Walk
To **Playa de la Arena** and return.

Access by car:
Drive through **Playa Quemada** as far as you can. At the far end of the settlement keep left to come onto a cul-de-sac on the seaward side of the houses where there is parking for 8-10 cars.

Access by bus:
N°25 (from **Costa Teguise** calling at **Arrecife** and **Puerto del Carmen**) to **Puerto Calero** and then follow Walk 2 'Coastal Discovery' to **Playa Quemada**. The start of Walk 22 is at the seaward end of the settlement.

The steep zigzag ascent

From beside the parking area (Wp.1 0M), a broad trail climbs up onto the headland to a cairn (Wp.2) above the first bay. This whole region is criss-crossed by a mixture of trails which can cause confusion, so we recommend staying on the main trail. Ahead, a clear trail zigzags up from the *barranco* behind **Playa la Arena** as we start curving into the *barranco* to a zigzag descent. Taking care on the slippery surface, we drop down to a path junction (8M) where most people go left and down to the **Playa de la Arena** beach. We continue straight on, to climb the steep zigzag ascent onto the next headland, taking it one zig or zag at a time.

Our ascent brings us up to a T-junction (16M) whose right hand branch is an alternative return route avoiding the descent and ascent through the *barranco*. Going left, we immediately hit another junction. Here the main path goes right to zigzag up the steep lomo to the *parapente* launch point, while we take the minor path straight ahead. We are now above the cliffs as we swing into a *barranco*, and ignoring a trace path descending, we stay on the narrow path to

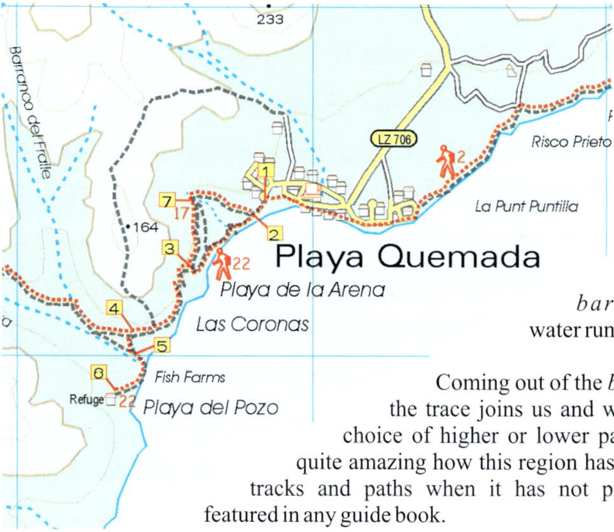

cross the *barranco*'s water runoff.

Coming out of the *barranco*, the trace joins us and we have a choice of higher or lower paths; it is quite amazing how this region has so many tracks and paths when it has not previously featured in any guide book.

Taking the higher path, we curve round into another *barranco*, and as our path runs out we find another couple of paths running into the *barranco*. In this myriad of traces we maintain altitude by stepping up onto the higher path off to our right (Wp.3 22M); our alternative return route winds inland, avoiding the steep ascents and descents by **Playa de la Arena**. Ignoring the many traces, we come along to cross the water runoff of the side *barranco*, then emerge from the side *barranco* and immediately curve around the main *barranco* to finally emerge above the cliffs and azure sea. Our route is very much into and out of *barrancos* interspersed with sea views, as we cross yet another small water runoff and stay on the best defined path out of this *barranco* from where our destination of **Playa del Pozo** comes into view (32M). It might look close, but there are still a few obstacles in the way. We turn into a small but precipitous *barranco* where the stone -littered path deserves careful footwork before crossing the water runoff; emerging, we have a choice of walking trail or dirt/stone track for our descent into **Barranco de la Higuera**.

The sculptor at work

Across from us on the opposite wall of the *barranco* is an enormous stone design, a maritime anchor-style design which was just being finished by the local sculptor when we were last on this route - if you look closely at the photo, you can just about make out the artist at the top right of his design. His presence gives a good impression of the size of his work.

Taking the walking trail, we descend until the path peters out and than transfer to the rubble-ised track. It looks as if we would have to go a long way up the ravine, but look for a walking trail leaving the track (Wp.4 40M). The narrow path drops us down towards the *barranco* floor, a cairn marking the last traverse before we come onto a track (Wp.5) running along the ravine floor.

The refuge at Playa del Pozo

Going left, we follow the track to the mouth of the *barranco*, where it swings right behind the boulder beach to bring us across to the refuge (Wp.6 62M) and *pozo* from which the beach takes its name. There is little, if any, shade at **Playa del Pozo** so make sure you are well protected against the sun.

Our return is a retracing of our outward route until we reach the junction at Wp.3 (46M) where we keep straight on instead of dropping into the *barranco*. Our path runs inland, and as is the way of this area, a second path parallels our route twenty metres lower down the *barranco*, gently descending slopes covered with goat traces. We are heading towards a junction of barren valleys that con-join inland of **Playa de la Arena**. At a faint junction (Wp.7) a trace goes ahead while our path turns right, its continuation is clearly seen across the valley, for us to join the second (lower) at the gravel-lined water course. Now we have a steady ascent up the grit-surfaced path, easier to ascend than descend, to come onto a faint track which runs along the *lomo*. We head back down the track towards the sea to rejoin our outward route.

PLAYA DEL POZO

It's thought that when the Normans invaded Lanzarote in 1402 under Jean de Béthencourt, the beach of **Playa del Pozo** became one of their first settlements. In the 1950s the Serra Ráfols brothers carried out archaeological investigations revealing the remains of a tower, a church, dwellings, wells, and a burial area. Other historians believe that the remains of the water channelling and well system, complete with triangular rock carvings, point to the Phoenicians as the first settlers. The *pozo* on the beach is a restoration of one of the original wells.

23 TEGUISE -THE ANCIENT CAPITAL

It's well worth strolling through this historic town, first established as a settlement by the island's original inhabitants, the *Mojos*. Cobbled streets lead between white buildings, many of which have a long and interesting history. You can visit the rather austere **Palacio Spinola** palace (open daily 10.00-17.00 in summer, until 09.00-15.00 in winter, entry fee payable) in **Plaza de la Constitución**. There are several churches, monasteries and museums worth a visit, including the prominent parish church, (16th century, with numerous later embellishments) **Iglesia de Nuestra Señora de Guadalupe**, and the old **Teatrillo Municipal de Teguise** which first opened its doors in 1825. Many of the old buildings have changed use over the years; ex-convents and erstwhile homes of the rich and influential now serve as art galleries, museums, shops and bar/restaurants while retaining original façades. At its busiest on Sunday mornings, **Teguise** street market is a magnet for both residents and visitors.

Overlooking the town on top of the peak of **Guanapay** (446 metres) perches the island's oldest castle, the 16th century **Castillo de Santa Bárbara**, rescued from dilapidation to house the **Museo del Emigrante Canario** which specialises in artefacts marking the history of migration by Lanzarote's inhabitants in their attempts to find fortune overseas. Enjoy panoramic views from the peak, or take a look inside (€3 adults, Sunday to Friday).

N.B. We have not included GPS information for this walk, as satellite coverage in the narrow streets is unreliable.

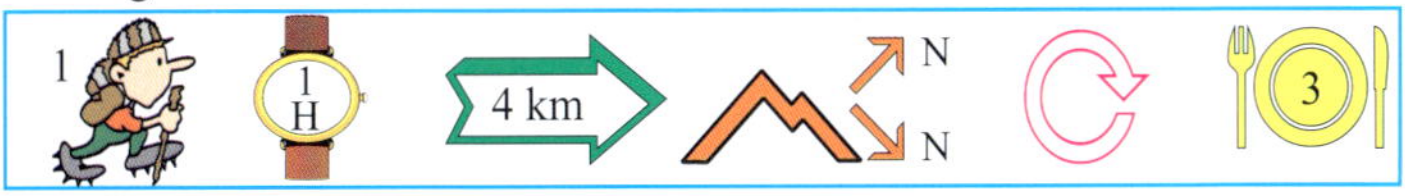

Access by car:
Parking in the **Plaza Spinola** and along the main road.

Access by bus:
In addition to the Sunday market day specials (Nºs 11, 12&13), Nºs 7, 9&10 all go via **Teguise**.

We suggest beginning this relaxed stroll with refreshments in one of the town's bars. If you arrive early, call in **Sejas Bar/Café** in **Plaza Doctor Alfonso Spínola** (06.00 until 20.00), which backs onto the old **Convento de San Francisco** (1534), no longer a convent, now housing Lanzarote's collection of religious art in the **Museo de Arte Sacro**. Leaving the bar, we turn right to walk through the *plaza,* named after the Teguise-born Doctor Spinola (1845-1905) who practiced in Lanzarote and Uruguay, where he was important in controlling a smallpox outbreak. Turning right at the north-east corner brings us onto **Calle Marqués de Herrera**, passing the **Casa del Marqués** on our left, and continuing on the few steps past the narrow street on our left to see the **Teatrillo Municipal de Teguise** which has given service as a church, hospital and children's hospice before becoming a theatre in 1825.

Doubling back, we take the narrow street which runs north on **Calle Espiritu Santu** to the great open space known as **Parque La Mareta**, although there's little evidence of greenery in this large public area. If you are fortunate enough

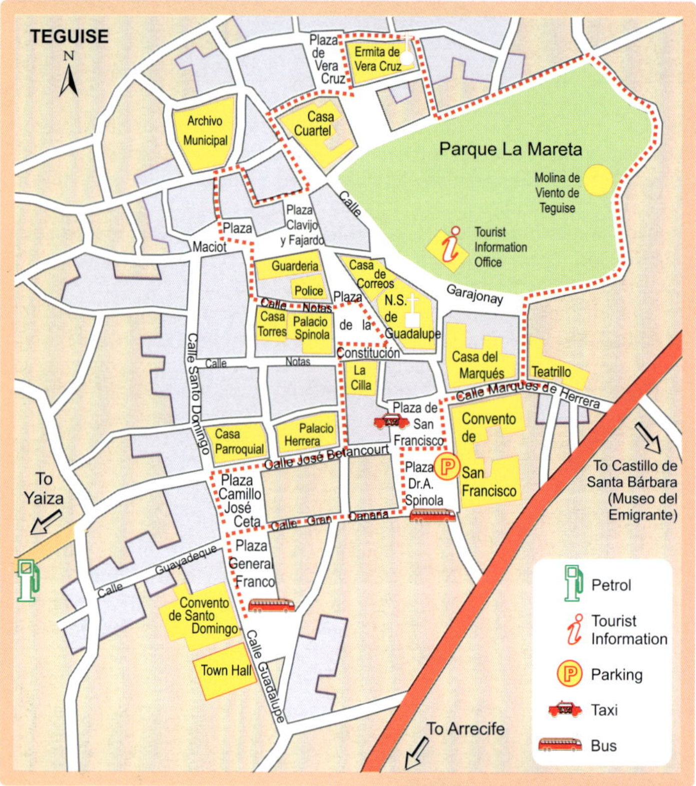

to be on the island on June 1, this square is transformed by colourful 'carpets' drawn with coloured salts.

Following its edge counter-clockwise brings us to a well preserved (except for some graffiti) windmill **Molino de Viento de Teguise**, the last remaining of twelve in this area which were used to grind cereal grains.

Parque La Mareta

El Molino de Viento de Teguise

We continue our circumnavigation of the *parque*, turning off north on the **Calle Princesa Ico** and into **Plaza de Vera Cruz** dominated by the **Ermita de Vera Cruz** with its magnificently huge doors. Leaving the *plaza* by its south-west corner, we walk to the next junction of streets where we go left (S), passing **Casa Cuartel** on our left, a former billet for

Casa Cuartel

soldiers, easily recognised by its old wooden balcony - rare on a largely treeless island.

Continuing ahead and taking a short dogleg right and left brings us into **Plaza de Clavijo y Fajardo**, where we turn right on a narrow street, at the end of which the **Archivo Municipal** faces us.

Turning left and immediately left again brings us into **Plaza Maciot**, which we walk through to leave by the narrow street in its south-east corner, then taking the next left with **Casa Torres** forming the corner, next door to the seventeenth century **Palacio Spínola** which became a museum in 1984, its walls on this side in the **Calle Notas** looking rather unstable, despite its reputation as the town's most important piee of architecture.. We step out into the main cobbled square of **Plaza de la Constitución**, the main façade and entrance to **Palacio Spínola** on its western side, and with the **Iglesia de Nuestra Señora de Guadalupe** on the opposite side, an imposing building standing out from the surrounding austere and simple architectural styles; on its north side is a building that once served as the post office, still known as **Casa de Correos** but now used by the Univerity of Las Palmas de Gran Canaria as a School of Medicine. By the south side of the church, the narrow lane **Calle Zonzamas** leads into the **Parque La Mareta**.

Cilla de Diezmos y Primicias

Also look for the seventeenth century **Caja Canarias**, on the southern edge of the square, one of the most attractive banks you are likely to see, housed in the **Cilla de Diezmos y Primicias** building once used to store grain paid as tithes - not too much of a change of use, then.

We leave the *plaza* by the street at its south-west corner, **Calle Leon y Castillo**, taking the second right onto **Calle José Betancort**, bringing us past the **Palacio Herrera** on our right - turn right around the building's corner to see its impressive wall plaque before retracing our steps back onto **Calle José Betancort** and continue in a westerly direction, passing the **Casa Paroquial** on our right. Turning left at the end of the street where it meets **Calle Guadalupe** at **Plaza Camillo José Cela** takes us past a small public garden and bus stop, opposite the **Convento de Santo Domingo** (1698), one of the town's largest buildings, and an important centre for local government offices and cultural activities in this region. It also houses the **Centro de Arte Santo Domingo** (open Mon-Fri 10.00 - 15.00, Sun 10.00-14.00). To return to our start point, backtrack to the first street right, **Calle Gran Canaria**, which leads us back to **Plaza Doctor Alfonso Spínola**.

24 THE FORGOTTEN TRAIL

If there's one route that you should walk on Lanzarote, this is it. Our route contains all the essentials for a top rate discovery and even the 280 metre ascent simply melts away as we climb a little-known donkey trail through the island's lushest vegetation. Originally a linear descent to **Haría**, we've now re-walked the route as an 'out and back' excursion, with basic refreshments taken at half way.

Short Route
Take a taxi to **Bar/Rest Los Helechos** and walk the route as a linear descent to **Haría**.

Stroll
Along the dirt road from **Haría**, as far as you like.

Access by bus:
N°7 from **Arrecife** calls at **Haría**; see appendices for details.

We start out from the centre of **Haría** outside **Bar Ney-Ha** on **Plaza de la Constitución** (Wp.1 0M) to go right in front of the *ayuntamiento* to stroll along to the **Eckholl** collection shop (Wp.2) where we go left on a small street lined with houses. It is gently uphill before going left to cross the stream bed and come up past a well (Wp.3) to a T-junction at the end of **Calle Angel**. Following the 'Deportivo' sign to the right, we start to leave the old village behind as we stroll along an avenue of palms. Fields replace houses on our left as we pass César Manrique's house (Wp.4) on our right, shortly before the tarmac swings right (Wp.5) towards the sports complex. Here we continue straight ahead, the tarmac changing to dirt (Wp.6 12M) as we pass a ruined cottage to finally leave the housing behind.

Ahead, the line of the donkey trail which climbs the ridge at the end of the valley is clearly visible, the buildings on top of the ridge making for a rather daunting prospect from down in the valley. We stroll along through a bucolic landscape of black *picon* cultivated plots interspersed with fallow fields populated with endemic flora. Coming to a junction (Wp.7) we take the minor dirt road to our front right. Our gentle uphill stroll becomes more serious as the road steepens, becoming grassier as it ascends in a slogging ascent towards the main road. Where the dirt road swings left up to the tarmac we take a donkey trail straight ahead to climb up onto the road (Wp.8 27M). Watching out for 'white knuckled' hire car drivers, we cross over onto the donkey trail's continuation on a long

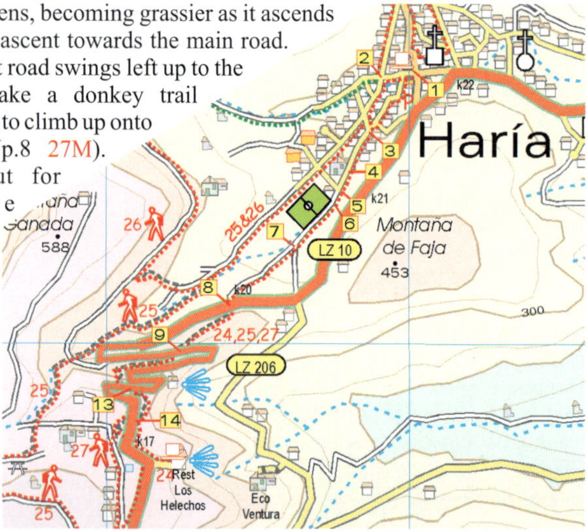

traverse across the slope. Endemic flora has narrowed the trail to path width as we climb up above a cultivated black *picon* plot which stands out amongst these long-

Surrounded by plant life, far above Haría

A boulder-cobbled section of the trail

abandoned terraces. At the end of the long climbing traverse, we come up to meet the main road again (Wp.9 40M) by the 'Val de Malpaiso' sign. Carefully over the road, we continue on the donkey trail in another climbing traverse. The plant growth on this steep hillside simply has to be seen to be believed; if you think of Lanzarote as 'grit and desert' then this floriferous setting will really surprise you. Giant sonchus, lavender, succulents and tamarisk cling to every available roothold.

A slogging ascent brings us up under massive buttresses which support the road, as a hairpin bend in the trail (Wp.10 43M) directs us towards another buttress. We come up to touching distance of the massive wall to zigzag steeply up alongside the tarmac (Wp.11) at a hairpin bend. Our trail, now mostly boulder-cobbled now, climbs steeply up through more zigzags to a hairpin bend (Wp.12) that directs us towards the **Mirador de Haría** building, a climbing traverse leading us up to the road again (Wp.13 48M). Carefully crossing the road, we find our trail's continuation 20 metres uphill where the path climbs up from a red rock dell, soon becoming boulder-laid again. As our trail curves right, we get views down the **Valle de Tenisía** as we push our way up through lush plant life to come up to the road again.

From here you could simply walk up the road to the Bar/Restaurant, but we cross the road to come onto the faintest section of the trail. Above us is a wooden cross which we use as a direction marker while climbing up over bare rock, before the trail resumes to take us past the cross (Wp.14). Twenty metres after the cross there is faint (easily missed) junction (Wp.15 55M), where our 'Capital Route' continues gently uphill to come onto a dirt road. At the junction we go left, to drop down the cobbled trail to the road (Wp.16).

Now it's an uphill stroll beside the crash barrier to turn into **Bar/Rest Los Helechos** (62M 570 metres), which may look closed from the road - but walk around the building to find a twee gift shop selling the usual tourist stuff and a large basic café geared up for the coach potato trade. It doesn't rate highly for refreshments, but it is a reasonably comfortable place to take a break and mix with the tourists and groups of lycra-clad cyclists who call in here.

We return by retracing our outward route, taking care on the steeper stretches of the donkey trail which can become very slippery in bad weather.

25 BARRANCO DEL MALPASO

Despite its unpromising name, **Malpaso** meaning 'bad pass/route', our new circular out of **Haría** is a Lanzarote classic combining the marvels of 'The Forgotten Trail'(Walk 24) with a hidden *barranco* stuffed with endemic flora and the possibility of seeing running water - a real rarity on Lanzarote. That's not all, add on the spectacular cliff-top views from **Mirador del Risco de Famara** plus a refreshment opportunity at another *mirador* - the scene is complete for a most memorable adventure.

It's longer, and tougher, than 'The Forgotten Trail' but still well within the compass of leisure walkers so if you only have time for one walk in the **Haría** region then make it our 'Barranco del Malpaso'; you won't regret it.

Access by car:
Either park in central **Haría** to follow the walk as described, or park at **Mirador del Risco de Famara** or **Restaurante Los Helechos** car parks to start our circular route at these options which give a unique view of our route and mid-walk refreshments in the centre of **Haría**.

Access by bus:
N°7 from **Arrecife** calls at **Haría**; see appendices for details.

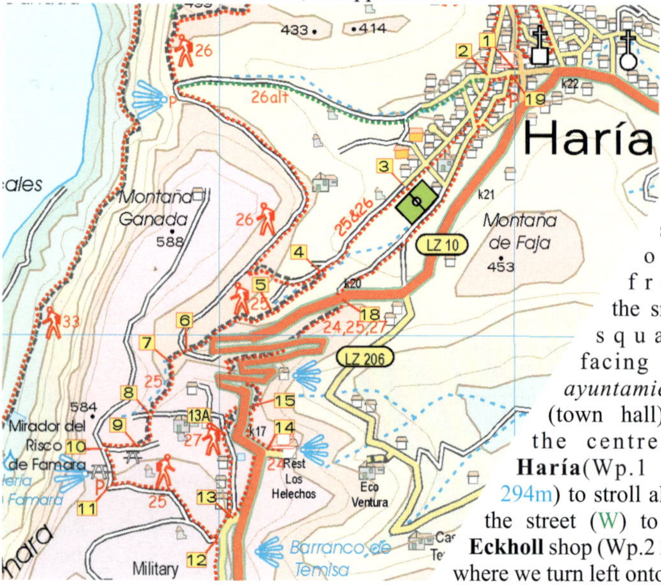

We start out from the small square facing the *ayuntamiento* (town hall) in the centre of **Haría**(Wp.1 0M 294m) to stroll along the street (W) to the **Eckholl** shop (Wp.2 3M) where we turn left onto the **Calle Angel Guerra** to start heading away from the town (SW) passing a mixture of houses and plots as we come gently up to pass the sports ground (Wp3 12M) where the tarmac street becomes a dirt track. Past the last house, new-ish but not named, we are out into the countryside walking between stone walled fields and plots while ahead we have the great swoops of the LZ10 framing our return descent 'The

Forgotten Trail'. It's easy strolling very gently uphill as we pass a section where a small stream has eroded the track down to trail width for a short section before we come up to pass a chained entrance on our right, followed by a chain across the main track just after it starts climbing up from the stream (Wp.4 21M 359m).

It's all been dreamily easy so far - but there's one tricky bit of wayfinding on this route and we are there now. Where the track moves away from the stream to run up past the chain into a large field (see Walk 26) there is no sign of any other route, but we need to follow the stream. After a few metres of stepping from stone to stone a trail emerges on the right side of the stream for us to snake up between stone walled terraces including vines. It's a narrow single-file path as it climbs above the watercourse for us to push past fennel and intense local endemics, passing another field of vines on our left before our path switches to the opposite side of the stream (Wp.5 30M). As we climb through the endemic flora the terraces gradually change from cultivated to abandoned so reverting to nature. Water erosion has collapsed a terrace wall and narrowed the already narrow path requiring careful footwork. We're climbing steadily above the stream, negotiating another eroded section, to come onto stone steps which bring us up onto a broad dirt track (Wp.6 42M 444m) where suitably sized boulders provide convenient rest points before tackling the next climb up the *barranco* proper.

Ascending the *barranco*

What a difference a track makes; our earlier 'stream in a gully' has become a fully-fledged steep-sided *barranco* (signed 'Barranco del Malpaso') as we climb up the narrow stone path to pass two 'netted rock'dams, there to prevent flash flooding sweeping away the rich soil down in the valley floor. After the steep climb to the second dam (Wp.7) our path crosses the watercourse as a sharp turn in the *barranco* takes **Haría** from sight behind us as we climb steeply up past trees to come up to the remains of a cistern and hut which mark the upper reaches of the *barranco*. As we continue upwards, cultivated fields come into view as the barranco finishes but our path continues uphill to a dirt track (Wp.8 60M 551m).

Across the track, our path continues up past stone-walled fields before swinging right to bring us onto another dirt track and the unexpected sight of picnic tables (Wp.9 66M 582m); after nearly three hundred metres of climbing ascent its almost as if divine providence has placed the tables here just for us. It's an easy stroll along (W) to meet the main track (Wp.10) where we turn left to follow the track uphill. You could clamber over the open ground to our west for views down the cliffs, but you'd be better advised to continue up the track, military camouflaged radomes coming into view as we reach the first access paths into the **Mirador del Risco de Famara Área Recreativa**. Alternatively, continue on to the recreation area's car park (Wp.11 74M 615m). In Lanzarote's largest *área recreativa* you'll find a sizeable children's playground along with enough picnic tables to seat the largest of extended families, plus of course the *mirador*. Arrive here on a weekend and you'll find the place bustling with Lanzarote families settling in for a day's relaxation complete with catering; on weekdays you could have the whole place to yourself. Missing at any time are tourist hire cars; seemingly this spectacular location is too far from the tarmac for visitors to consider, much to their loss.

From the car park entrance we still have some gentle uphill along the broad track before we pass a dirt track accessing a building on our left and then come down to a crossroads where we swing left to pass a farm on our left before coming to the tarmac lane (Wp.12 97M) serving the **Ermita de las Nieves**. Our stroll along this section of high ground provides increasing views over the **Haría** valley and east to **Tabayesco**, and there's evidence of cultivation returning to this previously abandoned farming area in the form of new fields and farmhouses under construction. Along the tarmac (NNE) we come to a dirt track (Wp.13) accessing houses before we reach the main LZ10 road.

If you plan to call at **Restaurant Los Helechos**, recommended for its view rather than its cuisine, then continue down to the LZ10 and carefully walk along the main road to the extensive car park (wildly over-optimistic in size compared to the numbers who call here) (Wp.14 102M). Should you prefer to eschew the restaurant's delights then take the dirt track (N) on the route of Walk 26 to the path (Wp.13A) that leads down past the cross to the LZ10 with our return route on 'The Forgotten Trail' continuing across the road.

We always call in at **Restaurant Los Helechos**, really because it's there but also to marvel at this waste of a golden opportunity. At best it's a cafe and gift shop with a massive car park in a spectacular location, after which any description goes as rapidly downhill as the LZ10. Food and drink seem palatable enough but the café is a depressing monument to featureless formica which even the spectacular view from its windows can't lighten. Its gift shop is a marvel of everything that might possibly count as Lanzarote tat, seemingly displayed on the basis that the visiting 'coach potatoes' will buy anything no matter how awful.

On the descent

We return from **Los Helechos** (0M) on our 'Forgotten Trail' route, taking care on the section of road walking until we meet the donkey trail (Wp.15), then enjoying the wonderful descent, taking extreme care at the road crossings (Wps. 16, 17 & 18) to come out on a dirt track running along the valley floor into **Haría**.

We stay on the dirt track which becomes a tarmac street after passing the sports ground, then it's Ceasar Manrique's house before the houses form up into long terraces, all different so quite the opposite of UK terraced houses. Easy strolling down the street, passing a couple of side streets and through a wiggle, brings us back onto our outward route at a T-junction just a few metres from our start point in the plaza (Wp.19 45M).

26 CIRCUIT OF HARÍA

The region around **Haría** contains quite a diversity of landscapes, ranging from lush valleys to barren hills and an unusual custom built *mirador* that nobody seems to know about. Our route is a complete mixture of a little tarmac, quite a lot of dirt road, a steep climb, a pathless section, breathtaking views; and the pleasure that comes from knowing that you wont have to share any of this with coach potatoes.

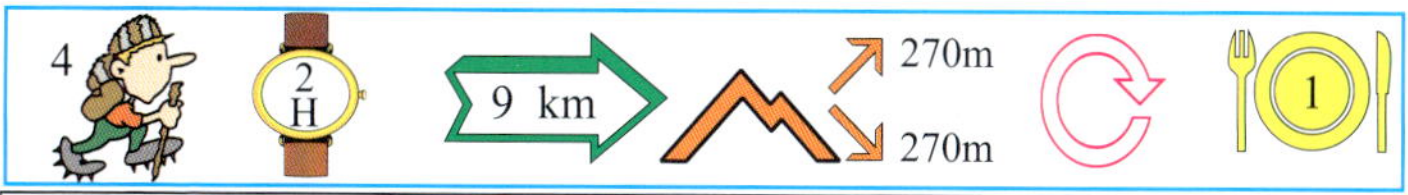

Stroll

From the **Eckholl** collection shop continue westwards on the street, which becomes the dirt road running up the valley to the *mirador* and return the same way.

Short Walk

Follow the route in reverse to the *mirador*, then continue on the dirt road back into **Haría**.

Access by car:
Park in **Haría**.

Access by bus:
N°7 from **Arrecife** calls at **Haría**; see appendices for details.

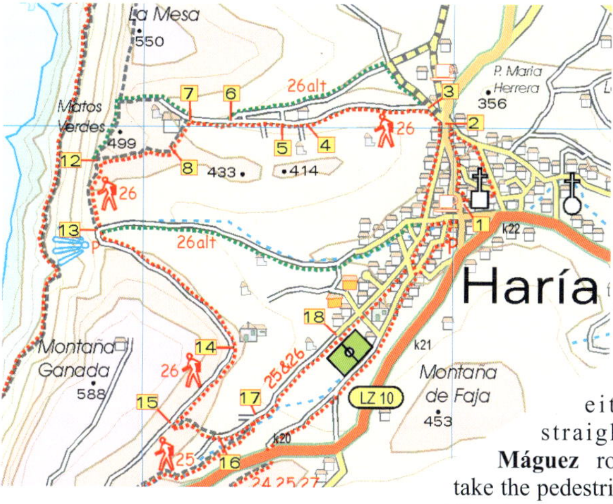

We start in the centre of **Haría** opposite **Bar Ney-Ha** (Wp.1 0M). Our first objective is the road junction at the top of the town. We can either walk straight up the **Máguez** road (N), or take the pedestrian street (E) past the church and then turn left (N) up the street; both options deal with the least pleasant part of the route as we slog up narrow streets. Both routes climb up the northern summit of the town, coming together at a junction (Wp.2) from which we head out on a country road on our front left (NE), **Calle Casa Atras**, rather a grand name for a smear of tarmac laid on a dirt road. Leaving the houses behind, we have views across the valley to a large quarry as we stroll down to a junction with a dirt road (Wp.3) going left (E).

Here we go left on the dirt road, though you could continue down the tarmac into the valley to go left on the next dirt road; it's a slightly longer and more energetic choice though, and with less extensive views. It's an easy stroll across the southern slope of the valley, passing through a patchwork of neatly cultivated plots and fallow fields being reclaimed by endemic plants.

We stroll past a squat house (Wp.4) surrounded by cultivated plots, and the dirt road becomes less used as we head up the valley. A steep dirt road drops down to the right linking our route with the longer alternative (Wp.5) before we crest a rise, then our road runs gently downhill to a junction with the alternative route (Wp.6). It is noticeable that the valley's southern slopes are more lush than the northern and mostly barren slopes, as we steadily ascend to come up to a breeze-block walled enclosure (Wp.7 33M).

Here we have another choice of route, our official route taking the faint track that climbs steeply up beside the enclosure. Another option is to continue on the dirt road to its end and follow a steep trail up over **Matos Verdes** to join our official route below the peak. The problem with this clifftop route is that it is usually extremely windy on all but the calmest days.

We take the faint track and start climbing steeply - and we do mean steeply - as the slope would benefit from having stairs cut into it.

The summit of the ridge, 40 minutes into the route

A 'puff and grunt' ascent takes us up past the top of the enclosure to reach the summit of the ridge by a gap in a stone wall (Wp.8 40M); after that exertion you have an excuse to stop and take in the extensive views over the **Haría** valley before continuing

Once through the wall, we swing right to follow it uphill towards a sad and lonely palm, the path is so little used we could think of this section as 'open ground' navigation. A small cairn (Wp.9) marks the spot where we move away from the wall and start to cross the long abandoned terraces to another gap in another stone wall (Wp.10). **La Caleta** and **Famara** come into view - and what a view it is - as we cross the terraces to a gap in another stone wall (Wp.11).

As we round the slopes below **Matos Verdes** we maintain altitude as we pass above a large stone storm-water wall which protects the lower valley, before coming to a path (Wp.12 52M) which runs down from the peak along the top of the cliffs; you'll notice that the wind's strength is multiplied several fold here near the cliff edge.

The path at 52 minutes

We pick our way down the path's gritty surface, which improves as we get lower, but it's still wiser to stop if you want to take in the impressive views. Our route runs down to join a dirt road beside an unusual structure (Wp.13 60M).

From above, this roofless structure resembles a very fancy grape vine cultivator, but from close to it is clearly a series of windbreaks for picnickers along with a parking area, so that they can enjoy the *mirador* views with some protection from the high winds; rather a shame that it does not feature on maps or in guide books, as visitors are most unlikely to stumble across this stunning location. While at the *mirador*, take the opportunity to look down the cliffs where you'll see a clear path cut across the cliff-face; this is part of our Walk 33 'Risco de Famara' route.

From the *mirador* you have a choice of either short-cutting down the dirt road running down the valley to **Haría**, or taking our official longer route exploring the **Haría** valley. Leaving the *mirador*, we head up the dirt road which runs below the slopes of **Montaña Ganada**. After a steady uphill the gradient eases for easy strolling between abandoned terraces above and below our route, more of **Haría** coming into sight ahead of us.

Views over the Haría valley as we descend

A pungent whiff announces a goat farm ahead as we pass the first cultivated plots, climbing a rise before the road turns right above the goat farm (Wp.14 74M), giving excellent views over the **Haría** valley. Now it's easy strolling towards **Valle de Malpaso**, our route lined with gigantic prickly pear in places as we walk above neatly cultivated plots to come to a junction (Wp.15 80M).

Going left, we leave the main dirt track to descend between the plots on a rough track, once a boulder-laid donkey trail but now much eroded and covered in *picon* grit in places, requiring careful footwork on our descent. The track narrows to a trail and then to a path, before it comes down to a track which runs along the valley floor (Wp.16 88M).

Gratefully, we turn left and head along the track as it runs gently downhill to come onto a better stabilised track by a chained entrance (Wp.17 91M). It's comfortable strolling, crossing a plant-choked water course before we reach civilisation in the form of the sports centre football ground (Wp.18), after which the houses start. Continuing down the tarmac street we turn right at its end, by the **Eckholl** collection shop, and walk along to the **Plaza de la Constitución** and the prospect of an *agua con gas* followed by a cold beer in **Bar Ney-Ha** (110M).

27 CAPITAL ROUTE - HARÍA TO TEGUISE

In far distant days **Teguise** was the capital of Lanzarote, and as is the way of things, all routes led to the capital. This long linear route is a relic of those times, when it provided the main route from **Haría** to the capital. Being a ridge-top route, it has survived the depredations of road building largely intact, and its elevation produces many spectacular views. There's a stiff climb through Lanzarote's most floriferous landscape, but you can divert to **Bar/Rest Los Helechos** for refreshments after completing most of the ascent. Once on the ridge - more a wide-backed *lomo* - it's easy striding with stops to take in the awesome cliff-top views. After those views, trailing down into **Teguise** is rather disappointing, but at least it makes for easy walking.

Access by car:
Park in **Haría**.

Short Walk.
See Walk 24, 'The Forgotten Trail'

Access by bus:
N°7 from **Arrecife** calls at **Haría**; see appendices for timetables.

We start out from the centre of **Haría**, following the directions for 'The Forgotten Trail', up to Wp.15 (55M). If, with most of the ascent behind you, you want to take a break, then follow 'The Forgotten Trail' road walk up to **Bar/Rest Los Helechos**. On leaving the bar, walk south along the road and take the first tarmac lane off to the right to meet our official route just before the military radar golf-balls. From Wp.15 we continue straight ahead to come onto a dirt road. Keeping straight on along the track, we come up past a

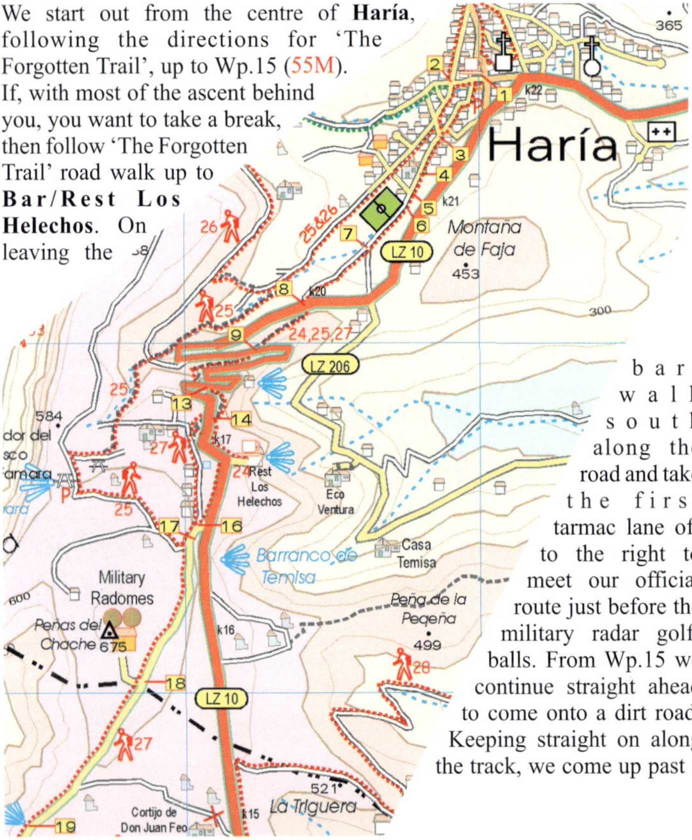

house, with **Bar/Rest Los Helechos** across a field on our left. We walk up past two more houses, the radar golf-balls coming into sight, before a section of the track goes left while we continue onto the tarmac lane (Wp.16) which serves the **Ermita de las Nieves**. We have an easy stroll along the narrow lane, ignoring a track to our front right (Wp.17), and passing the radar station entrance (Wp.18), with views opening up to our left (E) over the main road and down to the coastal plain.

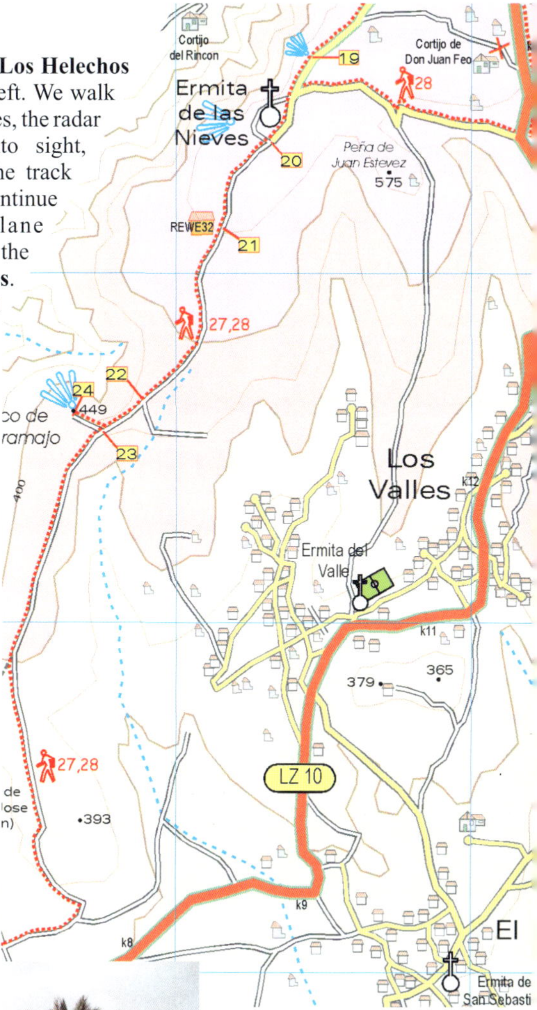

Over a small crest, and now the *ermita* comes into view ahead of us. This is easy striding country, so you might care to divert right to a *mirador* viewpoint at the top of the cliffs (Wp.19) before strolling over to arrive at the *ermita*'s walled courtyard (Wp.20 90M), where we take shelter from the wind inside its walled garden. From the **Ermita de las Nieves,** our route could not be more straightforward. We simply stroll south-west on the dirt road, passing '**REWE32**' (Wp.21), another military compound with aerials.

The pilgrims' well in the *ermita*'s garden

The dirt road, little-used by vehicles, makes for easy strolling as it runs gently downhill along the broad backed *lomo*; for more imposing views we can always divert right to the cliff top. We pass a track off to the left (Wp.22) before coming to a junction (Wp.23) where we go right to a *mirador* viewpoint overlooking a sharp cleft in the cliffs (Wp.24); beautiful views and even equipped with seat-height rocks to relax on.

... views, views ...

We come back to the main track to continue gently downhill with **Castillo de Santa Bárbara** dominating the view ahead. Our route curves towards the south and the first buildings of **Teguise** come into view. A black *picon* field stands out against the barren landscape, just before a small uphill section, after which our track starts to run down off the *lomo* towards a patchwork of cultivated fields., then curving down to a cross-roads of tracks (Wp.25). The main road is away on our left as we go straight ahead on the narrower track running between the plots directly towards the town. We pass a track off to the right (Wp.26) before strolling up behind the first buildings of the town at a track junction (Wp.27) then reaching the football ground (Wp.28) where we finally come onto town streets. Keeping the church tower as our direction finder we stroll down the quiet streets (on weekdays at least) to arrive in the main square (Wp.29).

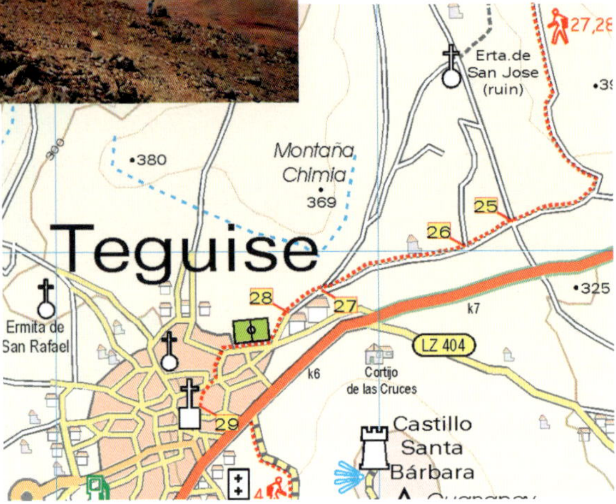

ERMITA DE LAS NIEVES

17th century **Ermita de las Nieves** (Chapel of the Snows) stands in isolation at Lanzarote's coldest, windiest and most exposed spot; visitors can shelter inside its surrounding walls, an oasis of relative calm away from the ferocity of the elements within which a garden thrives. Pilgrims of all sorts have paused here over the centuries, whether seeking spiritual sustenance or the quenching of thirst from its drinking water supply, though we can't vouch for its potability. The *ermita* itself is open on Saturdays (14.30 - 18.00) and on 5th August, its Saint's day.

The views from the cliffs near the *ermita* shouldn't be missed, but take great care, especially on windy days (unfortunately, in the majority). **Playa de Famara** lies below, while the island of **La Graciosa** will be visible on a clear day to your right, beyond the **Risco de Famara** cliff. You may also make out the further islands of **Montaña Clara** and beyond that, **Isla de Alegranza** when visibility allows. The highest point on the island (670 metres) is **Peñas del Chache** to the north-north east, standing 70 metres higher than the *ermita* and occupied by a military installation, so is off limits to visitors.

28 MALA TO TEGUISE

Another of Lanzarote's classic walking routes, all of which is on well stabilised dirt tracks or tarmac. The second half of the route, from **Ermita de las Nieves**, is common to Walks 27 and 28, so is not repeated again here. Our route has been only marginally affected by the LZ1 road which opened in March 2004 as our original track is now bridged over the new fast road. Our personal preference is for our **Haría-Teguise** route as the initial ascent simply melts away, but here it is always staring you in the face all the way up to the ridge. If you have an old Noel Rochford Landscapes (1998 edition) and a GPS, this is a good route to compare modern navigation techniques with a pre-GPS description.

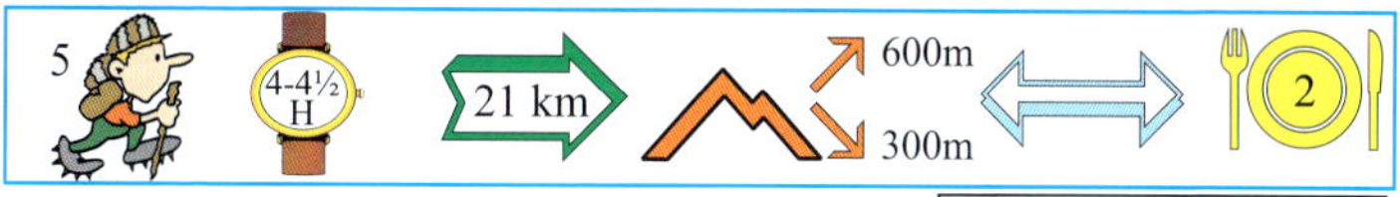

Access by bus:
N°9, and some of the N°7 buses to **Mala**; alight at the *farmacía*, then walk along the old main road (N) for 200 metres and just past the village school our route starts at the tarmac lane on the left (Wp.1).

Short Walk
To **Ermita de las Nieves** and return (3½ hours) and you get the benefit from your climb on the downhill return.

Access by car:
2CSK Route (see P.19)
Not really a car driver's route except by our '2CSK' approach. Park off the old main road in **Mala**, but on the main road in **Teguise**; it's easier to find a car on the main road than in the warren of town streets.

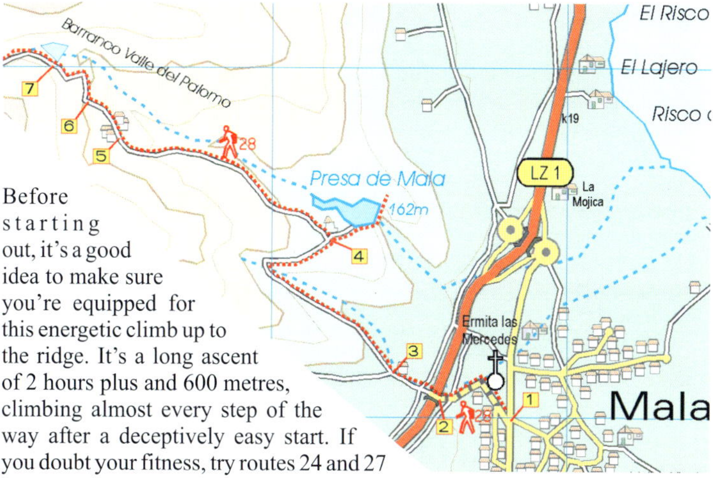

Before starting out, it's a good idea to make sure you're equipped for this energetic climb up to the ridge. It's a long ascent of 2 hours plus and 600 metres, climbing almost every step of the way after a deceptively easy start. If you doubt your fitness, try routes 24 and 27 first.

From the old main road (Wp.1 0M) we walk up the tarmac lane, keeping right to pass in front of **Ermita de la Merceo** where our lane swings left to head across the plain towards the distant ridge. The new LZ1 road presents no difficulty as our route climbs gently up to a bridge over the new road (Wp.2), but the plethora of 'Armco' crash barriers and new wide dirt roads has ruined a once tranquil landscape. Over the bridge, and we are heading towards rural tranquility as we come up to a pair of houses at a junction and take the right hand track (Wp.3).

Cochineal farming

We're now climbing steadily up the side of a valley to go through a hairpin bend across its watercourse which gives us views back over our outward route, and the fields devoted to the 'tunera' cactus and their 'crop' of Cochineal beetle which are still cultivated in this region. We come up onto the line of the ridge and a junction beside a ruin (Wp.4 26M) where a track goes off to our right. There is still plenty of climbing to come, so you might want to take a break by walking out along the track to see the **Presa de Mala** dam, only containing water after wet weather.

From the *presa* junction we continue up the track toward a distant hamlet, the ground around our route deeply scarred by storm water erosion, in contrast to the massively walled terraces along this section. A steady ascent brings us up to the hamlet (Wp.5 44M) to walk past an impressive stone wall (Wp.6) and the radomes come into view; known locally as the 'golf balls'. With the cliff wall at the head of the **Barranco Valle del Palomo** looming ahead of us, we start slicing our route up into our 'one step after another' approach with a dam in the *barranco* floor (Wp.7) giving us the chance for a 'Look at that' breather. Passing a ruin (Wp.8) gives another excuse, as does a small bridge (Wp.9 71M). Cultivated plots enclosed by well built walls have relieved

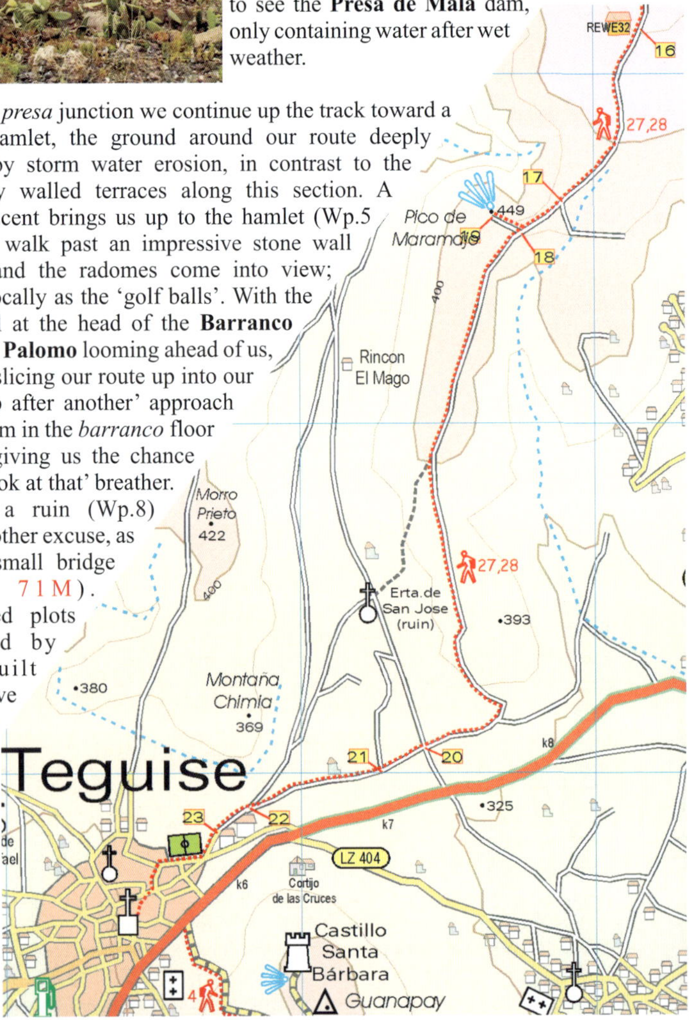

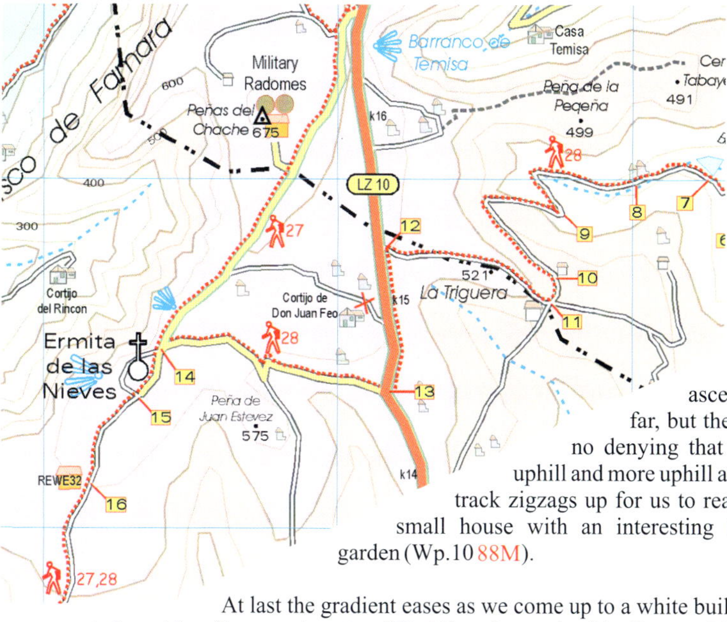

the ascent so far, but there is no denying that it is uphill and more uphill as our track zigzags up for us to reach a small house with an interesting back garden (Wp.10 88M).

At last the gradient eases as we come up to a white building set alongside a five-way junction (Wp.11) to the north of the **Parque Eólico** wind farm. Turning right to pass in front of the building, we have the luxury of a gentle uphill stroll to come onto the LZ10 road (Wp.12 105M), facing the radomes set on **Peñas del Chache**. Turning left down the road we head towards the wind farm to take the lane on the right (Wp.13) signed to the **Ermita de las Nieves**. Up the lane, we wriggle through a zigzag before coming up to meet the dirt track of Walk 26 (Wp.14). Left up the tarmac, or around the dirt track that runs around the western side, brings us up to a well earned break at the island's best known *ermita* (Wp.15 132M).

Famara and La Caleta, far below

Ermita de las Nieves (Chapel of the Snows) is a popular stopping off point for both walkers and drivers, and could be idyllic, if only someone would put in a little *tipico* bar to cater for the many visitors. Sitting on the well in the *ermita*'s courtyard is the most comfortable option, but we would not rely upon the it's water supply. If you've made the climb in hot weather (What other sort is there on Lanzarote?) you'll appreciate the cool shade given by the courtyard walls; before leaving, stroll west across the parking area to the edge of the escarpment for the best views down over **Famara** and **La Caleta**.

Our second stage of the route into **Teguise** is identical to Walk 27. GPS users should note that waypoints 16 to 23 are equivalent to waypoints 21 to 28 of Walk 27. Also note that the GPS waypoints are not identical, having been recorded on different days in very slightly different positions.

29 HELECHOS CIRCULAR

This interesting circular route takes in bucolic farmland, upland meadows (yes, meadows), stunning cliff-top views, a peak and one of Lanzarote's most impressive *calderas*; only refreshments are missing. Ascents are never steeper than steady, and the range of landscapes and views makes even these seem relatively gentle. All the route is on either narrow tarmac lanes or well-stabilised dirt tracks, so you could drive this route - but why would you want to?

Some guides describe the main circuit of this route in the opposite direction. This involves a mind-sapping relentless ascent right from the start which makes the route seem more penance than enjoyment.

Stroll	Short route
Drive up the route in reverse and make the ascent of **Helechos** on foot	Omit the four diversions off the main circuit, though you'll miss some of the most interesting features. **Alternative Short Route** Park just off the **Guinate** road by Wp.6. Follow official route to Wp.9 and go right to return to your car - see map.

Access by car: with on street parking in **Máguez**.

Access by bus:
Nº7 runs from **Arrecife** to **Máguez**; see appendices for timetables.

We start off in the centre of **Máguez** by house Nº16 (Wp.1 0M) by going (ENE) along a quiet street past the church on our left to come along to a cross roads (Wp.2) where we go left. A steady uphill stroll takes us past houses and vegetable plots, with **Helechos** on our front left. The street gets steeper and narrower before we go over the crest to leave **Calle las Casillas** on a well-used dirt track (Wp.3). After that steepish urban start we are now heading out (NE) into a bucolic landscape with the bulk of **Monte Corona** ahead of us. This is easy strolling between fallow and cultivated plots, passing tracks off to right and left, before coming to a junction (Wp.4) where we go left on the minor track.

Our track gently climbs past a rock outcrop towards a pair of buildings. The buildings resolve into a house and its garage as we come to the crest of the track to see the main road and **Guinate** junction ahead of us. Another easy stroll down through a meadow landscape (yes, this *is* Lanzarote) brings us to the main road opposite the **Mirador de Guinate** road (Wp.5).

Along the **Guinate** road, we turn off the tarmac onto a track (Wp.6). Now it is a steady climb round the slopes of **Helechos**, the effort partly relieved by the expanding views as we ascend past ancient walls and long abandoned plots. Past a cultivated field and a lichen-encrusted outcrop announces our arrival at a pass (453 metres) and a few metres further (Wp.7) we take a diversion to our right to follow a faint track (NW) to a viewpoint (Wp.8) at a stone wall overlooking the **Guinate** valley. Just beyond the wall, stone-walled, black *picon* plots of grape vines contrast with the meadows we've crossed.

The purple sheen of Viper's Bugloss

Back on the main track (Wp.7) we head up (WSW) through the waving grassland and meadow flowers towards another pass. Viper's Bugloss flowers give the slopes a gentle purple sheen as we come up to overlook the **Valle de Guinate**: the dirt road running along the valley is the route of our Alternative Short Walk. Now we stroll along overlooking the valley beside fallow meadow fields. On our front right is a remarkable 'bite' out of the ridge as though bitten by giant teeth; yes, you <u>could</u> drive this route, but how much more enjoyable to stroll through this wonderful landscape.

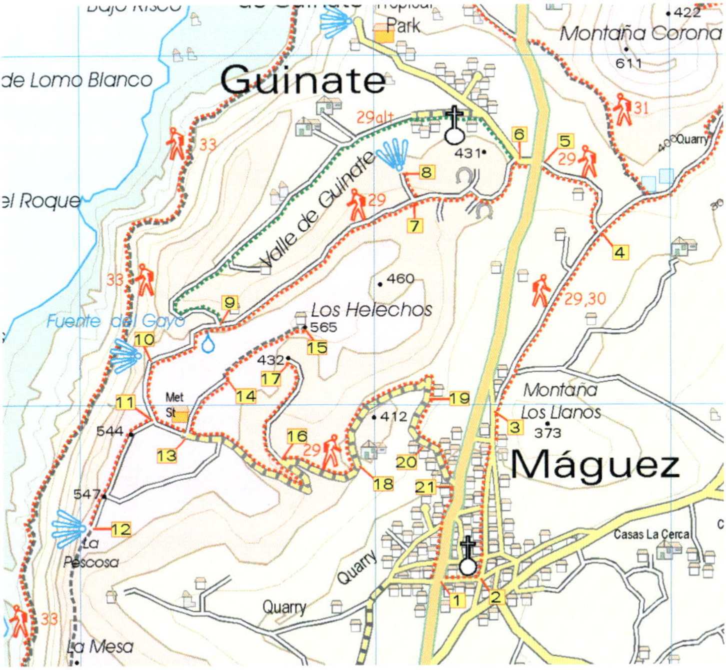

An uphill section takes us up past a house to a junction (Wp.9), where our Alternative Short Route goes right to drop down towards the valley floor.

Just past the junction we pass a pair of pits beside the track before reaching a Y-junction where we take the left fork; the two tracks soon coming together again. A valley drops steeply down on our right as we continue uphill to the top of the cliffs (Wp.10); take care if you approach the cliff edge as the winds are powerful. We stay on the track as it undulates along (SE) away from the cliffs to reach a junction (Wp.11).

Here we take the minor track (WSW) heading for the cliff tops at **La Pescosa**. We walk up past fields cut out of the meadows to come up onto the headland. This track ends at a storm-eroded area (Wp.12) from where we take in impressive views down over **El Risco de Famara** to **La Caleta** and the plain beyond.

Back at the main track (Wp.11) we head (E) past a white meteorological station, where the track becomes tarmacked, to another junction (Wp.13) where a track goes left (N). Taking to the track for our third diversion off the main circular route, we climb up onto a broad backed ridge which although only a few metres above our earlier route is almost barren with the exception of a black *picon* field. We walk along the rough track to swing left and right beside the field (Wp.14).

Ahead, the track leads us up the slope to the transmitter hut sitting on the top of **Helechos**, views opening up down over the **Valle de Guinate** from the saddle before the final walk up to the hut (Wp.15).

David just visible on the Helechos peak track

The rounded summit has plenty of plant life and the wreck of a transmitting tower blown down by ferocious winds. This is literally the high point of our route, so take your time enjoying the panoramic views before returning to our main route.

The *caldera* below Helechos peak

Back on the tarmac (Wp.13) we head (E) downhill, steadily at first and then steeply down through a hairpin bend to a junction (Wp.16) where a track heads off towards the **Helechos** peak from the second hairpin bend. By now you might well be dreaming of a cold beer in **Máguez** and be tempted to ignore this track, but stay with us for our fourth, and final, diversion off the main route. We walk out along the track, which is nothing special until it reaches a crest for us to find ourselves looking down into the *caldera* directly below the **Helechos** peak.

Our track continues down around the wall of the crater to reach the flat floor at the foot of sheer cliffs (Wp.17), giving us an impressive sense of scale in this soaring cliff landscape despite some rubbish dumping. Climbing back up the track out of the *caldera*, we arrive back at the tarmac. Now the return to **Máguez** is straightforward, as we simply walk down the tarmac lane, descending past cultivated fields, a farm (Wp.18) and an unusual dwelling set below the road (Wp.19). Houses start (Wp.20) shortly before we meet the main road (Wp.21) where we go right to walk down to our start point.

30 MÁGUEZ TO YÉ

A pleasing rural route, giving close up views of Lanzarote's agricultural region seldom seen by the average visitor. The range of different landscapes encountered on this moderate length route has to be seen to be believed. All the walking is on good dirt tracks or tarmac, technically driveable but much more fun on foot.

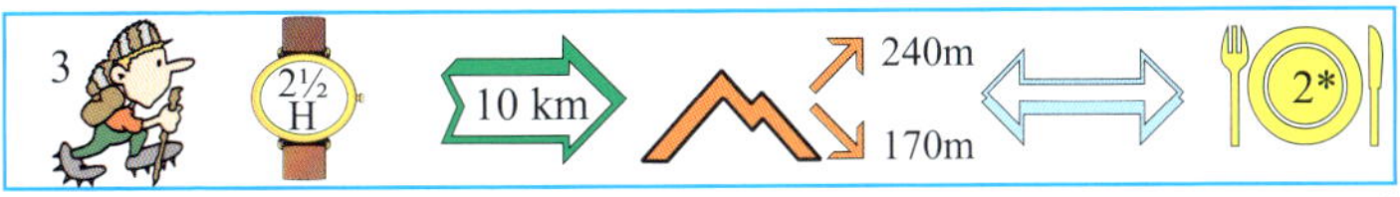

*in the **Centro Social Cultural de Yé** though they're not always open

Short Route
Park at **Yé** and walk back down the road (SE) until you come to the dirt track at Wp.7, then follow the main description for a circular route of 6.5 kilometres.

Access by bus:
Route Nº7 serves both **Máguez** and **Yé**, but not all departures call at **Yé**. See timetables for details.

Starting from the centre of **Máguez**, we follow the same route as Walk 29, 'Helechos Circular' until that route turns left at Wp.4. At this junction we keep straight ahead (NE) on the main track to walk gently uphill, as the bulk of **Monte Corona** starts to loom over us. Passing a water tank with blue door we come over a rise by a second water tank (Wp.5) to come into a *picon* landscape, much harsher than the earlier plain. Sturdy boulder walls criss-cross the land ahead as we pass a *picon* quarry, very different to the cultivated fields away on our right.

As our track wriggles through the moonscape, the top of the large mansion of **Torrecilla de Domingo** comes into view, gradually revealed as we come alongside cultivated plots and keep left at a junction, just before meeting the main road (Wp.6). Uphill, on or alongside the tarmac, we pass in front of the mock-fortified **Torrecilla de Domingo** to leave the road on a broad track (Wp.7) that drops down between stone walls. We head out into a 'walled' landscape - and we really do mean walled; there seem to be more walls than you would ever need to protect crops; not that this can be a consideration as the whole area is long abandoned.

Torrecilla de Domingo

Views over the Vega Grande valley

We stay on the main track, passing two tracks off right before coming over a rise, where the landscape ahead becomes more normal with cultivated plots. Strolling

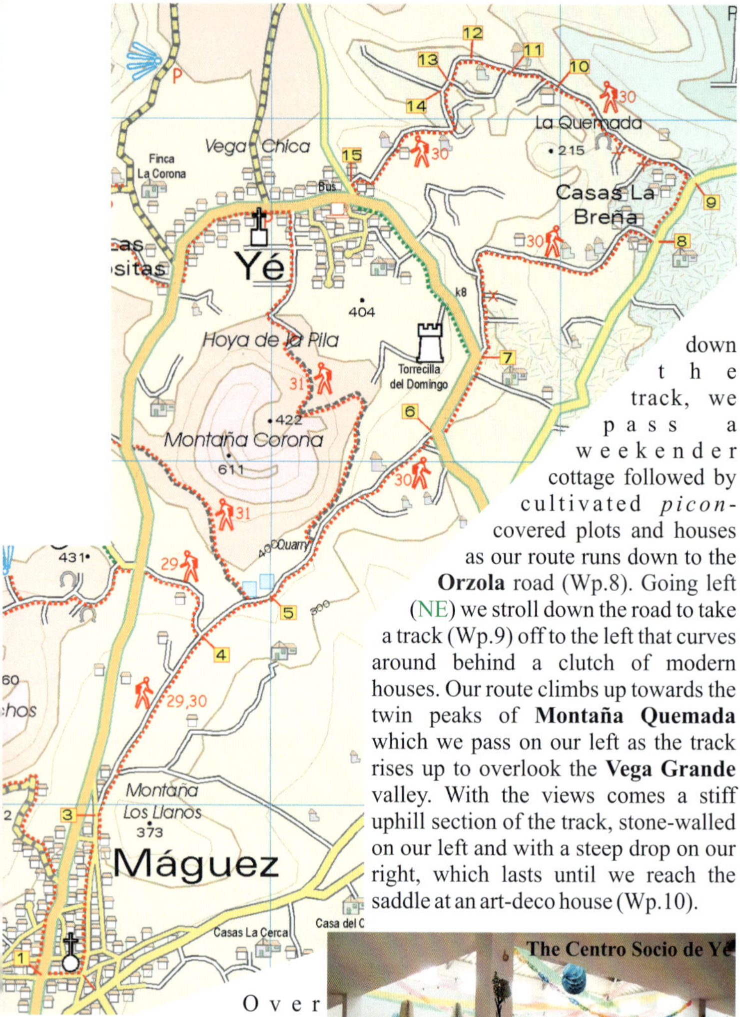

down the track, we pass a weekender cottage followed by cultivated *picon*-covered plots and houses as our route runs down to the **Orzola** road (Wp.8). Going left (NE) we stroll down the road to take a track (Wp.9) off to the left that curves around behind a clutch of modern houses. Our route climbs up towards the twin peaks of **Montaña Quemada** which we pass on our left as the track rises up to overlook the **Vega Grande** valley. With the views comes a stiff uphill section of the track, stone-walled on our left and with a steep drop on our right, which lasts until we reach the saddle at an art-deco house (Wp.10).

The Centro Socio de Yé

Over the saddle, we ignore a minor track left as we head down above cultivated fields in the valley below us, passing an old mill (Wp.11) and a ruin beside interesting rocks (Wp.12) before reaching cultivated fields which stretch up the valley on our right.

Passing a track off to the left (Wp.13) and one off to the right (Wp.14), we face a stiff climb up from the valley floor, passing another two tracks off to the left before the gradient eases beside walled grape vines. Passing a house on our left, we walk steadily uphill in a slogging ascent to the first houses of **Yé** (Wp.15) where we turn left to meet the main road. Do call in at the most unusual *tipico* bar on the island in the **Centro Socio Cultural de Yé** alongside the main bus stop, for coffee and to admire the murals.

31 CORONA'S NORTHERN TOUR

Approach the north of Lanzarote and one thing stands out - **Montaña Corona**, the classic volcanic cone peak that dominates the view ahead as you leave **Máguez**. We have great routes in the north (see walks 29, 30, 32 and 33) but somehow we'd never tackled the big northern mountain. Then came the happenstance of meeting Carmen Portella Ernest through Andreas at the **Bike Station** who invited us to join her group on a recently pioneered route taking in the mountain's *caldera* and **Famara** views as part of a northern tour. Carmen, a professional guide, pioneered this route; this, and the prospect of convivial walking companions combined with **Montaña Corona** was an opportunity too good to miss. As Carmen, surprisingly, did not know of the social centre theatre and bar in **Yé** (see Walk 29) we planned to add this surprise refreshment stop ending to the expedition.

The result is an interesting route taking in some amazing sights though as a new route paths are not the clearest and there is a risk of vertigo on the narrow path curving round below the peak.

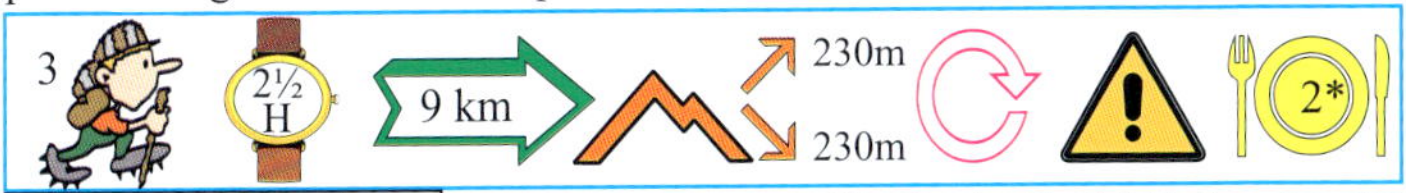

*in **Centro Social Cultural de Yé** though they're not always open

Short Walk A
Yé church to **Corona Caldera** and return (2 walker, 3kms, 1 hour).

Short Walk B
Famara cliffs and return, park on Camino de Guatifay and follow route to Wp.16 and return (2 Walker, 2.5kms, 1 hour).

Access by car:
Park in **Yé** church's extensive car park - avoid religious fiestas (not feasible by bus).

We start from the church car park entrance (Wp.1 0M) to walk along the road (E) for 150 metres where we take a dirt track (Wp.2 4M) heading (S) towards the mountain. Our track winds gently uphill through a *zoco*-cultivated area, grapes and almonds, side tracks accessing the fields as we steadily close with **Montaña Corona**. Gradually, cultivation gives out (Wp.3) as we continue gently uphill through abandoned fields and a shallow valley before ascending through lazy zigzags until our track runs out close to the mountain base (Wp.4 16M). A walking trail continues up past the end of the *zocos* to a stately palm where

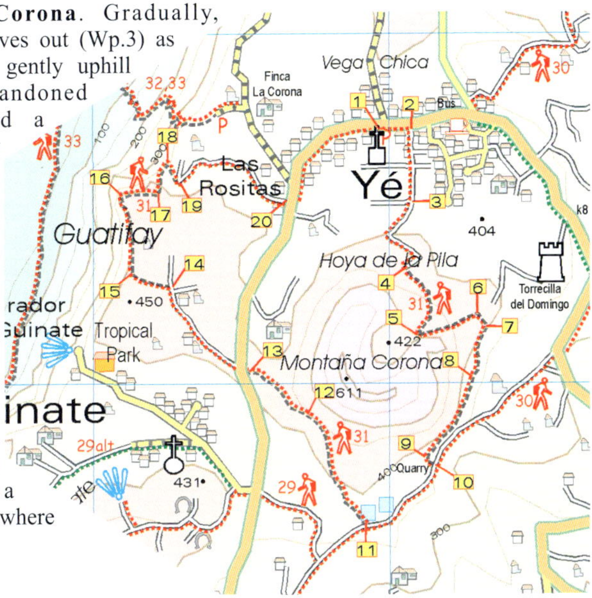

our narrow trail starts a more serious ascent through endemic plant life, passing a trail coming in from our right before going through a stone wall to continue up to the edge of the mountain's *caldera* (Wp.5 28M). It's an impressive *caldera*, the cone's southern section intact as seen in the view from **Máguez**, while the northern rim has collapsed giving us a 'rim-edge' view down to the caldera floor - don't go too close to the edge as the rocks are undercut - more collapses can be expected at any time! From the *caldera* we head west to follow an old stone wall. There's no path as such as we negotiate abandoned terraces, clambering from level to level through, and round, the vigorous plant life including prickly pear!

.. an impressive *caldera* ..

Don't think it's all like this; we're on the worst section of the route - as more walkers beat a path down beside the wall a reasonable walking trail will emerge. Finally we drop down an old terrace onto a faint path that brings us to a metal fence (Wp.6 40M) where a very broad stone wall goes right (SE). There is an onward path, but we go right onto the top of the broad stone wall for seventy metres before stepping down onto a narrow walking trail (Wp.7).

Our trail winds through an area of abandoned *zocos* before contouring round **Montaña Corona**. It's a narrow one-person path cutting across steep *picon* slopes which might give problems for vertigo sufferers until we come to a section of volcanic boulders and *vinagrera* plants (Wp.8). Past the boulders, we continue our gradual descent on the narrow *picon* path to arrive at the 'picon-cliff' edge of a quarry (Wp.9). Our path turns down by the edge of the quarry for a steep, skittery, slippery descent on the loose picon grit - consider going down on all fours (undignified but safe) while the adventurous might consider a 'scree-surf' descent to the quarry floor; both options bring us down onto the dirt road (of Walk 30, Wp.10 62M). After the narrow path this road is luxury; we stroll along to a pair of water cisterns set below the southern slopes of **Montaña Corona** (Wp.11 70M). Carmen declared a break at this point. We all consume the packed snack lunches she's provided, while showing us the cisterns' construction and explaining their key role in local agriculture.

On the trail after Wp.11

From the top of the second cistern (Wp.11 0M) we take a very faint trail heading up over the *picon* (NW) towards a saddle below the slopes of the mountain. From the saddle we walk up through an old terrace wall as we head towards a dark lava rock wall; it's easy uphill open ground walking but there's no defined path as we cross old terraces to step above the lava rock wall (Wp.12 15M). Here we walk above the wall, which reduces to nothing as we continue uphill across another wall to come onto a *picon* walking trail; following this brings us above another small quarry where we have another slip/slidey descent to come onto the road facing **Camino de Guatifay** (Wp.13 27M).

.. views ..

Carefully crossing the road we stroll up the **Camino de Guatifay** dirt road with views down over **Guinate** and the **Tropical Park** while passing a couple of houses on our left, complete with a 'Cliffs de Guinate' sign, before we come to a white cottage on our right,

.. more views ..

just past which a dirt track goes right while we turn left (Wp.14 38M) on an old track, now bouldered against vehicle access, to head directly towards the cliffs. As we've been walking only gently uphill since the road, the top of the **Famara** cliffs and the views (Wp.15) come on us suddenly - a pleasant 'suddenly' as the views are stupendous.

Swinging right, we walk gently downhill with **Las Salinas** and the island of **Graciosa** laid out below us, to pick up a cliff-top path (about four metres in from the edge); take your time on this section as the views, firstly back along the cliffs to the **Guinate** *mirador* and later (Wp.16 52M) over **Las Salinas** and **Graciosa** are some of Lanzarote's best - though remember to 'Stop, and look at the view'. Our route swings right (E) along the line of the cliffs over rough ground to step over a low wall (Wp.17) then swings left on a narrow walking trail descending towards fields in the valley floor. Where the path goes over a wall (Wp.18) to continue towards **Las Salinas** *mirador*, we go right to double back and descend towards the fields and a grey/blue gate. After crossing a gully on a 'cable-drum' bridge we pass the gate to come onto a dirt track (Wp.19 64M). It's an easy stroll along the dirt track which winds along the floor of a small valley literally stuffed with endemic flora until we come up to a house with noisy dogs (chained) at the junction with the road (Wp.20 76M). Striding out up the road, watching for traffic, we pass the outlying houses of **Yé** as we close with our start point at the church parking area (Wp.1 85M).

We haven't passed any opportunities for refreshment around the whole route so we could try our Walk 30 unusual *tipico* at **Yé** social centre; just continue along the road (E) towards the centre of the village - as much as the village has a centre - to the bus stop where we find the social centre. Inside is a theatre setting with wall murals and a café, and when we've found it open on all previous visits we were assured that all visitors will be most welcome - though a little bit of Spanish helps. This time, with Carmen and the walking tour in tow, we found the centre shut - most disappointing, though we hope this most unusual of Lanzarote *tipicos* will be open and welcoming when you call in.

32 SALINAS DEL RÍO

Yé is a sleepy farming village far removed from the excesses of Lanzarote's beach resorts. In addition to its rural tranquility, it boasts the most unusual *tipico* bar on the island in the **Centro Socio Cultural de Yé** alongside the main bus stop; do call in for coffee and admire the wall murals. Most visitors who discover **Yé** are simply passing through on their way to the 'pay on entry' sanitised **Mirador del Río**; once a simple gun emplacement dating from the civil war, but now upgraded to a 'tourist' attraction for the coach potatoes.

Less well known and largely undiscovered by the casual visitor is the *mirador* overlooking the **Salinas del Río**, where you'll not only enjoy similar views, but you'll be in the unusual situation of seeing your whole walking route laid out in front of you before you start out. Even if you don't plan to walk the **Salinas del Río**, or the 'Yé to La Caleta' cliff-face walk, you must visit this *mirador* if your visit to Lanzarote is to be complete.

Access by car (not feasible by bus)**:**
From **Máguez**, drive past the **Guinate** junction, and turn off the main road 1.7 kilometres further on, onto a narrow lane at **Las Rositas**. Drive carefully down the lane until the imposing **Finca La Corona** is on your right, and then turn left onto a stone-flagged road which widens into a car park.

From the car park (Wp.1 0M) we walk along the path past pleasant rocky scenery before starting to drop down a staired descent, views opening up over the straights to **Isla Graciosa**. The stairs bring us to a stone built *mirador* by an electricity pylon (Wp.2). Along with the beautiful views this is also your decision point. Far below us are the multi-hued *salinas* salt pans, while the path drops straight down

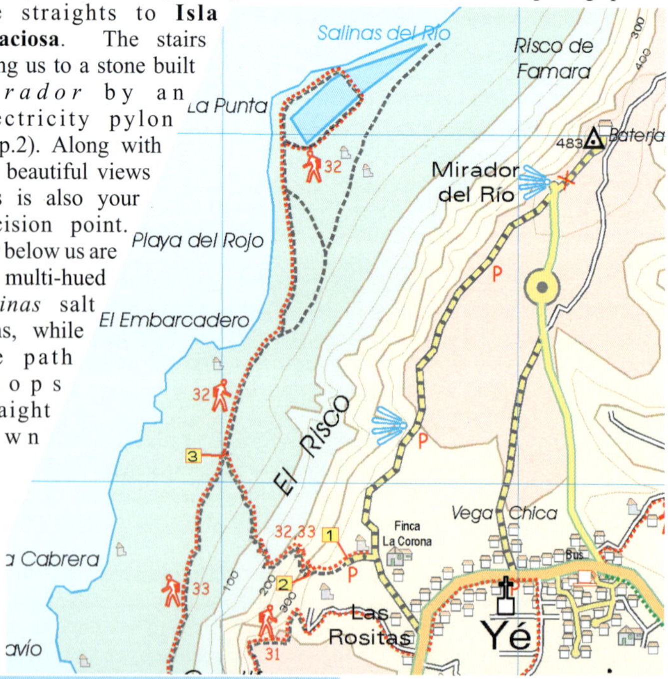

the cliffs; an intensely steep descent requiring careful footwork on the zigzagging trail, and an equally intense 'puff & grunt' ascent on your return.

Contemplating the descent

From the *mirador*, our whole route is laid out below us, and it is decision time. This is easily the steepest descent and ascent on the island, requiring concentration all the way down. Concentrating on where you are putting your feet helps combat any sense of vertigo, as does facing the cliff when taking breaks. However if it is windy, or any sign of bad weather, we would suggest you save this route for another day.

On the zigzag descent

We set off, stepping down through the small, steep zigzags in a near vertical descent. This continues down for over a hundred metres before there is any relaxation on a moderate slope, and then we tackle a second series of small, steep zigzags for another hundred metres of near-vertical descent. Finally, our trail comes to a steady descent, and a fainter trail goes left offering a short cut on our **Risco de Famara** route. Keeping straight on we are on easy walking to come down to a T-junction with a track (Wp.3 48M).

Having made the descent, we are now free to explore the beach and salt pans, either by keeping to the track (N) or using the tracery of small paths that have been walked. The track ends at an electricity transformer that sends power over to **La Graciosa** via a sea bed cable. **Salinas del Río** is no longer in production, but at least its 'pans' are still here, and the evaporating sea water creates some beautiful colours. Cozzie-optional swimming is popular at the beach of **Playa del Risco**, so do indulge yourself if you wish. This is a beautiful isolated region, where we usually see only eco-responsible walkers, so it's an unwelcome surprise to find so much litter, in particular broken bottles, detracting from its natural beauty.

At some stage we have to remember that civilisation in the form of our car is at the top of that cliff. Personally we prefer the ascent to the knee-jarring descent despite its 'puff & grunt' nature requiring a lot of recovery stops, but like it or hate it, it has got to be climbed. At least, when we get back to the *mirador* we certainly have a well-earned sense of achievement.

33 EL RISCO DE FAMARA

Lanzarote's classic walking route is not for the faint hearted, as it starts with that awesome descent used for our **Salinas del Río** route. The central part of the route is on an amazing path that has been hacked and dynamited out of the sheer cliff face of the **Famara** - quite why anyone should have undertaken such a labour is a mystery, but it has given us a route that is spectacular in any walker's lexicon. You can see a glimpse of this path from the **Mirador de Haría** on Walk 25; medium danger of vertigo on the descent and on the cliff face path. Best walked in the early morning, when most of the route is in shade from the cliffs.

If this route has a problem, it's because it is long and linear between two places not best served by public transport. Best approach is to use two cars between four to eight walkers. Park one car at **La Caleta** or **Famara** with half the party, and drive the other car to **Yé** and park at the end of the stone-flagged road as for Walk 32. When you meet up, remember to exchange car keys (see P.19 for a full explanation).

5 | 5½ H | 17 km | 100m 480m | 0

Access by car (bus access not feasible): Park at the end of the stone flagged road outside **Yé** (see Walk 32). When you reach **La Caleta** ask in the bars if they will call you a taxi for the trip back to **Yé**.

Short Walk

While not really a short walk, we suggest that you walk to **Punta del Roque** (Wp.5) and return. This is still four hours, but you do arrive back at your car.

Assuming we are in the downward group, we start off from the parking area (Wp.1 0M) outside **Yé** to walk down to the *mirador* (Wp.2) and tackle the descent down to the T-junction with the track (Wp.3 48M).

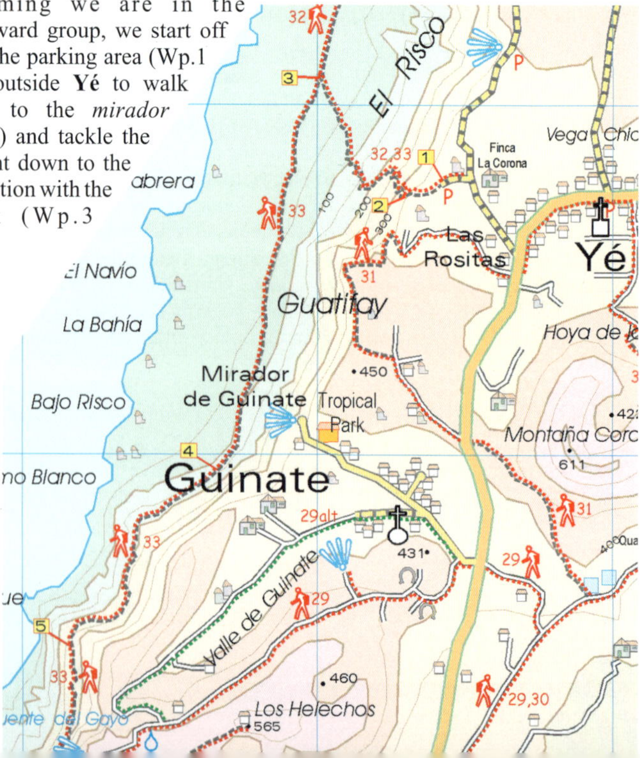

The descent to Wp.3

Here we turn left (S) to start the steady ascent up the old track, which climbs for a hundred metres to come back under the main cliffs (Wp.4 90M) and the cliff face section.

This path is remarkable, having been cut into the hardest rock on Lanzarote. We continue gradually uphill taking great care on any scree-covered sections, and whenever our route crosses gullies in the cliff face. It's steadily onwards and upwards until we cross a series of gullies

El Risco de Famara

to reach the trail's summit at **Punta del Roque** (Wp.5 126M) to be met by the spectacular view over **Famara** and **La Caleta**.

From **Punta del Roque** our trail slowly descends, but you are hardly likely to notice the gradient as we marvel at the path's construction, almost tunnelled along the cliff face in places, plus the views which are just spectacular. After what seems like a lifetime suspended alongside the **Risco de Famara**, our trail returns to normality (Wp.6 217M) as it becomes a scree-covered picky descent down towards a water tank and a house.

Down past the water tank, we come to the house (Wp.7 233M) set at the entrance of a tunnel that used to connect the pumping station to **Haría**. Until quite recently you could walk through the tunnel to **Haría**, but now it is closed off and locked.

On the beach at 244 minutes

From the 'tunnel' house we have a choice of routes to **La Caleta**. We could stay on the track running below the cliffs, our upward route on Walk 32, or take the track which runs down to the sea front pumping house which takes us to the abandoned structure (Wp.8 244M).

On Walk 34 we keep to the track which runs just inland of the beach, so this time we divert onto the beach for a sea-spray stroll along the very sea front to pass **Famara**'s unusual housing and arrive gratefully in **La Caleta** (Wp.9 320M).

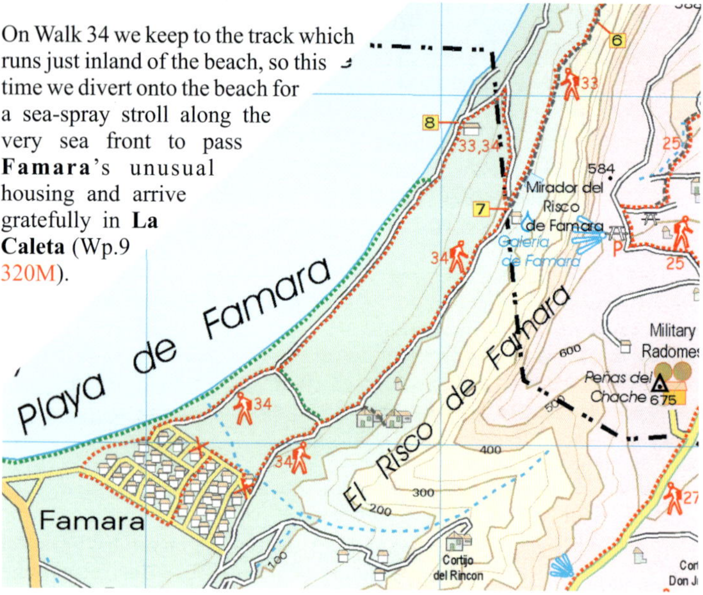

34 FAMARA CIRCULAR

El Risco de Famara provides a dramatic backdrop to this easy route along the base of the cliffs before descending to beach level and returning on an easy track. Easy that is, if the wind is not blowing. **Famara** is famous for its wind and when it blows, this easy beach-side walk is transformed into a struggle through a desert sandstorm.

If you walk this route in the morning, then the first half will be shaded by the tall cliffs. The earlier you start, the shadier the route is - much more refreshing than walking in the blazing intensity of the afternoon.

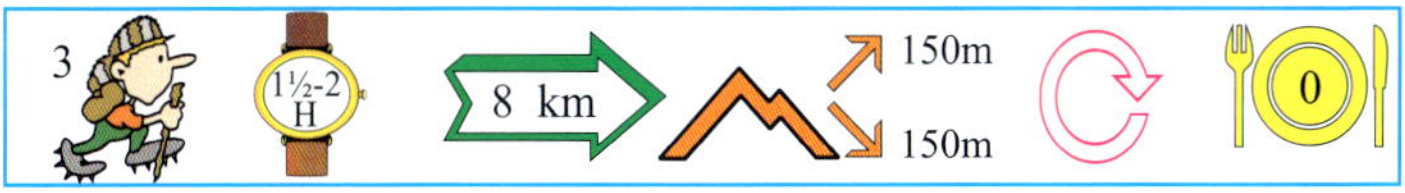

Access by car:
Park on the roadside just before reaching **Famara** bungalow development.

Access by bus:
Nº20 from **Arrecife** offers a limited service to **Caleta de Famara**; see appendices for timetables.

From the corner of the **Famara** development (Wp.1 0M) we head up the private road (SE) on an easy stroll past the walled squat bungalows. Ahead and above are the golf ball radomes on a ridge behind the main **Famara** cliffs as we come up to a sign for the reception (Wp.2). From here you could continue ahead, signed 'playa', to skirt the development, but our choice is to go left (NE) to walk between the square bungalows with curved walls. Past the reception, bar and shop, we reach the far side of the development (Wp.3 12M) where we go right (SE) to walk uphill, going right and left at the top of **Calle Aguamala** to come up between the houses and meet the beach road just beyond a barrier (Wp.4 17M). Interesting to note the change in architectural style between the lower and higher bungalows; below reception are square houses with curved walls, while above reception, the houses are curved with straight walls.

Going left on the broad dirt track (NE), we're back to easy strolling as we come down past little gobbets of lava rock beside the route; insignificant beside the impressive cliffs, but nevertheless large rocks in their own right. When the main track swings towards the beach (Wp.5 25M) - a short stroll option - we continue straight ahead on a steady ascent that brings us up to pass an old farmstead in the course of restoration (Wp.6 27M), and on our right a cobbled trail leads up to a second house and its veritable oasis of a walled

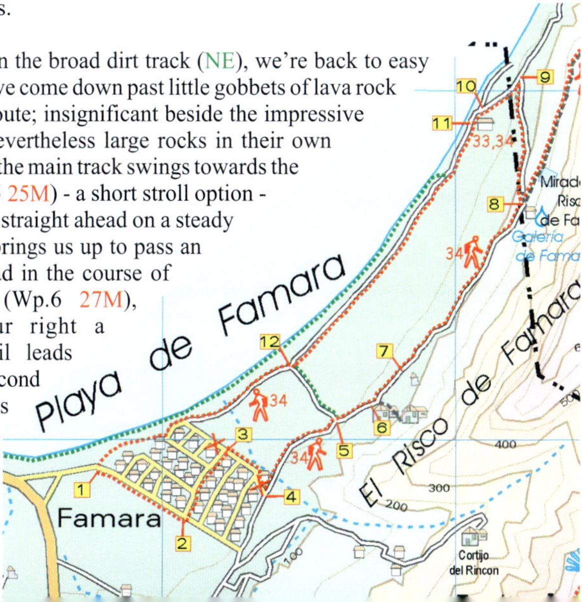

garden amongst this barren wilderness. Along the track, we pass a walled threshing circle before coming below an old ruin (Wp.7), the track getting rougher as we ascend. It is steadily uphill towards an intriguing white building that peeks out from behind the ridges which run down from the towering cliffs. As we move along below the cliffs, the surroundings become more floriferous, the slopes becoming covered in *tabaiba* and other endemic plants; even the giant dandelion-like *sonchus* thrives here, showing that this is a 'wet' area compared to the barren land earlier in the route.

Round a small headland, the house comes back into view, a large spoil heap giving a clue as to what lies ahead. We come up beside the little house (Wp.8 47M 136 metres) to find that it sits at the entrance to a tunnel into the cliffs. In this unusual elevated position we can appreciate both the towering cliffs and the beach curving around to **La Caleta**. A track leads up behind the house past an old white water tank (NNE), the cliff face route to **Yé**. Down below us beside the beach track stands a white building which is our next destination.

Wonderful views from the spoil heap

.. the aquamarine sea crashes onto rock 'pimples' ..

We take the downhill track behind the house (N), more a path than a dirt road with a rubble-ised surface requiring careful footwork. As we pick our way down, the aquamarine sea crashes onto rock 'pimples', and the beach raises its own sea mist. Our track becomes increasingly rubble-strewn as we pass a steep path down to our left, a possible short cut to miss a loop of the track, while we stay on the track to drop down to a junction (Wp.9 60M). Going left (SW) we continue dropping down towards the white building on the rubble-strewn track. Passing the lower end of the short cut path, we pick our way down to a junction (Wp.10) with the *playa* track. At last we're back to comfortable strolling towards the old pumping house and a beach-side pillbox (Wp.11 68M).

The final section needs hardly any description. You could walk along the pebble beach, but our choice is to take the *playa* track for an easy stroll (SE). Easy that is, if it isn't windy, when it can be more like fighting our way through a desert storm than an easy stroll. When the *playa* track swings inland (Wp.12), keep straight ahead on a minor track (SE) which almost peters out before reaching the corner of the bungalows. Here, you could cut through the houses or keep to the sand dunes and beach before curving round the beach side of **Famara** to come onto the road near your car (100M).

35 CALDERA BLANCA

It's a new edition of Walk! Lanzarote so we've saved the best for last - not that it was the last route walked and 'best' is our personal opinion - which includes experiencing the 'lava sea' followed by climbing the crater rim of the *caldera* along with a surprising sight to go with superb views from the rim. There are no refreshments (a short drive away) but then, no route is completely perfect!

This is one of the new routes encouraged by the island government, who have opened up and improved the path through the lava sea to reach the **Caldereta** and **Blanca** *calderas*; previously you could only approach them from the north after a lengthy off-tarmac drive which would negate your hire car insurance, so more congratulations to the authorities for encouraging walking through improved access.

Walking along the crater rim, we overlook steep (very) slopes down to the floor of the *caldera* which might upset vertigo sufferers, plus you should only undertake this route in good weather conditions - dry and with low windspeeds.

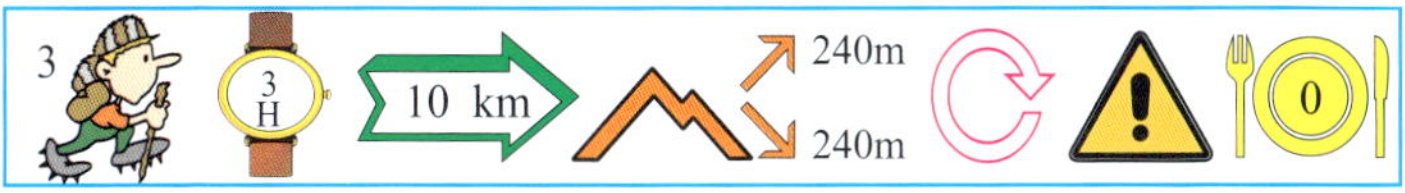

Access by car:
Depending from which direction you arrive, you'll be looking for the LZ67 road signed to 'Visitors' Centre'. Normally you'll be turning off the LZ56 main road in **Mancha Blanca**. As you leave **Mancha Blanca** houses behind, look for a tarmac lane on your right, after which you want to take the next dirt track on your right. If you reach a tarmac lane on your left you've gone too far; if you reach the **Visitors' Centre** you've gone way too far. Take the dirt track, easily driveable, to its end at a small parking area for a dozen cars and a 'Caldera Blanca' (official walk number 4) signboard. If the parking area is full go back to **Mancha Blanca**, park and walk in; don't park on the dirt track as it is in regular use by farmers.

From the end of the car park (Wp.1 0M) we continue on the track, bouldered against vehicle access, which in a few metres peters out for us to come onto the new path cut through the lava field. While the path is well made, just look each side to see what conditions would be like without it. It is mighty stony underfoot giving us a rocking gait as we slowly progress towards **Caldereta** which shields the bulk of **Montaña Blanca** from this viewpoint.

Any thoughts that this is a calm lava sea are dispelled as we drop into a valley formed between waves of lava - it's quite surreal to think that this was molten magma that set into the shapes we now see. After winding across the floor our path climbs out of the valley into a seriously disrupted landscape of peaks and holes like an angry sea frozen in rock formations. Our path guides us through this wild barren landscape to a junction (Wp.2 18M), the path to our right having stones across it; keeping to the main path, we snake our way through the lava, passing a small tree growing in the centre of the path, unusual in this barren waste.

As we curve around the north of **Caldereta** we leave the lava sea (Wp.3 25M)

.. flower-bedecked slopes ..

for the luxury of a dirt path and flower-bedecked slopes (in February) as we come up to the entrance to **Caldereta** (Wp.4 31M). Just a few steps off the main trail brings us to the view into the *caldera*; and what looked like a small cone compared to **Montaña Blanca** is a most impressive sight; from the entrance there's a tempting option to follow a steep path ascending to the *caldera*'s rim.

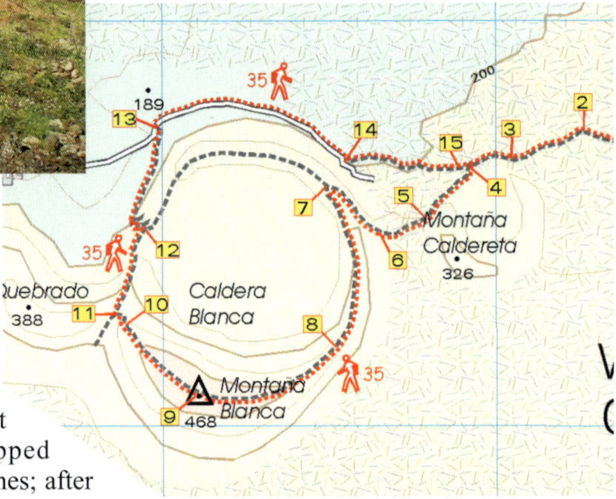

Back on the main trail, we climb steadily until, approximately half way up **Caldereta**, our trail turns to cross the lava (Wp.5). If the previous lava was an angry sea, then this is a furious torrent of tortured rock trapped between two volcanic cones; after the manicured paths so far we're now on bare pathless rock, following cairns for our route across the torrent; if in doubt about the route then scan ahead for the next cairn before heading off.

After twisting, turning and clambering from cairn to cairn we're across the lava to come onto a dirt path (Wp.6 42M) and a junction where we go right so that in thirty metres we are angling up towards the **Caldera Blanca** rim from beside a loose rock shelter. A traverse across the slope on the faint worn path, including going through a rock channel, brings us up onto the lowest point of the crater rim (Wp.7 55M) to find that it consists of a broad top up to five metres wide, before it rolls off to near vertical slopes dropping to the *caldera* floor.

.. the *caldera* way below us ..

Surprisingly, the floor of the *caldera* way below us is covered in abundant vegetation, a direct contrast to the landscape outside the volcanic cone. What we first take to be dots resolves into a large flock of goats apparently enjoying the rich grazing found in this verdant and unlikely oasis.

Buoyed by the views, we set off up the great curving slope of the rim towards the summit, the views expanding over the southern lava fields as we climb while to the north over the crater rim we look out over the lava and **Montaña Teneza** to the Atlantic Ocean. The first third of the ascent is easy uphill walking until we come to wind-sculpted rock ledges providing amphitheatre style seating when we take a break (Wp.8 75M). Now the climbing becomes more serious as we climb from ledge to ledge before the final ascent on the narrowing rim to the summit cairn and trig point (Wp.9 89M 468m).

On the summit (Wp.9)

The views have to be seen to be believed, the goats really are dots down on the *caldera* floor, while looking down the southern face we find that Lanzarote's outdoor artists have been at work creating giant footprints and a huge mouse/rat from lava rocks at the base of the mountain.

From the summit the only way is down as we carefully pick our way around the western rim to come down onto a goat trail whose loose surface again needs careful concentration before a path finally emerges (Wp.10) to take us down to the saddle between **Montaña Blanca** and **Risco Quegrado**. Down on the saddle we pick up the path (Wp.11 115M) running between the two volcanic cones as an alternative to picking our way down the rocky nose of the *caldera* rim.

Down below it is surprising to see so many cultivated fields on the *islotes* (islands) set amongst the lava sea. Our path follows the rim until we come to a zigzag descent (Wp.12) down the western slope on the remains of a stone-laid donkey trail. At the end of the zigzags we are onto a 'normal' dirt walking trail interspersed with tricky rock sections running down to meet with a dirt track (Wp.13). Now we are into relaxed walking round the northern base of the *caldera* to pick up the path across the lava (Wp.14) just below some newly constructed corrals at the end of dirt track. Now it is back onto a rocking gait until we come to the far side of the lava 'torrent' (Wp.15) just after which we meet up with our outward trail.

We retrace our outward route back through the lava 'angry sea' landscape to the parking area by which time, after that bobbly rocking gait finish, we're glad to be thinking of finding some suitable refreshments to celebrate a compact but spectacular route.

GPS Waypoints are quoted for the WGS84 datum used on the Lanzarote Tour & Trail Map 2nd ed (2009), from which the map sections used in Walk! Lanzarote are taken. WGS84 is the default datum for GPS units by the main GPS manufacturers.

To input the waypoints into your GPS, set the 'location format' to 'hdddº .mm.mmm'. While we quote waypoints to four places of decimals, as recorded during our research, you might only be able to input to three places of decimals, depending on your GPS unit.

PNFs (Personal Navigator Files) of the GPS tracks and waypoints from all of DWG's walking research is available on CD. See our website for details:
www.walking.demon.co.uk

1 PUERTO DEL CARMEN - ARRECIFE

Wp	N	W
1	28 55.7784	13 37.4574
2	28 55.8612	13 37.2504
3	28 55.9446	13 36.9666
4	28 56.0916	13 36.5916
5	28 56.9088	13 35.9034
6	28 56.9898	13 35.8086
7	28 57.0816	13 35.0952
8	28 57.2856	13 34.3308
9	28 57.3696	13 33.7494
10	28 57.3834	13 33.5700
11	28 57.4746	13 33.6510

2 COASTAL DISCOVERY

Wp	N	W
1	28 55.3054	13 40.3590
2	28 55.3086	13 40.5930
3	28 55.2738	13 40.8042
4	28 55.2180	13 40.9848
5	28 55.1795	13 41.1429
6	28 55.1040	13 41.9988
7	28 55.1142	13 42.2082
8	28 54.9531	13 42.5937
9	28 54.9734	13 42.7114
10	28 54.4982	13 43.5339
11	28 54.4255	13 43.8788

3 COASTAL PROMENADE - COSTA TEGUISE

Wp	N	W
1	28 59.2956	13 30.2214
2	28 59.4792	13 29.8614
3	28 59.6070	13 29.6916
4	28 59.6190	13 29.6046
5	28 59.5692	13 29.4198
6	28 59.5644	13 29.2356
7	28 59.6910	13 29.2206
8	28 59.8428	13 29.3466
9	29 00.0090	13 29.2134
10	28 59.9712	13 29.0178
11	28 59.9976	13 28.9224
12	29 00.1476	13 28.9014
13	29 00.2988	13 28.6896
14	29 00.4524	13 28.8138
15	29 00.0984	13 29.1720

4 SUNDAY MARKET SPECIAL - CAMINO EL CHARCO

Wp	N	W
1	29 03.5790	13 33.3996
2	29 03.2880	13 33.0660
3	29 03.0792	13 32.7906
4	29 03.1560	13 32.2680
5	29 03.3072	13 32.1474
6	29 03.2520	13 31.9608
7	29 03.2760	13 31.8714
8	19 03.3102	13 31.7568
9	29 03.2736	13 31.6764
10	29 03.2556	13 31.6614
11	29 03.1680	13 31.5354
12	29 02.9652	13 31.0548
13	29 02.7798	13 30.8622
14	29 02.6370	13 30.5766
15	29 02.7906	13 30.3978
16	29 02.6376	13 30.5586
17	29 02.5308	13 30.4698
18	29 02.2290	13 30.1542
19	29 02.1492	13 30.0234
20	29 01.9638	13 29.8140
21	29 01.6770	13 29.6016
22	29 00.8634	13 29.1954
23	29 00.7056	13 29.3358

5 MONTAÑA CORONA

Wp	N	W
1	29 00.7386	13 29.3538
2	29 00.7764	13 29.6724
3	29 00.8946	13 29.7312
4	29 00.9936	13 29.7774
5	29 01.0536	13 29.8152
6	29 01.1040	13 29.8482
7	29 01.1502	13 29.8932
8	29 01.2582	13 30.0450
9	29 01.3470	13 30.0498
10	29 01.4760	13 29.9676
11	29 01.4814	13 29.9172
12	29 01.4142	13 29.8194
13	29 01.3698	13 29.7360
14	29 01.4298	13 29.7426
15	29 01.4118	13 29.6568
16	29 01.3836	13 29.6226
17	29 01.2990	13 29.6022
18	29 01.2792	13 29.5938
19	29 01.2534	13 29.6010
20	29 01.2270	13 29.6208
21	29 01.0548	13 29.6622
22	29 01.0722	13 29.6124
23	29 00.9198	13 29.4996
24	29 00.8874	13 29.4456
25	29 00.8712	13 29.4030

6 COASTAL PROMENADE - PLAYA BLANCA WEST

Wp	N	W
1	28 51.5382	13 50.1492
2	28 51.3792	13 50.4150
3	28 51.4992	13 50.5920
4	28 51.7212	13 51.2130
5	28 51.7236	13 51.2910
6	28 51.6624	13 51.4254
7	28 51.6900	13 51.6156
8	28 51.5634	13 51.9204

7

COASTAL PROMENADE - PLAYA BLANCA EAST

Wp	N	W
1	28 51.5802	13 48.1140
2	28 51.4476	13 48.2712
3	28 51.4104	13 48.6348
4	28 51.3966	13 48.7152
5	28 51.5370	13 48.7962
6	28 51.5694	13 48.9504
7	28 51.6918	13 49.1454
8	28 51.7134	13 49.2762
9	28 51.6606	13 50.0670

8

MONTAÑA ROJA

Wp	N	W
1	28 52.1772	13 50.9028
2	28 52.2126	13 50.9280
3	28 52.2390	13 51.0324
4	28 52.2348	13 51.2202
5	28 52.1298	13 51.2226
6	28 52.0962	13 51.3006
7	28 52.0950	13 51.4020
8	28 52.1196	13 51.4656

9

PAPAGAYO BEACH

Wp	N	W
1	28 51.6354	13 47.8392
2	28 51.5640	13 47.8296
3	28 51.4374	13 47.6958
4	28 51.3756	13 47.6772
5	28 51.2886	13 47.6082
6	28 51.1992	13 47.5188
7	28 50.9922	13 47.4180
8	28 50.9418	13 47.4126
9	28 50.8032	13 47.3406
10	28 50.6862	13 47.2710
11	28 50.5992	13 47.2974
12	28 50.9148	13 47.3148
13	28 51.3330	13 47.4870

10

PEÑA DEL RUBICÓN

Wp	N	W
1	28 51.5616	13 51.9180
2	28 51.3432	13 52.3422
3	28 51.3708	13 52.3992
4	28 51.4458	13 52.4586
5	28 51.6396	13 52.5480
6	28 51.9384	13 52.5462
7	28 52.3242	13 52.4760
8	28 52.7202	13 52.5750
9	28 52.8954	13 52.7370
10	28 53.0340	13 52.8030
11	28 53.5134	13 52.4148
12	28 53.4828	13 52.0170
13	28 53.6724	13 51.7302
14	28 53.8116	13 51.4356
15	28 54.1464	13 51.3438
16	28 54.3432	13 51.1296
17	28 54.4128	13 51.2040
18	28 55.2876	13 50.1750
19	28 55.3206	13 50.1282
20	28 55.3884	13 50.0448
21	28 55.5750	13 49.9164
22	28 55.8510	13 49.7130
23	28 55.6392	13 49.4448
24	28 56.3088	13 48.8166

11

YAIZA'S VOLCANIC GARDENS

Wp	N	W
1	28 57.1410	13 45.9192
2	28 57.0414	13 45.9360
3	28 57.0438	13 46.0560
4	28 56.9694	13 46.2180
5	28 57.0780	13 46.2762
6	28 57.2034	13 46.3368
7	28 57.0762	13 46.6104
8	28 57.2508	13 46.3632

12

ATALAYA DE FEMÉS LINEAR

Wp	N	W
1	28 57.1338	13 45.9162
2	28 57.0246	13 45.9030
3	28 56.9070	13 45.7248
4	28 56.4696	13 45.4554
5	28 56.1540	13 45.5940
6	28 56.0400	13 45.7068
7	28 55.2858	13 46.8558
8	28 55.1304	13 47.0358
9	28 55.0458	13 46.7460
10	28 55.0032	13 46.5828
11	28 54.7962	13 46.7544
12	28 55.2738	13 46.1304
13	28 55.4652	13 45.9888
14	28 55.7400	13 45.8166
15	28 55.8360	13 45.7344
16	28 55.8696	13 45.6636
17	28 55.9482	13 45.7308

13

ATALAYA DE FEMÉS CIRCUIT

Wp	N	W
1	28 54.7962	13 46.7544
2	28 55.2738	13 46.1304
3	28 55.4652	13 45.9888
4	28 55.7400	13 45.8166
5	28 55.8360	13 45.7344
6	28 55.8696	13 45.6636
7	28 55.9482	13 45.7308
8	28 55.9737	13 45.8436
9	28 55.2858	13 46.8558
10	28 55.1304	13 47.0358
11	28 55.0458	13 46.7460
12	28 55.0032	13 46.5828

14

THE HIDDEN BARRANCOS

Wp	N	W
1	28 54.7722	13 46.7508
2	28 54.6264	13 46.6518
3	28 54.4326	13 46.6428
4	28 54.3720	13 46.3938
5	28 54.1752	13 45.9768
6	28 54.1308	13 45.9804
7	28 54.0942	13 45.7020
8	28 54.0588	13 45.6354
9	28 53.9238	13 46.0734
10	28 53.8681	13 46.2052
11	28 53.7258	13 46.2732
12	28 53.8014	13 46.4400
13	28 53.9118	13 46.7382
14	28 53.9874	13 46.8018
15	28 54.3096	13 46.8060
16	28 54.5154	13 46.7928

15

FEMÉS RIDGE

Wp	N	W
1	28 54.7818	13 46.7658
2	28 54.6492	13 46.6500
3	28 54.6414	13 46.4868
4	28 54.7020	13 46.3152
5	28 54.8688	13 46.0194
6	28 55.1322	13 45.7026
7	28 55.0278	13 45.5796
8	28 54.8970	13 45.4830
9	28 54.7608	13 45.3798
10	28 54.8112	13 45.5652
11	28 54.4398	13 45.6072
12	28 54.3858	13 45.9054
13	28 54.3750	13 46.1766
14	28 54.4128	13 46.4532
15	28 54.4326	13 46.6410

16

FEMÉS TO PLAYA BLANCA

Wp	N	W
1	28 54.7974	13 46.7460
2	28 54.6210	13 46.7010
3	28 54.3168	13 46.8060
4	28 53.9838	13 46.8054
5	28 53.9280	13 46.9218
6	28 53.3592	13 46.2918
7	28 53.0748	13 45.7950
8	28 52.7880	13 45.2412
9	28 52.3602	13 45.7458
10	28 51.7578	13 46.2258
11	28 51.6612	13 46.2954
12	28 50.6544	13 47.2590

17

FEMÉS TO PLAYA QUEMADA

Wp	N	W
1	28 54.7962	13 46.7418
2	28 54.6306	13 46.6548
3	28 54.4314	13 46.6476
4	28 54.4344	13 45.6294
5	28 54.2772	13 45.2256
6	28 54.1554	13 44.8500
7	28 54.0714	13 44.7486
8	28 54.0846	13 44.5596
9	28 54.3324	13 44.4234
10	28 54.3978	13 44.2416
11	28 54.4362	13 44.1924
12	28 54.4338	13 43.8804

18

TREMESANA GUIIDED WALK

Wp	N	W
1	28 59.1494	13 47.9747
2	28 58.0119	13 46.1206

19

MONTAÑA CUERVO - A GEM IN LANZAROTE'S CROWN

Wp	N	W
1	28 59.5674	13 41.1024
2	28 59.4894	13 41.3808
3	28 59.5830	13 41.4894
4	28 59.5230	13 41.5170
5	28 59.5800	13 41.6406
6	28 59.4960	13 41.7438
7	28 59.4480	13 41.8572
8	28 59.3520	13 41.7294
9	28 59.4414	13 41.4534
10	28 59.5075	13 41.3105

20

A PATH BETWEEN TWO SEAS - THE TIMANFAYA COASTAL PATH

Wp	N	W
1	29 03.7390	13 46.4203
2	29 59.5442	13 49.0825
3	28 59.3694	13 49.0306
4	28 59.1605	13 48.8771

21

LA GÉRIA

Wp	N	W
1	28 56.9490	13 44.6406
2	28 56.9082	13 44.4868
3	28 57.1602	13 44.2506
4	28 57.4074	13 42.9570
5	28 57.3552	13 42.7032
6	28 57.3702	13 42.5586
7	28 57.4482	13 42.3774
8	28 57.0852	13 41.9934
9	28 56.9886	13 41.9568
10	28 56.9190	13 41.8002
11	28 56.7797	13 41.7152
12	28 56.6199	13 41.6631
13	28 56.4030	13 41.6262
14	28 56.2356	13 41.4546
15	28 56.1666	13 41.1354
16	28 55.5420	13 41.2680
17	28 55.1922	13 41.2540
18	28 55.2911	13 40.3503

21A

LA GERIA, TINASORIA

Wp	N	W
1	28 56.9580	13 44.6466
2	28 56.9052	13 44.4900
3	28 569874	13 44.3916
4	28 57.1602	13 44.2506
5	28 57.1686	13 44.1042
6	28 57.4884	13 43.2810
7	28 57.3498	13 42.6318
8	28 57.3702	13 42.5586
9	28 57.7660	13 42.3932
10	28 57.2808	13 42.6894
11	28 57.1590	13 42.7530
12	28 57.0138	13 43.0368
13	28 57.2814	13 42.9828
14	28 57.3288	13 42.9732
15	28 57.3912	13 42.8778

22

PLAYA DEL POZO

Wp	N	W
1	28 54.4590	13 44.1822
2	28 54.3984	13 44.2452
3	28 54.2670	13 44.4552
4	28 54.0618	13 44.6184
5	28 53.9904	13 44.6244
6	28 53.8986	13 44.6874
7	28 54.4458	13 44.4360

24

THE FORGOTTEN TRAIL

Wp	N	W
1	29 08.7678	13 29.9988
2	29 08.7456	13 30.0744
3	29 08.6010	13 30.1500
4	29 08.4858	13 30.2130
5	29 08.4294	13 30.2448
6	29 08.4096	13 30.2562
7	29 08.2836	13 30.3738
8	29 08.0988	13 30.6180
9	29 07.9668	13 30.8070
10	29 07.9062	13 30.9534
11	29 07.8930	13 30.9390
12	29 07.8852	13 30.9684
13	29 07.8690	13 30.9342
14	29 07.7880	13 30.9240
15	29 07.7775	13 30.9324
16	29 07.7598	13 30.9282

25

BARRANCO DEL MALPASO

Wp	N	W
1	29 08.7678	13 29.9982
2	29 08.7444	13 30.0798
3	29 08.4318	13 30.3798
4	29 08.1936	13 30.6516
5	29 08.0592	13 30.8598
6	29 07.9638	13 31.0986
7	29 07.9320	13 31.1670
8	29 07.7748	13 31.2354
9	29 07.6950	13 31.2894
10	29 07.6854	13 31.4004
11	29 07.5612	13 31.3776
12	29 07.4286	13 30.9582
13	29 07.5126	13 30.9210
13A	29 07.7742	13 30.9324
14	29 07.6326	13 30.8658
15	29 07.8096	13 30.9174
16	29 07.8684	13 30.9234
17	29 07.9614	13 30.8100
18	29 08.0970	13 30.6162
19	29 08.7420	13 30.0282

26

CIRCUIT OF HARÍA

Wp	N	W
1	29 08.7936	13 29.9598
2	29 09.0114	13 30.0264
3	29 09.0516	13 30.0888
4	29 09.0210	13 30.4848
5	29 09.0270	13 30.5490
6	29 09.0138	13 30.7182
7	29 09.0264	13 30.8598
8	29 08.9466	13 30.9246
9	29 08.9508	13 30.9666
10	29 08.9460	13 30.9792
11	29 08.9358	13 31.0074
12	29 08.9070	13 31.1544
13	29 08.7138	13 31.1562
14	29 08.4042	13 30.7092
15	29 08.1906	13 30.9204
16	29 08.1504	13 30.7242
17	29 08.1948	13 30.6504
18	29 08.4402	13 30.3720

27

CAPITAL ROUTE - HARÍA TO TEGUISE

Wp	N	W
1	29 08.7678	13 29.9988
2	29 08.7456	13 30.0744
3	29 08.6010	13 30.1500
4	29 08.4858	13 30.2130
5	29 08.4294	13 30.2448

6	29 08.4096	13 30.2562
7	29 08.2836	13 30.3738
8	29 08.0988	13 30.6180
9	29 07.9668	13 30.8070
10	29 07.9062	13 30.9534
11	29 07.8930	13 30.9390
12	29 07.8852	13 30.9684
13	29 07.8690	13 30.9342
14	29 07.7880	13 30.9240
15	29 07.7741	13 30.9324
16	29 07.4886	13 30.9396
17	29 07.4394	13 30.9552
18	29 07.0350	13 31.1352
19	29 06.6072	13 31.5444
20	29 06.3840	13 31.6944
21	29 06.1320	13 31.8360
22	29 05.6268	13 32.1180
23	29 05.5470	13 32.2386
24	29 05.5860	13 32.3610
25	29 04.0938	13 32.5686
26	29 04.0164	13 32.7570
27	29 03.9072	13 33.1830
28	29 03.8346	13 33.2928
29	29 03.6012	13 33.5844

28

MALA TO TEGUISE

Wp	N	W
1	29 05.9916	13 28.1850
2	29 06.0528	13 28.4394
3	29 06.1104	13 28.6014
4	29 06.4836	13 28.8054
5	29 06.7968	13 29.5212
6	29 06.8898	13 29.6172
7	29 07.0068	13 29.7510
8	29 06.9798	13 29.9910
9	29 06.9108	13 30.2424
10	29 06.7188	13 30.2616
11	29 06.6402	13 30.2760
12	29 06.8028	13 30.8574
13	29 06.3990	13 30.8346
14	29 06.5034	13 31.6002
15	29 06.3840	13 31.6944
16	29 06.1266	13 31.8384
17	29 05.6364	13 32.0998
18	29 05.5471	13 32.2412
19	29 05.5881	13 32.3472
20	29 04.0901	13 32.5734
21	29 04.0271	13 32.7363
22	29 03.9169	13 33.1760
23	29 03.8277	13 33.2938

29

HELECHOS CIRCULAR

Wp	N	W
1	29 09.5460	13 29.7720
2	29 09.5520	13 29.6370
3	29 09.9276	13 29.5998
4	29 10.4832	13 29.2278
5	29 10.6932	13 29.4306
6	29 10.7082	13 29.4882
7	29 10.5864	13 29.8536
8	29 10.6566	13 29.9034
9	29 10.2198	13 30.5382
10	29 10.1388	13 30.7698
11	29 09.9600	13 30.7512
12	29 09.6582	13 30.9720
13	29 09.8976	13 30.6258
14	29 10.0686	13 30.5022
15	29 10.2090	13 30.2346
16	29 09.8328	13 30.3432
17	29 10.1106	13 30.2772
18	29 09.8340	13 30.0474
19	29 10.0068	13 29.8308
20	29 09.8790	13 29.8308
21	29 09.7536	13 29.7354

30

MÁGUEZ TO YÉ

Wp	N	W
1	29 09.5460	13 29.7720
2	29 09.5520	13 29.6370
3	29 09.9276	13 29.5998
4	29 10.4832	13 29.2278
5	29 10.5972	13 28.9944
6	29 11.0976	13 28.4106
7	29 11.3196	13 28.2594
8	29 11.6424	13 27.6408
9	29 11.8230	13 27.5166
10	29 12.0852	13 28.0080
11	29 12.1368	13 28.1652
12	29 12.1578	13 28.3086
13	29 12.0780	13 28.3908
14	29 12.0456	13 28.4088
15	29 11.8122	13 28.7070

31

CORONA'S NORTHERN TOUR

Wp	N	W
1	29 11.7336	13 29.0268
2	29 11.7366	13 28.9356
3	29 11.5266	13 28.9302
4	29 11.3430	13 28.9524
5	29 11.1408	13 28.9020
6	29 11.2008	13 28.7004
7	29 11.1684	13 28.6758
8	29 11.0292	13 28.7178
9	29 10.7820	13 28.8648
10	29 10.7802	13 28.8444
11	29 10.5750	13 29.0574
12	29 10.9086	13 29.2938
13	29 11.0298	13 29.4732
14	29 11.2866	13 29.7588
15	29 11.3166	13 29.8734
16	29 11.5332	13 29.9178
17	29 11.5452	13 29.7744
18	29 11.6274	13 29.7606
19	29 11.5842	13 29.7198
20	29 11.5170	13 29.3082

32

SALINAS DEL RÍO

Wp	N	W
1	29 11.7906	13 29.5470
2	29 11.7414	13 29.6994
3	29 12.0804	13 29.9976

33

RISCO DE FAMARA

Wp	N	W
1	29 11.7906	13 29.5470
2	29 11.7414	13 29.6994
3	29 12.0804	13 29.9976
4	29 10.9554	13 30.3438
5	29 10.4394	13 30.8418
6	29 08.2074	13 31.4580
7	29 07.6584	13 31.7838
8	29 07.9290	13 31.9416
9	29 07.0080	13 33.8346

34

FAMARA CIRCULAR

Wp	N	W
1	29 06.9132	13 33.2004
2	29 06.7764	13 32.9256
3	29 06.9558	13 32.7828
4	29 06.8388	13 32.6418
5	29 07.0236	13 32.4132
6	29 07.0878	13 32.2944
7	29 07.1922	13 32.1792
8	29 07.6482	13 31.7868
9	29 08.0502	13 31.7706
10	29 07.9458	13 31.9014
11	29 07.9110	13 31.9494
12	29 07.2078	13 32.5614

35

CALDERA BLANCA

Wp	N	W
1	29 02.6280	13 42.0972
2	29 02.7300	13 42.7572
3	29 02.6586	13 42.9522
4	29 02.6322	13 43.1154
5	29 02.5104	13 43.2222
6	29 02.4666	13 43.3566
7	29 02.5896	13 43.4994
8	29 02.2068	13 43.4838
9	29 02.0670	13 43.9050
10	29 02.2512	13 44.1006
11	29 02.2674	13 44.1390
12	29 02.4954	13 44.0256
13	29 02.7606	13 43.9770
14	29 02.6610	13 43.4418
15	29 02.6358	13 43.1274

HIDDEN BARRANCOS - ADDITIONAL WALKING

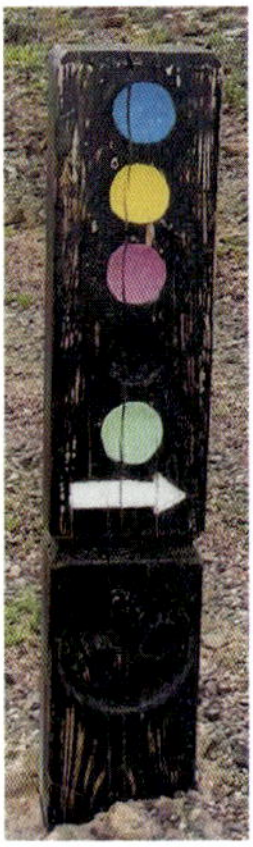

Having pioneered the first published walking route for this previously unknown region, 'The Hidden Barrancos' in Lanzarote Walking Guide 1995, it is very pleasing to see an increasing number of walkers discovering these landscapes. By the time we produced Walk! Lanzarote (2004) new refuges had been built on the route overlooking **Barranco de la Casita** and at **Playa del Pozo**, cozzie-optional bathers had discovered **Playa de la Arena** to be only a short hike from Quemada, and there was increasing interest from serious hikers in the **Femés - Papagayo - Playa Blanca** trek. With five walking routes published in Walk! Lanzarote, this previously empty landscape started to fill with walkers. This popularity for this wild landscape was noticed by the local authorities who decided to install a unique system of colour coded wayposts as their guide to people following the walking trails. Such an initiative is to be applauded even if the system of wayposts is completely different to the 'classic' system used by the *Cabildo* (island government) for the **La Geria** region.

Unfortunately, the leaflet explaining the wayposted routes was not available from the tourist information offices we visited; it seems the leaflet ran out some time ago, so the only reference materials are the 'Red de Senderos de Los Ajaches' notice boards at the entry points to the 'Hidden Barrancos'. You could take a digital photo of the board and refer to this but the map is 'freehand' and your image too small for accurate navigation, or establishing where you are, so we have superimposed the 'Los Ajaches' routes as shown on the notice boards onto a section of our Lanzarote Tour & Trail Map which gives more information, and is more portable than a notice board, but is still subject to the 'freehand' accuracy of the artist.

Seven walking routes are shown on notice boards and wayposts, which we interpret as:-

WHITE ROUTE
Femés - Quemada is our Walk 17 'The Missing Link'.

PINK ROUTE
Femés circular back to **Femés** is our Walk 14 'The Hidden Barrancos'.

LILAC/PURPLE ROUTE
Femés - Playa Quemada is a variation linking our Walk 14 and Walk 17 routes. Basically, follow Walk 14 to the path junction at waypoint 5, then take the path down into the **Barranco de la Higuera** to link with Walk 17 inland of **Playa del Pozo** then Walk 17 to **Playa Quemada**.

BLACK ROUTE
Playa Quemada - Casitas de Femés is part of Walk 17 (in reverse and 22) until waypoint 6 where you turn off to walk up the **Barranco del Frailes**. At the top of the barranco you come onto a dirt track taking you into the hamlet of **Casita de Femés**.

BLUE ROUTE

Femes - Casitas de Femés - Playa Quemada is our Walk 15 'Femes Ridge' but taking the easier but longer alternative route (staying on the walking trail) to the dirt track accessing **Casita de Femés**, the route does not go into the hamlet, and continues on the alternative route walking trail to come into **Valle del Pozo**. Where Walk 15 (Wp.11) meets Walk 17 (Wp.4) we turn down the valley following Walk 17 to **Playa Quemada**.

RED ROUTE

Femés - inland of **Playa Blanca East** is our Walk 16 'Femés to Playa Blanca' following the dirt track all the way to waypoint 11 where the Red Route takes the main track inland, our Alt route, then turns right at the next main junction to finish on the dirt track T-junction inland of **Playa Mujeres**.

DEEP PURPLE ROUTE

Circular route from **Playa Blanca East** to **Papagayo** and the eastern beaches before striking inland to join the Red Route, then turning left at the T-junction to meet its outward route at **Playa Mujeres**. This is a combination of our Walk 9 'Papagayo Beach' then Walk 16 in reverse to **El Pasito** then inland to join the dirt tracks in the desert.

2nd BLUE ROUTE

Playa Quemada - inland of **Playa Blanca East**. An interesting route initially following our Walk 22 'Playa del Pozo' route and then striking over the headland to head up the **Barranco de la Casita** before crossing the next ridge into the **Barranco de los Dises** to come down towards the coast before heading south-west to link up with our Walk 16 and Red Route. Personally we would much prefer our Walk 16 route as a way of reaching **Papagayo** and **Playa Blanca**, but this more coastal route does mean that you can walk from **Playa Quemada** to **Playa Blanca** by a relatively coastal route - it also means that you could walk, assuming you ever wanted to, all the way from **Arrecife** to **Puerto del Carmen** to **Puerto Calero** to **Papagayo** to **Playa Blanca** and on round the coast as far as **Las Salinas** on clearly identifiable walking trails and pavements/promenades. Now we've hinted at it, then its only a matter of time before we get reports of masochistic long distance walkers completing this 55 kilometre challenge.

Note that the 'Los Ajaches' walking routes overlaid on this map are based on the noticeboard sketchs and are at best approximations of the routes.

LA GERIA - ADDITIONAL WALKING

Thanks to a *Cabildo* (island government) initiative a series of linked walking routes have been wayposted for the **La Geria** region. These **La Geria** routes are detailed (in Spanish) in the colour leaflet 'PR LZ 40 Red de senderos La Geria' available from tourist offices - though when we had collected ours the office was having to colour photocopy a master as the printed editions had run out. On the back page of the leaflet the walk leader for the group is Carmen Portella Ernest - see Acknowledgements and Walk 31.

PR LZ 40 routes; 40.1, 40.2, 40.3, 40.4, are marked with wayposts with standard GR/PR symbols but in the local colours.

The *Cabildo* leaflet uses Google Earth mapping with the walking routes and some roads overlaid, but it is not the easiest mapping to follow so we reproduced the LZ 40 routes on the section of our Lanzarote Tour & Trail Map which covers the region, and which you might find easier to use for route finding.

The main route PR LZ 40.1 (red, ~16 kilometres)
- starts in **Uga** and follows the route of Walk 21 until we turn right at waypoint 7 to head towards the coast while 40.1 continues straight ahead towards **Asomada** before heading north between **Guardilama** and **Gaida** after which it curves round to cross the LZ502 on its way towards **Cerro de Tegoyo**.

Next is a section of road walking through **Vegas de Tegoyo** before setting off cross country for a small peak before arriving on the LZ503 to walk north-east along the road until turning off towards **Montaña Tersa** and then heading south between **Tersa** and **Montañeta** to pick up the dirt road linking **Conil** to the northern outskirts of **Tías** where we follow the streets to pass the **Iglesia de la Candelaria** church before finishing at a roundabout north of the motorway.

PR LZ 40.2 (yellow, ~6 kilometres)
- leaves the LZ 40.1, and our Walk 21, at our **Guardilama** option then heads north to cross the LZ30 before turning right taking in a stretch of road walking before reverting to dirt tracks to meet the main 40.1 route just west of **Vegas de Tegoyo**. An interesting extension of the main route or could be the basis of a circular route based on **La Asomada**.

PR LZ 40.3 (blue, ~6 kilometres)
- forms an extension between 40.2 and the main 40.1 route. Leaving the 40.2 at the end of the LZ30 road walking section it heads north-east towards **Montaña Cuervo** (Walk 19, which you should include in your itinerary) before south-east to meet the LZ30 for a short road walk (SW) before taking a dirt track to meet the main 40.1 route on the LZ503 just above **Conil**.

PR LZ 40.4 (green, ~2 kilometres)
- is simply a road walk on a *camino rural* and the LZ502 through **La Asomada** that gives bus access and cuts off a loop of the 40.1.

LA GERIA - ADDITIONAL WALKING

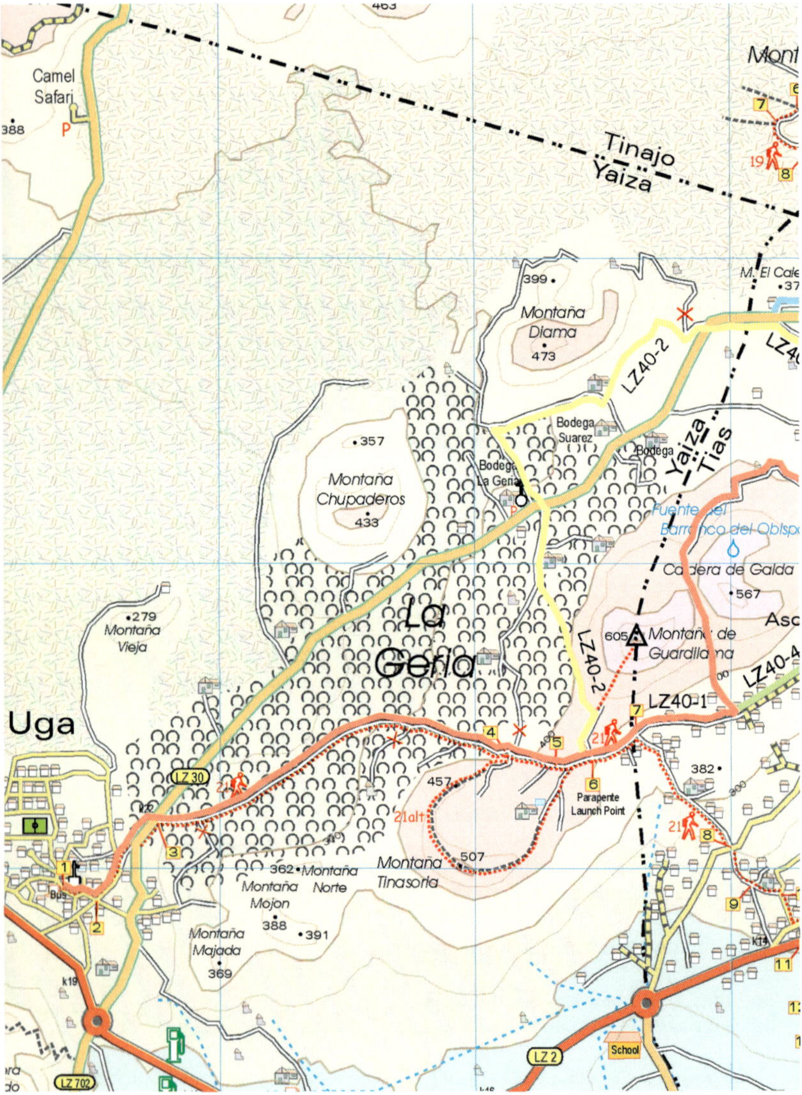

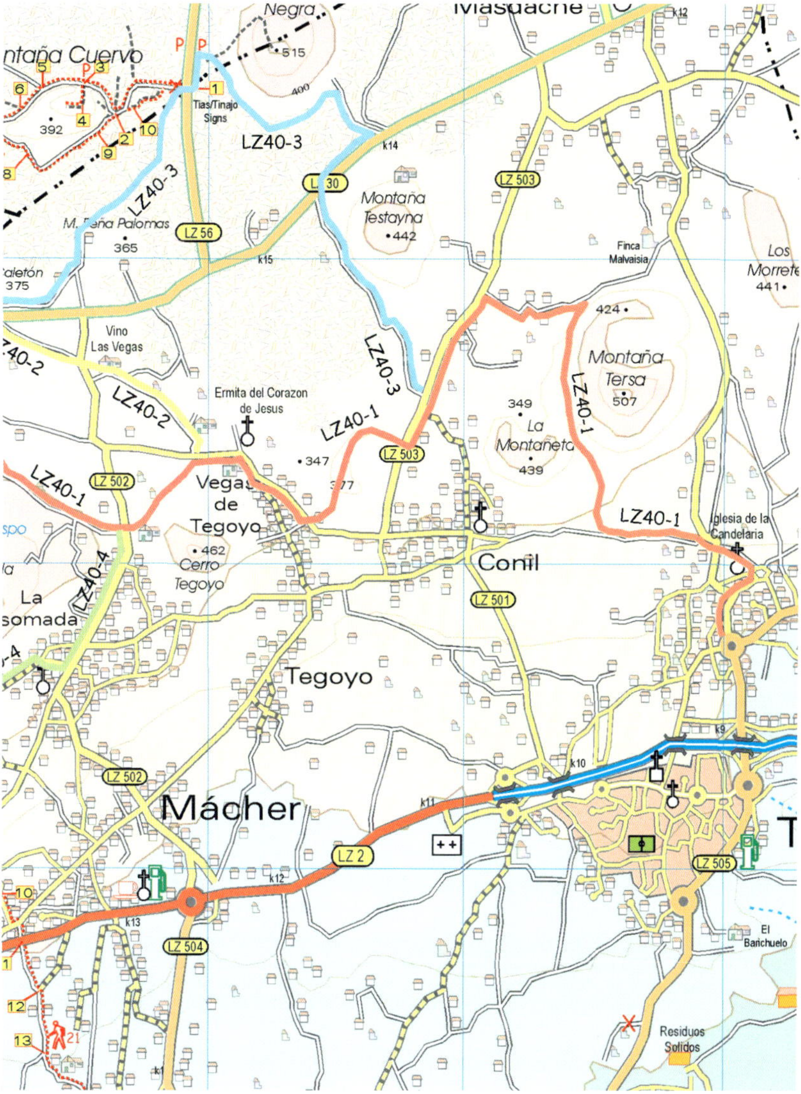
Negra
Masdache
Montaña Cuervo
515
400
392
Tias/Tinajo Signs
LZ40-3
k14
LZ 30
LZ 503
Montaña Testayna
442
M. Peña Palomas
LZ 56
365
k15
Finca Malvaisia
Los Morrete
441
375
424
Vino Las Vegas
Montaña Tersa
507
LZ40-2
Ermita del Corazon de Jesus
349
La Montañeta
439
LZ40-1
347
LZ 502
Vegas de Tegoyo
377
LZ40-1
Iglesia de la Candelaria
462
Cerro Tegoyo
Conil
LZ 501
La
LZ40-4
Tegoyo
k9
k10
LZ 502
Mácher
k11
LZ 2
k12
LZ 505
k13
LZ 504
El Barichuelo
Residuos Solidos

Walks 25, 31 & 35

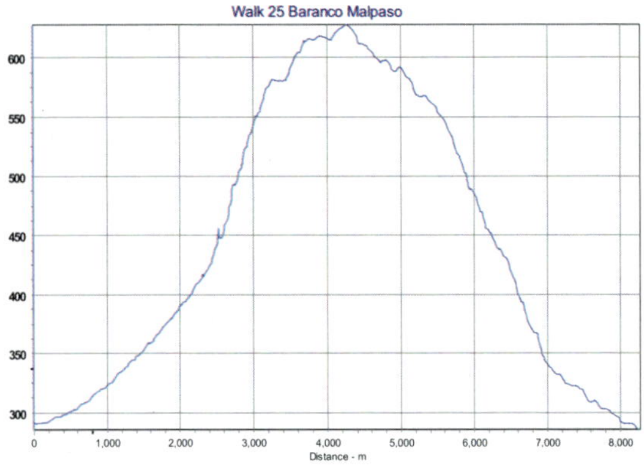

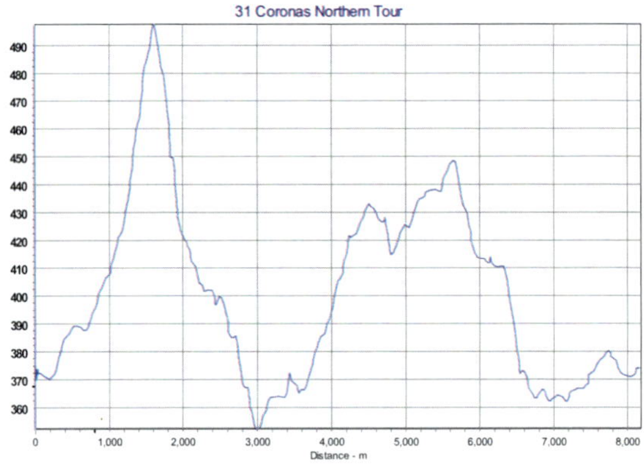

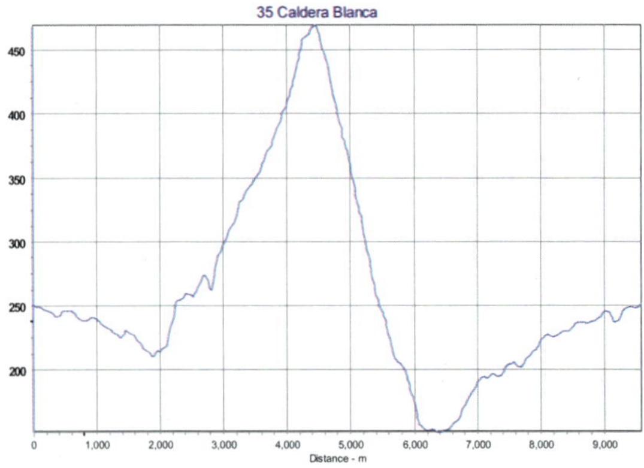

MAPS

Lanzarote is awash with cheap tourist maps of dubious accuracy, none of which are of any help to the walker. The route maps used in this book are taken from our new Lanzarote Tour & Trail Map, available in two versions; **Lanzarote Tour & Trail Super-Durable Map** (ISBN 9781904946540) and **Lanzarote Tour & Trail Map** printed on Map-Paper (ISBN 9781904946588) which cover the whole island at 1:40,000 scale; naturally, we recommend our own maps as the best, but when you see ours we believe you'll agree that they are remarkable maps.

IGN 1:25,000 and 1:50,000 scale official Ministerio de Fomento maps are available from **Libreria Villalobos** in **Arrecife** at the reasonable price of €3.20 each. Surprisingly, the 1:25,000 scale maps have very little information on them of use to walkers, as they do not show tracks or footpaths. And as a complete island set of these maps would cost you €32.00, you'll be better off with one of our maps at £5.99 for the Map-Paper version or £8.99 for our Super-Durable version; they are far more detailed and up-to-date; the Super-Durable version is tough, waterproof and virtually tear-proof.

WALKING BOOKS & INFORMATION

It's funny how many walking guide books deliberately ignore all the other walking guide books. as though there was no other walking information available. Well, not us. We seek out everything there is to find concerning walking for our destinations. Admittedly, on Lanzarote this is not a lot, but here is our opinion on what books are available - and please remember this is *our* opinion on these publications.

Ruta de Caballos (Ayuntamiento de Yaiza Dept. of Educación y Cultura. Free)

These six photocopied sheets first introduced us to the region between **Playa Quemada** and **Femés** for our 'Hidden Barrancos' route back in '95. All these routes are now incorporated into **Walk! Lanzarote**, but do call in for a copy, so that the department realises just how important walking is to Lanzarote tourism; they are trying to attract riders for the local stables industry, hence the *caballos* (for horse riders) and not *senderismos* (walking routes). Collect.

Red de Senderos(Cabildo de Lanzarote (Island Government)

Free leaflets have been produced for some of the official waymarked PR LZ trails and include walk descriptions and basic (very basic) maps. Not always available in English, though ask in Tourist Information Offices.

Guía Oficial de Senderos de Lanzarote (Cabildo de Lanzarote (Island Government) 2002 €15)

160 pages (in Spanish) plus a box of route maps is a commendable effort by the island government to promote walking. Maps are good on technicality giving height profiles, distances, walking surface, gradients. However, we

would argue with their 'difficulty' grading when they rate the easy track down to **Papagayo** as 'medium' but the far trickier path around **Pico Redondo** as 'easy'.

Researched and written by three lads exploring the island, the book has a good feel, but is let down by having no contents page or index. There are only 16 main routes, and that includes **Yaiza** and **San Bartolomé** town walks, but our main comment is on the choice of routes. No thought has been given to accessibility. Most routes involve a long linear hike, often well away from bus routes. Their only real circular route is **Yaiza - El Golfo - Yaiza** - all along tarmac roads! Some routes seem to have little point to them, except to cover the ground.

Having been quite damning so far (and one book shop told us they refused to stock the book because the routes were so bad!) we would nevertheless recommend this book if you speak a little Spanish. Bits and pieces of routes can be used, and the book has good background information on the island. Buy.

Landscapes of Lanzarote (Sunflower Books 2000 £9.99 128 pages, and 4th edition 2007 £12.99 128 pages but see below)

128 pages plus pull-out map. One of the infamous 'blue book' series, supposedly by the equally infamous (in the Canary Islands anyway) Noel Rochford. Noel originally researched the Landscapes Canary Islands titles in the mid/late 80s, and those early editions were renowned for walking times so fast, you thought he had used a motorcycle. For the 2000 editions John Underwood has produced his own mapping, much clearer than the old edition. Updates are carried out by local walkers, Noel now being long gone from the islands, and the whole book style modernised.

What we said in 2004
"Generally, you won't go far wrong with this book. If we have a criticism, it is that the five separate coastal walks included as '16 Coastal walks' deserve more description, and that when a book appears in a brand new cover we would expect a lot of new content inside that cover. Hopefully, the next edition will benefit from having GPS Waypoints to go with the routes."

Well, we purchased the latest 2007 edition in 2009 and feel we've been done; this book has exactly the same number of pages and the same routes (17) yet costs £3 more! There's virtually nothing new in the book at all, so if you can get hold of an old 2000 edition then don't waste your money on a supposedly 'new' edition.

Walking in the Canary Islands: 2 East (Cicerone Press £12.00 2002)
235 pages, but only 55 of these relate to Lanzarote. Paddy Dillon is an experienced walking writer and Cicerone Press publish a massive pile of walking guide books; so why do we not like this one, and its companion **Walking in the Canary Islands 1: West**

Firstly, why carry 180 redundant pages around with you? Secondly, the mapping (in both books) is not worthy of the name and does not deserve to be called 'mapping'. If you had to navigate from these sketches, you would soon be in trouble.

With such truly awful maps, you would expect the detailed walk descriptions to make up for the lack of mapping, but they don't. Descriptions are fairly minimalist. There is not even one route timing included in any walk description, no compass directions at trail junctions, and certainly no GPS navigation. Routes seem to have been chosen on the basis of going on a big hike, typically in the range of 17 to 29 kilometres in length; one exception to this is the three page section given to the 3 kilometre **Timanfaya** guided walk.

No thought has been given to accessibility; we presume Paddy was dropped at his start point and picked up again at his finish point, but for us mortals getting back to our hire car is very important, and we would have liked to hear how he got back again, and not just leave us 29 kilometres from our start point! Paddy's route, **La Hoya** to **Yaiza** via **El Golfo** is 17 kilometres of tarmac roads - not what we would call a 'walking route'.

Rather like some of the routes, 'pointless' is our conclusion for a book that purports to cover three islands in detail but fails on all of them.

REFERENCE BOOKS

Flores Silvestres de las Islas Canarias
This is the serious plantsperson must-have publication. David and Zoë Bramwell's impressive and comprehensive tome, published in Spanish by Editorial Rueda, is usually available in **Libreria Villalobos** in **Arrecife**. There is an English translation which was published in 2001 (ISBN 8472071294 £35), but not always available on the island.

Volcanoes

Los Volcanes de las Islas Canarias (II) Lanzarote y Fuerteventura
There is nothing in English which goes into much detail about Lanzarote's volcanoes, but the enthusiast might look for this publication by Araña, Vicente and Carracedo, published by Editorial Rueda. Ask in **Libreria Villalobos** in **Arrecife**.

César Manrique

Fundación de César Manrique
If you want to know more about the man and his legacy, you need this publication (author Simon Marchan Fiz, published by Opus £25). It's available in English translation and can be found on amazon.co.uk., or may be in the **Libreria Villalobos** in **Arrecife**.

Coastline Guide

Coastline Aeroguide Eastern Canary Islands
This is one of a fascinating series of books combining aerial photographs with background information on various island destinations. **Coastline Aeroguide Eastern Canary Islands** covers Gran Canaria, Fuerteventura and Lanzarote. An English translation is Published by Geoplaneta (ISBN 8-40803165-1 1999 around £25) Not easy to get hold of, but look in the **Arrecife Airport** bookshop (airside newsagents) or try in **Libreria Villalobos** in **Arrecife**.

GLOSSARY

This glossary contains Spanish and Canarian words found in the text (shown in *italics*), plus other local words that you may encounter.

a	
abandonado	abandoned
abierto	open
acantilado	cliff
agua	water
agua no potable	water (not drinkable)
agua potable	drinking water
aljibe	sunken water tank
alto	high
aparcamiento	parking
arepa/arepera	deep fried savoury snack/bar specialising in arepas
autopista	main road, motorway
ayuntamiento	town hall
b	
bajo	low
barranco	ravine
bocadillo	bread roll
bodegón	inn
buceo	scuba diving
c	
cabezo	peak, summit
cabra	goat
café	coffee
caldera	collapsed cone (volcanic area)
calima	suspended dust brought in by hot east winds
calle	street
camino	trail, path, track
camino particular	private road
camino real	old donkey trail (lit. royal road)
carne	meat
carretera	main road
casa	house
casa rural	country house accommodation to let
caserío	hamlet, village
castillo	castle
cementario	cemetery
centro comercial	shopping centre
cerrado	closed
cerveza (caña, jarra, presión, lata)	beer (small, large, draught, can)
charco	pool
choza	shelter
clinica	clinic, hospital
colmena	bee hive
comida	food
conquistador	conqueror
cordillera	mountain range
correos	post office
cortijo	farmstead
costa	coast
coto privado de caza	private hunting area
Cruz Roja	Red Cross (medical aid)
cuesta	slope
cueva	cave
cumbre	summit
d	
degollado	pass
derecha	right (direction)
desayuno	breakfast
desprendimiento	landslide
e	
ermita	chapel
Espacio Naturaleza Protegido	protected area of natural beauty
estación de autobus/ guagua	bus station
este	east
f	
farmacia	chemist
faro	lighthouse
fiesta	holiday, celebration
finca	farm, country house
g	
gasolinera	petrol station
gofio	flour made from roasted maize, wheat or barley
guagua	bus
Guardia Civil	police
guia	guide
h	
hornito	lava bubble
hostal	hostel, accommodation
hoya	depression (geological)
huevos	eggs
i	
iglesia	church
información	information

isla	island
izquierda	left (direction)
j	
jameo	volcanic tube
jamón	ham
l	
librería	bookshop
llano	plain
lluvioso	rainy
lomo	broad-backed ridge
m	
Majos/Mahos	Lazarote's original inhabitants
malpais	'bad lands' wild, barren countryside
malvasia	Malmsey grapes and wine
mapa	map
mareta	raised water collection tank
mariscos	shellfish
mercado	market
mirador	lookout/viewing point
mojo	spicy sauce based on olive oil, tomatoes and chillis
montaña	mountain
museo	museum
n	
norte	north
nublado	cloudy
o	
oeste	west
oficina de turismo	tourist office
p	
paella	rice dish, usually with seafood or meat
panadería	bakery
papas arrugadas	wrinkled potatoes (small potatoes in their skins cooked in salt water)
parapente	hang-glider
parque eólico	wind farm
pastelería	cake shop
peligro	danger
pensión	guesthouse
pescado	fish
pico	peak
picon	black volcanic rock/sand
pista	dirt road/track
pista (forestal)	forest road/track
playa	beach
plaza	square
policia	police
postre	dessert
potaje	thick soup
pozo	well
prohibido el paso	no entry
puente	bridge
puerto	port, mountain pass
q	
queso	cheese
r	
risco	cliff
roque	rock
ruta	route
s	
salida	exit
salinas	salt pans
sangría	wine with fruit punch served in a jug of ice
senda	path, track
sendero	foot path
sin salida	no through road/route
sirocco	hot, dust-laden wind from Africa
sur	south
t	
tapas	bar snacks
té	tea
tienda	shop
tipico	traditional bar/eating place
tormentoso	stormy
torre	tower
tubería	water pipe
v	
valle	valley
vega	meadow
ventoso	windy
vino (blanco, tinto, rosado)	wine (white, red, rosé)
volcán	volcano
z	
zocos	crescent shaped vine enclosures (as seen in La Geria)
zona recreativa	recreation area
zumo/zumería	freshly pressed fruit juice/juice bar

CYCLING ON LANZAROTE

Lanzarote is a surprisingly varied island; you cycle up steep valleys through green palm trees and black *picon* fields. Once you reach the ridge, you head down to the coast where the Atlantic bursts onto black lava-cliffs, descending through brown and sandy landscapes. In winter it's at its most interesting, full of colour as flowers, crops and plants burst from the otherwise desert-like terrain.

Lanzarote is becoming better known as a mountain biking destination and is perfect for winter training; there's also the sports complex of Club La Santa open all year. Sporting competitions such as Lanzarote Ironman (in May each year) attract more and more participants. Lanzarote is perfect for both off-road and on-road cycling; leisure cyclists too enjoy following coastal paths, quiet roads and beach promenades.

For the mountain biker, Lanzarote can be divided into three regions; the north where you ride along the coast or through steep green valleys, either on quiet country roads or over rocky trails and single tracks; the centre of the island, less hilly - but far away from being flat, and the south which is again steep and very rocky, but less green. This section offers high mountain dirt tracks and gentle gradients along the coast or through lava fields.

- **What the cyclist won't find** on Lanzarote includes forests, grass trails, high altitude climbs and, unfortunately, cycle lanes. However, some are in plan and the roads are quiet enough to enjoy.

- **What the cyclist will find only occasionally** - but usually can avoid - wet conditions.

- **What might surprise you** - going faster climbing up than rolling down - due to the wind.

- **What might amaze you** - stunning views all over the island.

- **What you have to see** - the landscape around Timanfaya National Park - unforgettable!

If you bring your own bike, bear in mind that some of local tracks and roads, and getting your bike here, might cause your kit to be damaged.

Other useful information:-

- In winter bring a windbreaker, maybe zip-on-sleeves and you'll need sun protection all year round.

- It's the law to wear a bike helmet on Lanzarote. One will be included in your cycle hire from all reputable rental companies on the island.

- Take your **Lanzarote Super-Durable Tour & Trail Map** (published by Discovery Walking Guides), the best map you can get.

- When riding off-road please respect local signs and don't leave trails or pistes as this can damage the island's delicate ecosystems.

- Be alert to loose or abandoned dogs - they might view you as escaping goats.

If you need any further advice or want to join us on one of our guided rides don't hesitate to contact us via email:

bike@mylanzarote.com info@tommys-bikes.com
info@bikelanzarote.com

Our shops in **Costa Teguise** (**Bike Station** and **Tommy's BIKES**) stock all kind of bicycles individually adjusted to your needs. We carry spares and biking equipment and also offer guided excursions and useful tips. We've been running our bike excursions for many years and we know all the hidden corners of the island. Our team offers you easy rides for the whole family on quiet roads and trails, with loads of information about traditions and local history of Lanzarote as well as hardcore trails for the serious rider.

Currently local authorities are designing signposted MTB-routes for Lanzarote - please contact us for the latest news.

Andreas Kern
www.mylanzarote.com
www.tommys-bikes.com

- Bus times change; ask for the latest version on arrival. The Biosphere Information Office (almost faces you on emerging from Arrecife airport baggage hall) usually has free copies or ask in the Puerto del Carmen Information office (near the beach).
- www.arrecifebus.com is the official website, parts of which can be viewed in English.
- Occasionally buses showing numbers other than that designated for the route will arrive at the stop; ask the driver if he is going to your destination.
- Don't rely on catching the last bus back. It is advisable to carry taxi phone numbers and a mobile phone, just in case. Most villages have a public phone, otherwise, try a bar.

01 ARRECIFE - COSTA TEGUISE - ARRECIFE

Playa de Reducto - Juzgados - Bus Station - Los Alonso - Los Mármoles - Las Caletas (Costa Teguise) - Hotel Oasis - Playa Roca - Playa Bastián - Pueblo Marinero - Hotel Salinas

MONDAY TO FRIDAY (excluding holidays)

From Arrecife Bus Station to Costa Teguise: 06:40 07:00 07:40 08:00 08:20 then every 20 mins until 21:20 22:00 22:20 22:40 23:50 00:50 01:50 02:50 03:50 04:50 05:50

From Costa Teguise to Arrecife: 07:20 07:20 08:00 08:20 then every 20 mins until 21:20 22:00 22:20 22:40 23:00 24:10 01:10 02:10 03:10 04:10 05:10 06:10

SATURDAY, SUNDAY & HOLIDAYS

From Arrecife Bus Station to Costa Teguise: 06:40 07:40 08:40 09:10 09:40 then at 10 past and 40 past every hour until 23:10 23:50 00:50 01:50 02:50 03:50 04:50 05:50

From Costa Teguise to Arrecife: 07:00 08:00 09:00 09:30 10:00 10:30 then at 10 and 30 mins past every hour until 23:30 24:10 01:10 02:10 03:10 04:10 05:10 06:10

02 ARRECIFE - PUERTO DEL CARMEN

Los Alonso - Bus Station - Rotonda S Fco Javier/Juzgado on return journey - Playa del Reducto - Poligono Playa Honda - Matagorda - Hotel Jameos - Costa Mar - Hotel San Antonio - C C Welcome See - La Peñita - C C Arena Dorada - Apart. Los Fariones - C C Biosfera - Balcón del Mar

MONDAY TO FRIDAY (excluding holidays)

From Bus Station to Puerto del Carmen: 06:20 06:40 07:00 07:40 08:00 then at 20 past, 40 past and on the hour until 21:40 22:20 23:20 24:30 01:30 02:30 03:30 04:30 05:30

From Puerto del Carmen to Arrecife Bus Station: 07:00 07:20 07:40 then on the hour, 20 past and 40 past each hour until 22:20 23:10 24:10 01:10 02:10 03:10 04:10 05:10 06:10

SATURDAY, SUNDAY & HOLIDAYS

From Bus Station to Puerto del Carmen: 06:20 07:20 07:50 08:20 09:20 09:50 then at 20 and 50 mins past every hour until 22:20 23:20 00:30 01:30 02:30 04:30 05:30

From Puerto del Carmen to Arrecife Bus Station: 07:00 08:00 08:30 09:30 10:00 11:00 then at 30 past the hour and on the hour until 22:30 23:10 24:10 01:10 02:10 03:10 04:10 05:10 06:10

03 COSTA TEGUISE - PUERTO DEL CARMEN

Hotel Salinas (Costa Teguise) - Lanzarote Gardens - Pueblo Marinero - Playa Bastián - Playa Roca - Hotel Oasis - Las Caletas - Los Marmoles - Los Alonso - Arrecife Bus Station - Rotonda S Fco Javier - Playa del Reducto - Poligono P Honda Matagorda (Pto del Carmen) - Costa Mar - Hotel San Antonio - C C Welcome See - La Peñita - C C Arena Dorada - Apart Los Fariones - C C Biosfera - Balcón del Mar

MONDAY TO FRIDAY (excluding holidays)

From Costa Teguise to Puerto del Carmen: 07:00 07:20 08:00 08:20 08:40 09:00 then at 20 and 40 mins past each hour and on the hour until 21:00 21:20 22:00 23:00 24:10 01:10 02:10 03:10 04:10 05:10

From Puerto del Carmen to Costa Teguise: 07:00 07:20 07:40 08:00 then at 20 and 40 mins past each hour and on the hour until 20:00 20:20 20:40 21:20 22:00 23:10 24:10 01:10 02:10 03:10 04:10 05:10

SATURDAY, SUNDAY & HOLIDAYS

From Costa Teguise to Puerto del Carmen: 07:00 08:00 09:00 09:30 10:00 then at 30 past the hour and on the hour until 20:30 21:00 22:00 22:30 23:10 24:10 01:10 02:10 03:10 04:10 05:10

From Puerto del Carmen to Costa Teguise: 07:00 08:00 08:30 09:00 10:00 then at 30 past the hour and on the hour until 22:00 22:30 23:10 24:10 01:10 02:10 03:10 04:10 05:10

05 ARRECIFE - FEMÉS

Arrecife Bus Station - Rotonda S Fco Javier - Playa del Reducto - Poligono P Honda - Ferretería de Tías - Tías centre - Los Lirios - Iglesia de Coníl - Coníl centre - Palmera Asomada - La Asomada centre - Mácher Petrol Station - Palmera de Mácher - Puerto Calero crossroads - Las Casitas (Femés) El Puente de Femés - Femés church

MONDAY TO FRIDAY only (excluding holidays)

From Arrecife Bus Station: 08:00 14:00 17:45

From Femés: 09:00 18:30

06 PUERTO DEL CARMEN - PLAYA BLANCA (N.B. this route commences from Arrecife Bus Station approximately 30 mins before arriving in Puerto del Carmen)

C C Biosfera - Balcón del Mar - La Finca de Mácher - Mácher Petrol Station - Palmera de Mácher - Puerto Calero crossroads - Uga church - Yaiza supermarket - Aljibe de Yaiza - Centro de Salud de Yaiza - Rotonda La Hoya - Playa Blanca Bus Station - Playa Blanca port (muelle)

MONDAY TO FRIDAY (excluding holidays)

From Puerto del Carmen to Playa Blanca: 06:26 08:38 09:46 10:44 11:45 12:48 14:31 15:47 16:22 17:27 18:59 20:54 21:56

From Playa Blanca to Puerto del Carmen: 07:00 09:30 10:30 11:45 12:45 13:30 15:30 17:15 18:15 19:45 21:30 22:30

SATURDAY, SUNDAY AND HOLIDAYS

From Puerto del Carmen to Playa Blanca: 07:17 08:26 (only on Sundays) 09:38 12:31 13:57 (on bus N°13 Sundays only) 14:58 17:16 20:09

From Playa Blanca to Puerto del Carmen: 08:00 09:10 (on bus N°13 Sundays only) 10:20 13:10 14:40 (only on Sundays) 15:40 18:30 20:50

07 ARRECIFE - MÁGUEZ

Arrecife Bus Station - Altavista - Cuesta del Gallo (Tahiche) - El Jamonal - César Manrique crossroads - Tahiche - Las Cabreras - Nazaret - Teguise town hall (ayuntamiento) - Centro de Salud de Teguise - Teguise church - Teseguite de Abajo - El Mojón crossroads - Plaza de Guatiza - Jardín de Cactus - Centro de Salud de Mala - Mala post office (correos) - Mala de Abajo - Tabayesco - Arrieta - Los Morros - Punta Mujeres - Bar Palenque - Calle San Juan, Haría - La Plaza, Haría - La Cruz, Haría - La Molina de Máguez - Sociedad de Maguez

MONDAY TO FRIDAY (excluding holidays)

From Arrecife Bus Station to Máguez: 08:00 10:00 12:30 14:30 18:00 20:00

From Máguez to Arrecife Bus Station: 06:55 09:00 11:30 13:30 15:30 19:00

SATURDAY

From Arrecife Bus Station to Máguez: 08:00 12:00 14:00 20:00

From Máguez to Arrecife Bus Station: 07:00 09:00 13:00 21:00

SUNDAY AND HOLIDAYS

From Arrecife Bus Station to Máguez: 07:30 13:30 20:00

From Máguez to Arrecife Bus Station: 08:45 14:30 21:00

08 ARRECIFE - PLAYA BLANCA

Arrecife Bus Station - Rto S Fco Javier - Playa del Reducto - Poligonon Playa Honda - Ferretería de Tías - Tías centre - Los Lirios - football ground, Tías - C C Biosfera, Pto del Carmen - Balcón del Mar - La Finca de Mácher - Mácher petrol station - Palmera de Mácher - Puerto Calero crossroads - Uga church - Supermercado de Yaiza - Aljibe de Yaiza - Centro de Salud de Yaiza - Rotónda La Hoya - - Las Breñas 123 - Playa Blanca Bus Station - Playa Blanca port (muelle)

MONDAY TO FRIDAY only (excluding holidays)

From Arrecife Bus Station to Playa Blanca: 07:00 08:30 13:00 19:30

From Playa Blanca to Arrecife Bus Station: 07:45 09:15 14:00 16:30 20:30

09 ARRECIFE - ÓRZOLA

Arrecife Bus Station - Altavista - Cuesta de Gallo (Tahiche) - César Manrique crossro

Tahiche - Las Cabreras - Nazaret - Teguise town hall (ayuntamiento) - Centro de Salud de Teguise - Teguise church - Teseguite de Abajo - El Mojón crossroads - Plaza de Guatiza - Jardín de Cactus - Centro de Salud de Mala - Mala post office (correos) - Mala de Abajo - Tabayesco - Arrieta - Los Morros - Punta Mujeres - Bar Palenque - El Callao - Órzola port (muelle)

MONDAY TO FRIDAY (excluding holidays)

From Arrecife Bus Station: 07:40 10:30 15:30

From Órzola: 08:30 11:30 16:30

SATURDAY, SUNDAY AND HOLIDAYS

From Arrecife Bus Station: 07:40 15:30

From Órzola: 08:30 16:30

10 ARRECIFE - LOS VALLES

Arrecife Bus Station - Altavista - Cuesta de Gallo (Tahiche) - El Jamonal - César Manrique crossroads - Tahiche - Las Cabreras - Nazaret - Teguise town hall (ayuntamiento) - Centro de Salud de Teguise - Teguise church - Teseguite de Abajo - El Mojón - Sociedad de Los Valles - Valle Arriba

MONDAY TO FRIDAY only (excluding holidays)

From Arrecife Bus Station: 10:00 14:00 19:00

From Los Valles: 07:00 11:50 15:50 19:45

11 COSTA TEGUISE - TEGUISE MARKET

Hotel Salinas - Lanzarote Gardens - Pueblo Marinero - Playa Bastián - Playa Roca - Hotel Oasis - Teguise market

SUNDAY only

From Costa Teguise: 09:00 09:30 10:00 10:30 11:00

From Teguise market: 12:00 12:30 13:00 13:15 14:00

12 PUERTO DEL CARMEN - TEGUISE MARKET

Balcón del Mar - Las Vistas - Apart Los Fariones - C C Arena Dorada - La Peñita - C C Welcome See - Hotel San Antonio - Costa Mar - Hotel Jameos - Matagorda - Teguise market

SUNDAY only

From Puerto del Carmen to Teguise market: 09:00 09:30 10:00 10:30 11:00

From Teguise market to Puerto del Carmen: 12:00 12:30 13:00 13:15 14:00

13 PLAYA BLANCA - TEGUISE MARKET

Playa Blanca port (muelle) - Playa Blanca Bus Station - Rotonda La Hoya - Centro de Salud de Yaiza - Aljibe de Yaiza - Yaiza Supermarket - Uga church - Puerto Calero crossroads - Palmera de Mácher - Mácher petrol station - La Finca de Mácher - El Toro - Balcón del Mar - C C Biosfera - Football ground - Los Lirios - Tías centre - Ferreteria de Tías - Poligono Playa Honda - Playa del Reducto - Juzgados - Arrecife bus station - Teguise market

SUNDAY only

From Playa Blanca to Teguise market: 09:10

From Teguise market to Playa Blanca: 13:00

14 ARRECIFE - MONTAÑA BLANCA - GÜIME

Arrecife Bus Station - Registro- Rotonda S Fco Javier - Playa del Reducto - Poligono Playa Honda - Calle Mayor, Playa Honda - Instituto Playa Honda - Calle San Borondón, Playa Honda - Avda de Las Palmeras, San Bartolomé - El Islote/Güime - Masdache - Montaña Blanca

MONDAY TO FRIDAY only (excluding holidays)

From Arrecife Bus Station to Montaña Blanca/Güime: 07:00 13:50 18:30

From Montaña Blanca to Arrecife Bus Station: 07:40 14:20 19:15

16 … - LA SANTA

…tion - General Hospital - Avda de las Palmeras, San Bartolomé - San …ds - Mozaga post office (correos) - La Caseta de Tao - La Tienda de …post office (correos) - Curva La Vegueta - Las Cadenas - Los Dolores - …b Mancha Blanca - Guigua (Tinajo) - Tajaste - El Calvario - Cine de

Tinajo - La Plaza de Tinajo - La Cañada - El Cuchillo - La Santa - La Santa Sport
MONDAY TO FRIDAY (excluding holidays)
From Arrecife Bus Station to La Santa: 06:15 08:00 10:00 12:00 14:00 16:00 18:00 20:00
From La Santa to Arrecife Bus Station: 07:00 09:00 11:00 13:00 15:00 17:00 19:00
SATURDAY
From Arrecife Bus Station to La Santa: 07:45 09:15 11:50 13:50 18:00
From La Santa to Arrecife Bus Station: 07:00 08:30 10:00 12:50 18:45
SUNDAY AND HOLIDAYS
From Arrecife Bus Station to La Santa: 07:45 13:30 18:00
From La Santa to Arrecife Bus Station: 07:00 08:30 18:45

19 ARRECIFE - LA ASOMADA
Arrecife Bus Station - Rto S Fco Javier - Playa del Reducto - Poligonon Playa Honda - Ferretería de Tías - Tías centre - Los Lirios - Conil church - Conil centre - Palmera Asomada - La Asomada centre - Mácher petrol station - Palmera de Mácher - Puerto Calero crossroads
MONDAY TO FRIDAY only (excluding holidays)
From Arrecife Bus Station: 07:00 08:00 14:00 17:45
From La Asomada: 07:25 09:15 18:45

20 ARRECIFE - CALETA FAMARA
Arrecife Bus Station - General Hospital - Avda Las Palmeras (San Bartolomé) - San Bartolomé crossroads - Mozaga post office (correos) - La Caseta de Tao - La Tienda de Tiagua - Sociedad de Muñique - Soo - Caleta Famara
MONDAY TO FRIDAY only (excluding holidays)
From Arrecife Bus Station to Caleta Famara: 06:30 07:45 14:15 16:00 20:00
From Caleta Famara to Arrecife Bus Station: 07:00 08:40 15:00 17:00 20:45

21 ARRECIFE - PLAYA HONDA
OUTWARD JOURNEY Arrecife Bus Station - Registro - Rotonda S Fco Javier - Playa del Reducto - Poligono Playa Honda - Calle Mayor, Playa Honda - Instituto Playa Honda
INWARD JOURNEY Calle San Borondón, Playa Honda - Princess Ico - Rotonda Playa Reducto - Gran Hotel - Casino - Parque Viejo - Escuela de Pesca - Policia Nacional - Los Alonso - Arrecife Bus Station
MONDAY TO FRIDAY only (excluding holidays)
From Arrecife Bus Station to Playa Honda: 06:50 07:00 08:10 08:40 08:55 09:25 09:40 10:10 10:25 10:55 11:10 11:40 11:55 12:25 12:40 13:10 13:25 13:50 13:55 14:10 14:40 15:25 15:40 16:25 16:55 17:10 17:40 17:55 18:25 18:40 19:10 19:25 19:55 20:10 20:40 20:55 21:25 21:40 22:10
From Playa Honda to Arrecife Bus Station: 07:05 07:50 08:25 08:55 09:10 09:40 09:55 10:25 10:40 11:10 11:25 11:55 12:10 12:40 12:55 13:25 13:40 14:10 14:25 14:40 14:55 15:40 15:55 16:40 17:10 17:25 17:55 18:10 18:40 18:55 19:25 19:40 20:10 20:25 20:55 21:10 21:40 21:55 22:25

22 ARRECIFE - AIRPORT
OUTWARD JOURNEY Arrecife Bus Station - Registro - Rotonda S Fco Javier - Playa del Reducto - Poligono Playa Honda - Airport terminal 1 - Airport terminal 2
INWARD JOURNEY Airport terminal 2 - Esq Calle Mástil, Playa Honda - Deiland, Playa Honda - Playa del Reducto - Juzgados - Arrecife Bus Station
MONDAY TO FRIDAY only (excluding holidays)
Arrecife Bus Station to Airport: 06:50 07:30 08:00 08:30 09:00 09:30 10:00 10:45 11:15 11:45 12:15 12:45 13:15 14:00 14:30 15:30 16:00 16:30 17:00 17:30 18:15 18:45 19:15 19:45 20:15 20:45 21:15 21:45 22:15
Airport to Arrecife Bus Station: 07:00 07:40 08:10 08:40 09:10 09:40 10:10 10:55 11:25 11:55 12:25 12:55 13:25 14:10 14:40 15:40 16:10 16:40 17:10 17:40 18:25 18:55 19:25 19:55 20:25 20:55 21:25 21:55 22:25

23 ARRECIFE - PLAYA HONDA - AIRPORT
OUTWARD JOURNEY Arrecife Bus Station - Registro - Rotonda S Fco Javier - Playa del Reducto - Poligono Playa Honda - Airport terminal 1 - Airport terminal 2

INWARD JOURNEY Airport terminal 2 - Esq Calle Mástil, Playa Honda - Calle Mayor, Playa Honda - Calle San Borondón - Princesa Ico - Rotonda Playa Reducto - Gran Hotel - Casino - Parque Viejo - Escuela de Pesca - Policia Nacional - Los Alonso - Arrecife Bus Station

SATURDAY, SUNDAY AND HOLIDAYS only

From Arrecife Bus Station to Airport: 08:50 09:35 10:20 11:05 11:50 12:35 13:20 14:05 14:50 15:35 17:00 17:45 18:30 19:15 20:00 20:45 21:30 22:15

From Airport terminal 1 to Arrecife Bus Station: 09:00 09:45 10:30 11:15 12:00 12:45 13:30 14:15 15:00 15:45 17:10 17:55 18:40 19:25 20:10 20:55 21:40 22:25

24 ARRECIFE - PUERTO CALERO

OUTWARD JOURNEY Los Alonso - Arrecife Bus Station - Rotonda s Fco Javier - Playa del Reducto - Poligono Playa Honda - Matagorda (Puerto del Carmen) - Hotel Jameos - Costa Mar - Hotel San Antonio - CC Welcome See - La Peñita - C C Arena Dorada - Apart Los Fariones - C C Biosfera - Balcón del Mar - Puerto Calero

INWARD JOURNEY Puerto Calero - Balcón del Mar - Las Vistas - Apart Los Fariones - CC Arena Dorada - La Peñita - C C Welcome See - Hotel San Antonio - Costa Mar - Hotel Jameos - Matagorda - Esq Calle Mástil, Playa Honda - Deiland - Playa del Reducto - Juzjados - Arrecife Bus Station - Los Alonso

MONDAY TO FRIDAY only (excluding holidays)

From Alonso, Arrecife to Puerto Calero: 07:00 09:00 11:20 15:00 19:40 23:20

From Puerto Calero to Alonso, Arrecife: 07:30 09:30 11:50 15:30 20:10 24:00

SATURDAY, SUNDAY & HOLIDAYS

From Alonso, Arrecife to Puerto Calero: 07:20 10:20 11:50 14:50 19:50 23:20

From Puerto Calero to Alonso, Arrecife: 07:50 10:50 12:20 15:20 20:20 24:00

25 COSTA TEGUISE - PUERTO CALERO

OUTWARD JOURNEY Hotel Salinas, Costa Teguise - Lanzarote Gardens - Pueblo Marinero - Playa Bastián - Playa Roca - Hotel Oasis - Las Caletas - Los Marmoles - Los Alonso - Arrecife Bus Station - Rotonda s Fco Javier - Playa del Reducto - Poligono Playa Honda - Matagorda (Puerto del Carmen) - Hotel Jameos - Costa Mar - Hotel San Antonio - CC Welcome See - La Peñita - C C Arena Dorada - Apart Los Fariones - C C Biosfera - Balcón del Mar - Puerto Calero

INWARD JOURNEY Puerto Calero - Balcón del Mar - Las Vistas - Apart Los Fariones - CC Arena Dorada - La Peñita - C C Welcome See - Hotel San Antonio - Costa Mar - Hotel Jameos - Matagorda - Esq Calle Mástil, Playa Honda - Deiland - Playa del Reducto - Juzjados - Arrecife Bus Station - Los Alonso - Los Marmoles - Las Caletas, Costa Teguise - Hotel Oasis - Playa Roca - Playa Bastián - Pueblo Marinero - Hotel Salinas

MONDAY TO FRIDAY only (excluding holidays)

From Costa Teguise to Puerto Calero: 08:40 11:00 14:40 19:20 23:00

From Puerto Calero to Costa Teguise: 07:30 09:30 11:50 15:30 20:10 24:00

SATURDAY, SUNDAY & HOLIDAYS

From Costa Teguise to Puerto Calero: 07:00 10:00 11:30 14:30 19:30 23:00

From Puerto Calero to Costa Teguise: 07:50 10:50 12:20 15:20 20:20 24:00

26 ARRECIFE - YÉ

OUTWARD JOURNEY Arrecife Bus Station - Altavista - Cuesta del Gallo/Tahiche - El Jamonal - Cesar Manrique crossroads - Tahiche - Las Cabreras - Nazaret - Teguise town hall (ayuntamiento) - Centro Salud de Teguise - Teseguite church - Teseguite de Abajo - El Mojón crossroads - Plaza de Guatiza - Cactus Garden - Centro Salad de Mala - Mala de Abajo - Tabayesco - Arrieta - Los Morros - Punta Mujeres - Bar Palenque, Punta Mujeres - Calle San Juan, Haría - La Plaza, Haría - La Cruz, Haría - La Molina de Máguez - Sociedad de Máguez - Guinate crossroads - Yé

INWARD JOURNEY Yé - Sociedad de Máguez - La Cruz, Haría - La Plaza, Haría - Calle San Juan, Haría - Guardia Civil - Bar Palenque, Punta Mujeres - Punta Mujeres - Los Moros, Altavista - Arrieta - Tabayesco - Mala de Abajo - Mala post office (correos) - Centro Salud de Mala - Cactus Garden - Plaza Guatiza - El Mojón crossroads - Teseguite de abajo - Teseguite church - Centro Salud Teguise - Teguise town hall (ayuntamiento) - Nazaret - Las Cabreras - Tahiche - Cesar Manrique crossroads - El Jamonal, Tahiche - Cuesta del Gallo - Altavista - Arrecife Bus Station

MONDAY TO FRIDAY only (excluding holidays)
From Arrecife Bus Station to Yé: 18:00
From Yé to Arrecife Bus Station: 06:50

27 ARRECIFE - MÁGUEZ

OUTWARD JOURNEY Arrecife Bus Station - Altavista - Cuesta del Gallo/Tahiche - El Jamonal - Cesar Manrique crossroads - Tahiche - Las Cabreras - Nazaret - Teguise town hall (ayuntamiento) - Centro Salud de Teguise - Teseguite church - Teseguite de Abajo - El Mojón - Sociedad de Los Valles - Valle Arriba - Calle San Juan, Haría - La Cruz, Haría - La Molina de Máguez - Sociedad de Máguez
INWARD JOURNEY Sociedad de Máguez - La Cruz, Haría - La Plaza, Haría - Calle San Juan, Haría - Guardia Civil de Haría - Valle Arriba - Sociedad de Los Valles - El Mojón - El Mojón crossroads - Teseguite de Abajo - Teseguite church - Centro Salud Teguise - Teguise town hall (ayuntamiento) - Nazaret - Las Cabreras - Tahiche - Cesar Manrique crossroads - El Jamonal, Tahiche - Cuesta del Gallo - Altavista - Arrecife Bus Station
MONDAY TO FRIDAY only (excluding holidays)
From Arrecife Bus Station to Máguez: 10:00
From Máguez to Arrecife Bus Station: 11:30 15:30

30 PLAYA BLANCA

(There are two itineraries around Playa Blanca - check with the driver for the journey you require)
Itinerary 1
Playa Blanca Bus Staion - Beach Sun - C C Papagayo - Princesa Yaiza - Castillo del Aguila - Ciudad Jardin 2 - San MArcial 2 - Las Coloradas - San Marcial 1 - Ciudad Jardin 1 - Marina Rubicón - Playa Dorada - Lanzarote Princess - El Aulagar - Playa Blanca port (muelle) - Flamingo - Volcanes 2 - Volcanes 1 - Natura Palace - Rubicón Palace - La Goleta 2
Itinerary 2
Playa Blanca Bus Station - Casas del Sol - Playa Limones - Las Margaritas - La Perla 1 - College (school) - El Pueblito - Virginia Park - Jardín del Sol - Bajo Los Riscos - Los Arcos - La Goleta 1 - Faro Park
DAILY SERVICE
06:30 07:00 07:30 then on the hour and 30 mins past the hour until last service at 22:00

A
Airport 11, 14, 30, 145, 150, 153, 154
Archivo Municipal 98, 99
Arrecife 3, 6, 10, 12, 15, 21, 28, 29, 31, 32, 34, 36, 38, 43, 46, 50, 55, 62, 66, 68, 72, 76, 79, 94, 98, 100, 102, 105, 108, 114, 127, 132, 138, 143, 145, 150,155
Arrieta 10, 151, 152, 154
Asomada 88, 90, 91, 139, 151, 153
Atalaya de Femés 4, 34, 62, 66, 133
Atlante del Sol Hotel 7, 47, 55, 56, 58
Avenida Faro de Pechiguera 50

B
Bar Femés 65, 67, 71, 72, 75, 76, 79
Bar NeyHa 100
Bar/Café Sejas 97
Bar/Restaurant 7 Islas 35
Bar/Restaurant El Campo 60, 61
Bar/Restaurant Gregorio 63, 88
Bar/Restaurant La Casita 35
Bar/Restaurant Los Helechos 100, 102, 104, 108, 109
Bar/Restaurant Mercedes 30
Bar/Restaurant Mesana 30
Bar/Restaurant The Sunburnt Arms 38
Bar/Restaurant Villa Toldeo 37
Barceló Suites Hotel 36
Barranco de la Casita 70, 136, 137
Barranco de la Higuera 12, 50, 55, 68, 69, 71, 72, 75, 79, 80, 94, 95, 136
Barranco de los Dises 70, 76, 137
Barranco de Quiquere 6, 7, 32, 33, 90
Barranco del Fraile 80, 136
Barranco del Malpaso 5, 7, 28, 102, 103, 107, 134
Barranco Parrado 77
Barranco Valle del Palomo 112
Beatrix Hotel 42

C
Cactus Garden 10, 12, 17
Caldera Blanca 2, 6, 7, 28, 129, 130, 135
Caldereta 129, 130
Caleta de Famara 127, 153
Calimera Hotel Club 47
Calle Agonal 29
Calle Angel Guerra 102
Calle de los Volcánes 37, 38
Camino Barranco de Quiquere 90
Camino del Mesón 90
Camino el Charco 3, 39, 40, 41, 132
Camino la Caldarina 90
Camino las Casanas 90
Camino los Olivos 90
Casa Cuartel 98, 99
Casa de Correos 99
Casa del Marqués 97
Casa la Helice 90
Casa Paroquial 99
Casa Torres 99
Casitas de Femés 13, 74, 136, 137
Castillo Coloradas 49
Castillo de Santa Bárbara 39, 97, 98, 110
Castillo del Aguila 155
Centro de Arte Santo Domingo 99
Centro de Visitantes 15, 81, 129
Centro Socio Cultural de Yé 118, 122
Cerro de Tegoyo 139
Charco de los Clicos 18
Cilla de Diezmos y Primicias 99
Club La Santa 14, 148
Commercial Centre Cucharas 38
Commercial Centre Limones 46

Commercial Centre Neptuno 37
Commercial Centre Pueblo Marinero 38
Conil 139, 153
Convento de San Francisco 97
Convento de Santo Domingo 99
Costa Teguise 3, 6, 7, 11, 12, 14, 17, 28, 32, 34, 36, 38, 40, 43, 79, 94, 132, 149, 152, 154
Cucharas Commercial Centre 38
Cucharas Commercial Centre 38
Cueva de los Verdes 17

D

Degollada del Portugués 76

E

Eckholl Collection Shop 100, 102, 105, 107
El Cable 12
El Cable Yacht Club 30
El Cuchillo 153
El Golfo 18, 20, 25, 87, 144, 145
El Islote 152
El Mojón 151, 152, 154, 155
El Pasito 78, 137
El Risco de Famara 18, 102, 103, 116, 124, 125, 127
El Rubicón 4, 55, 133
El Veradero 32
Ermita de la Merceo 111
Ermita de las Nieves 39, 104, 109, 111, 113
Ermita de Vera Cruz 98
Eruption Gardens 4, 60, 6163, 133

F

Famara 5, 18, 102, 103, 106, 107, 110, 113, 116, 119, 121, 123, 128, 135, 153
Faro de Pechiguera 55
Faro Park (development) 46, 55, 155
Femés 4, 13, 19, 20, 27, 28, 34, 62, 69, 71, 74, 76, 77, 79, 80, 94, 133, 134, 136, 137, 143, 151
Femés Ridge 4, 27, 72, 79, 80, 133
Femés Valley 63
Finca de Mácher 151, 152
Finca La Corona 122
Finca Lomos Altos 90
FInca Luna 40
Finistere (development) 55
Fundación de César Manrique 15, 145

G

Gaida 139
Graciosa 6, 17, 110, 121, 123
Gran Arrecife Hotel 31
Guanapay (peak) 97
Guatiza 10, 12, 16, 151, 152, 154
Güime 152
Guinate 114116, 121, 122, 154

H

Hacha Grande 71, 76
Haría 5, 18, 39, 100, 108, 111, 124, 125, 134, 151, 154, 155
Helga's Patisserie 38
Hespería Hotel 34
Hotel Atlante del Sol 7, 47, 55, 56, 58
Hotel Barceló Suites 36
Hotel Beatrix 42
Hotel Club Calimera 47
Hotel Gran Arrecife 31
Hotel Hespería 34
Hotel Iberostar Papagayo 49
Hotel Lanzarote Park 46
Hotel Las Coronas 37
Hotel Natura Palace 47, 155
Hotel Papagayo Arena 53, 78
Hotel Paradise Island Club 50, 53
Hotel Rubicón Palace 155
Hotel Sol Lanzarote 7, 29
Hotel Timanfaya Palace 46
Hotel Volcán Lanzarote 49

I

Iberostar Papagayo Hotel 49

Iglesia de Nuestra Señora de Guadalupe 97, 99
Isla de Alegranza 110
Islote de Hilario 15

J

Jameos del Agua 12, 15, 17
Janubio 16, 17
Jardín de Cactus 12, 15, 17, 151, 152

K

Kamezi Villas 46, 47, 55

L

La Asomada 88, 90, 91, 139, 151, 153
La Caleta 106, 113, 116, 122, 124, 126, 128
La Degollada 62, 63
La Finca 61
La Finca de Macher 151, 152
La Geria 2, 5, 7, 9, 18, 34, 88, 93, 134, 136, 139, 140
La Hoya 7, 55, 57, 59, 85, 145, 151, 152
La Isla Graciosa 6, 17, 110, 121, 123
La Pescosa 116
La Santa 14, 148, 152, 153
La Vegueta 152
Laguna de Janubio 16
Lanzarote Park Hotel 46
Las Breñas 13, 151
Las Coronas Hotel 37
Las Rositas 122
Limones Commercial Centre 46
Los Clavelles 50
Los Cocoteros 16
Los Helechos 5, 28, 100, 102, 104, 108, 109, 114, 116, 117, 135
Los Hervideros 17
Los Valles 152, 155

M

Mácher 151, 153
Máguez 5, 105, 114, 116, 117, 119, 120, 122, 135, 151, 154, 155
Mala 5, 16, 39, 111, 112, 127, 135, 151, 152, 154
Mancha Blanca 15, 81, 129 152
Masdache 152
Matagorda 7, 10, 11, 29, 150, 152, 154
Matos Verdes 106
Mirador de Guinate 114
Mirador de Haría 101, 124
Mirador del Río 15, 17, 122
Mirador del Risco de Famara 102, 103
Molino de Viento de Teguise 98
Montaña Baja (development) 50
Montaña Blanca 2, 129, 131, 152
Montaña Cinta 60, 61
Montaña Clara 110
Montaña Corona (nr. Costa Teguise) 2, 3, 40, 41, 43, 44, 132
Montaña Corona (nr. Yé) 6, 7, 119, 120, 135
Montaña Cuervo 4, 6, 28, 83, 134, 139
Montaña de Guardilama 34, 88
Montaña de Saga 45
Montaña Ganada 107
Montaña Guardilama 34, 89
Montaña Halcones 86
Montaña Quemada 87, 118
Montaña Roja 4, 6, 7, 28, 43, 47, 50, 51, 133
Montaña Teneza 131
Montaña Tersa 139
Montaña Tinasoria 88, 91, 92, 134
Montañas del Fuego 15, 17, 73
Morro de la Loma del Pozo 69
Mozaga 152, 153
Muñique 153
Museo de Emigrante Canario 97, 98

N

Natura Palace Hotel 47, 155
Nautilus Apartments 37
Nazaret 151, 152, 154, 155
Neptuno Commercial Centre 37
Nuevo del Fuego 9

O

Orzola 17, 118

P

Palacio Doctor Alfonso Spinola 97, 99
Papagayo 4, 28, 48, 49, 51, 54, 56, 71, 76, 78, 133, 136, 138, 144, 155
Papagayo Arena Hotel 53, 78
Paradise Island Club Hotel 50, 53

Parque Eólico 113
Parque la Mareta 97, 98
Parque Nacional de Timanfaya 3, 4, 9, 15, 17, 19, 60, 62, 72, 73, 81, 86, 89, 90, 92, 134, 145, 148
Peña del Rubicón 4, 55, 133
Peñas del Chache 9, 110, 113
Pico Aceituna 69, 70, 76, 79
Pico Oveja 72, 74
Pico Redondo 70, 71, 76, 144
Playa (de la) Madera 20, 85, 86
Playa Bastián 37, 38, 150, 152, 154
Playa Blanca 4, 7, 14, 17, 28, 32, 36, 39, 43, 46, 47, 48, 50, 55, 57, 59, 71, 76, 78, 132, 133, 136, 138, 151, 152, 155
Playa Coloradas 49
Playa Congrio 52
Playa Cucharas 3638
Playa de Famara 110
Playa de Guasimeta 30
Playa de la Arena 94, 96, 136
Playa de los Charcos 38
Playa de Papagayo 52
Playa del Afe 48, 49, 78
Playa del Pozo 5, 28, 54, 75, 79, 80, 94, 96, 136, 137
Playa del Risco 123
Playa Familia 47
Playa Flamingo 46
Playa Honda 10, 29, 30, 150, 154
Playa Limones 155
Playa Mujeres 52, 54, 137
Playa Quemada 4, 32, 34, 35, 69, 79, 80, 94, 136, 137, 143
Playa Real 47
Playa Reducto 31, 153, 154
Plaza de la Constitución (Haría) 100, 107
Plaza de la Constitución (Teguise) 9799
Plaza de Vera Cruz 98
Plaza Maciot 99
Presa de Mala 112
Pueblo Marinero Commercial Centre 38
Puerto Calero 32, 34, 35, 43, 69, 79, 80, 90, 94, 138, 151, 154
Puerto del Carmen 3, 6, 7, 14, 28, 29, 32, 34, 36, 39, 43, 46, 50, 65, 67, 76, 79, 88, 90, 91, 94, 132, 138, 150, 152, 154
Punta del Roque 125
Punta Jabillo 37
Punta Mujeres 12, 151, 152, 154

R

REWE32 109
Rincón Apartments 32
Risco Quegrado 131
Rte. del Diablo 15
Rubicón 9, 20, 28, 34, 46, 47, 49, 52, 55, 56, 66, 71, 76, 77, 133, 155
Rubicón Marina 49
Rubicón Palace Hotel 155

S

Salinas del Agujero 16
Salinas del Janubio 16
Salinas del Río 5, 16, 122, 124, 135
Salinas El Charco 39
San Bartolomé 144, 152, 153
Sands Beach Villas 38
Sands Beach Villas 38
Sol Lanzarote Hotel 7, 29

T

Tahiche 11, 15, 39, 41, 151, 152, 154, 155
Tajaste 152
Tao 9, 152, 153
Taro de Tahiche 15
Teatrillo Municipal 97
Tegoyo 139
Teguise 3, 57, 912, 14, 17, 28, 32, 34, 36, 38, 43, 45, 79, 88, 91, 94, 97, 98, 108, 110, 111, 113, 132, 134, 135, 149, 152, 154, 155
Tenesar 85
Teseguite 39, 40, 151, 152, 154, 155
Tiagua 152, 153
Tías 83, 139, 151, 152, 153
Timanfaya 3, 4, 9, 15, 17, 19, 60, 62, 72, 73, 81, 86, 89, 90, 92, 134, 145, 148
Timanfaya Palace Hotel 46
Tinajo 81, 83, 85, 152, 153
Tinasoria 88, 91, 92, 134

Tinguatón 9
Torrecilla de
Domingo 117
Tremesana 4, 15, 19, 81, 134
U
Uga 19, 20, 6267, 85, 88, 91, 93, 139, 147, 151, 152
V
Valle de Fena 63
Valle de Guinate 115, 116
Valle de Malpaso 107
Valle de Tenisía 101
Valle del Pozo 74, 80, 137
Vega Grande 117, 118
Vegas de Tegoyo 139
Villa Vistas 90
Villas Kamezi 47, 55
Visitor's Centre 15, 81, 129
Volcán Lanzarote
Hotel 49
Volcanic Gardens 4, 60, 61, 63, 133
Y
Yaiza 4, 13, 19, 20, 60, 67, 79, 81, 85, 87, 88, 98, 133, 143, 145, 151, 152, 155
Yé 2, 5, 117, 119, 121, 122, 124, 128, 135, 154, 155